Preserving Your Past

Preserving Your Past

A PAINLESS GUIDE
TO WRITING
YOUR AUTOBIOGRAPHY
AND FAMILY HISTORY

Janice T. Dixon
and Dora D. Flack

DOUBLEDAY & COMPANY, INC.
GARDEN CITY, NEW YORK

Library of Congress Cataloging in Publication Data

Dixon, Janice T
Preserving your past.

Bibliography: p. 331.
1. Autobiography. 2. Genealogy. I. Flack, Dora,
joint author. II. Title.
CT25.D58   809
ISBN: 0-385-12817-7
Library of Congress Catalog Card Number 76–56278

Dedicated to
Willard and LeGrand

Preface

No sooner had we set up our tent, pounded in the stakes and lifted the canvas high enough so we could almost stand tall, than our new neighbors from a nearby campsite dropped over to visit.

"Where ya from?"

"Utah. What about you?"

"California. What's your business?"

"Chemistry," my husband said. "And my wife is a writer."

"No kidding!" our new neighbor said. "A writer! Ya know, I've had a story I've been wanting to write. Happened to me a couple a years ago. I'll tell it to you, and you can write it down."

This is not an isolated incident. It happens all the time at parties, classes, PTA meetings, and other social functions. The only problem is that the stories told to me are not my stories. They belong to the teller. If I did eventually break down and write one of these stories, then it would become my story and no longer belong to the person who told it to me. No one can write your story except you. You have a story inside; everyone does. Sometimes you have many stories: stories that happened to you, to your family, to your parents or grandparents that are waiting to be told.

"I don't know how to write," and "How do I start?" are the two most commonly heard laments. This book attempts to solve these two problems.

Dora and I decided to guide you on a step-by-step approach to the same method we used to write our own personal and family histories. We start with the research. To be accurate we have to have records. We have included all the helps we could in suggesting places you could look for your records and what information was available on those records, including public, military, service, and religious organizations. We found addresses for many of these organizations and direct you where to search for others. This information should give you a basic nudge in the right direction.

Now that you have all these records gathered, how do you organize and use them? We have included suggestions for a filing system, charts, ancestral charts and organizational helps where you can see at a glance exactly what needs to be done and where to find the needed information. You can quickly refer back to verify dates and places if you follow the simple directions.

The actual writing process stops many would-be writers, but in the first three sections we have provided simple basic ideas you can use. Outline one story at a time, add background, details, and feelings until finally you are re-creating your story the same way you have told it a hundred times. The only difference is that now you've written it down and it will not be forgotten. The major portion of the book is concerned with the writing. With this guide to direct you, you'll find that this is the most enjoyable part of putting your own book together.

When those stories are finally written and polished, Section Four suggests ways of reproducing your stories for family members, preserving your records, and keeping a continuing family record.

While we did concur on what would be included in the book overall, we did decide it would be more sensible to split the writing chores, making it easier for the reader to follow our own experiences in our writing. Dora wrote Section Four, and is the "I" in that part of the book, while I am the "I" of the first three sections.

We have tried to cover all the problems we encountered and a few others besides. That's what makes this book so long—we tried to cover situations that most of us never run into. We've also given alternate suggestions; after all, there are many ways to write a book, and we've tried to cover as many as possible. In other words, we have systematically guided you through the writing process from the research, organization, writing, editing, reproducing, and preserving processes.

Next time you meet a writer you won't have to say, "I have a great story, will you write it for me?" Instead you can smile smugly and show them your own personal and family histories.

Janice Dixon
January 1977

Acknowledgments

During the writing of this manuscript, encouragement and technical experience has been offered by a number of individuals whose services and interest are deeply appreciated. Among them are Dr. Lucile M. Thorne, Librarian at the Brigham Young University; Peg Nichols, professional writer and critic; Dr. Glen M. Leonard, William G. Hartley, and Conservationist Paul Foulger, of the Historical Department of The Church of Jesus Christ of Latter-day Saints; Dr. Jay M. Haymond, Co-ordinator of Records, Utah State Historical Society; Cheri Smith, Roberta L. Lindsay, Elizabeth L. Nichols, Accredited Genealogists; and the members of the Manuscripters who have served as audience and critics.

J.T.D. and D.D.F.

Contents

Section Four
Searching, Organizing, and Preserving
the Material

Appendix

Section One

WRITING
YOUR AUTOBIOGRAPHY

We all love to reminisce. We all love to tell others what we have done, what we have thought, what we have dreamed. Some of us confide most readily in our close friends; some of us, oddly enough, confide in strangers. Others of us again find it impossible to talk of ourselves except in a letter, a diary, or an outright narrative addressed to a general audience. But whatever form it may take, our desire to reminisce and to confess is bound to have expression for it arises from our sense of the unity of human life. We know that we are alone: we are at the same time part of a group. There is, we are sure, a very real connection between our life and the lives of others. And just as we are driven to confess our innermost secrets in the hope of establishing contact with others, so we find interesting all of the words of those who have written their autobiographies.

Richard D. Mallery
Masterworks of Autobiography

Chapter 1

WHY SHOULD YOU WRITE YOUR AUTOBIOGRAPHY?

My father died thirty-six years ago when I was eight years old. He gave me life, a few pictures, and fewer memories. I wish he had written something of his life, so that I could know him better.

It is the same for you and me. You have your family and are remembered by them, but your memories fade and so will those of your children. You remember your parents well, but you are less sure of your grandparents. Your great grandparents are fading even farther from your mind. As each generation replaces the next, those memories dim unless a written record is kept.

John Quincy Adams recorded his feelings on this matter September 20, 1823:

> I walked in the burying-yard, and viewed the granite tombstones erected over the graves of my ancestors . . . four generations, of whom very little more is known than is recorded upon these stones. There are three succeeding generations of us now living. Pass another century, and we shall all be mouldering in the same dust or resolved into the same elements. Who then of our posterity shall then visit this yard? And what shall be read engraved upon the stones?[1]

Histories record the story of nations, and biographies and autobiographies record the stories of individuals. Few people, unless they are quite famous, have a biographer willing and anxious to write their story. It is, therefore, necessary for each person to write his own personal history.

It is more than vanity that makes you want to tell your stories. You have lived many years and have learned many things. It is

[1] Philip Dunaway and Mel Evans, A *Treasury of the World's Great Diaries* (Garden City: Doubleday & Company, Inc., 1957), p. 198.

only natural that you should want to share these experiences and
truths. This is one of the reasons artists paint, sculptors sculpt,
or writers write—so they can leave something they have created.
They want to leave some bit of truth captured in capsule form in
their art.

You have that same privilege. You can write your autobiography and in it will be your truth. As you write your stories and
your goals, you will find your life being put into perspective. After
all, that person you were ten years ago . . . or twenty . . . is a
different person from today. You can look objectively at him and
understand him. As you write your stories you may find that each
time there was a decision to be made, you chose a certain way. A
pattern emerges, and you understand yourself better than you ever
have.

Annie Clark Tanner, a woman who lived from 1864–1941,
wrote the story of her life. When finished she evaluated her personal history. She says:

> True, this biography has made me live again so many of the
> joys and sorrows of the past. Yet it has been very fascinating to
> look more carefully at my life as a whole and in a way that has
> been objective as well. With a distant perspective one can more
> easily see the funny side of life. It is interesting to compare this
> past with the present, especially if by doing it one can create
> something that will prove interesting for the future, as this book
> may. It has also been somewhat of a relief for me to think out the
> reason for the unhappy events of the past. All censure is now ob-
> literated and one can appreciate the efforts even of those who
> made mistakes. After all, most people do their best. All self-cen-
> sure, too, is laid aside and one sees there is "good in everything."[2]

But even more important is the fact that you are recording a
small part of history. As you write your history, you give the testimony of your life and of your family. Joined with many lives and
many records your story becomes part of the history of your people.

Samuel Pepys wrote a diary in 1660 and continued it for nine
years. Through his writings we are able to look into the lives and

[2] Annie Clark Tanner, *A Mormon Mother*, published by Tanner Trust Fund,
University of Utah Library, Salt Lake City, Utah, 1976, p. 333.

habits of a common man in England. Samuel Pepys was not especially important, although he was educated and held a good position. The most significant thing about him is the diary he left telling of his life. He wrote anecdotes of himself, his friends, and royalty. He was honest in telling how he felt. When he was successful, he bragged about his success; when he failed, he tried to console himself. He discussed his weaknesses, his frustrations, and his happiness. He has become an important man in history who would have been unknown except for his diary.

History is made up of individual men and women who have written of their lives. That's all history is, the interwoven stories of many people. These people have recorded the happenings of the day and the significance it held for them. Your autobiography should include the significant events in your life and how you feel about them.

Edgar Johnson explains the value of personal histories and the rich interweaving it plays with our lives:

> . . . In letters, in diaries, in table-talk, memoirs, and autobiographies, men have recorded how the passing current of their lives and feelings seemed to them, what they thought of their friends and enemies, and all the things that colored the passing current of their days. Therein, sometimes with no thought of being a witness to future generations, they have exclaimed over the trivia of their existences, aired their quarrels, jotted down a comment on their pleasures. What a rich fragrance of the life and personality of the past arises out of these records! As we read them, the dust that has sifted down over the far-away is blown from its surface by a wind of life; and the dried yellow pages that have been so hard and shriveled gradually open, expand, and take on bright colorings, like those tight little pellets of paper that placed in water unfold into flowers and trees and fountains and tiny castles . . .[3]

Your autobiography is a witness to future generations. There is no self-serving here. You are adding your comments, your feelings, your experiences, your observations about the important things in your world.

[3] Edgar Johnson, *One Mighty Torrent* (New York: The Macmillan Company, 1955), p. 29.

The entire story of mankind has come to us from individual voices from the past. Each person who has written has contributed a small portion of the knowledge we have today. Without the written stories, ideas, and feelings of individuals, we would have no history and a very barren future.

Your life is as important to the making of future history as that of a senator or President or general, but it loses its significance unless it is written down. You are telling the people who follow after you, the people you love, just what life has meant to you. No one else can do it.

You want to write your autobiography, but you don't know where to start? You have lived twenty-three years, forty-five years, sixty-six years, seventy-seven years . . . it doesn't matter how many years or how few, it is still a long time, and the paper in front of you is very white and just as empty. You have given yourself every excuse not to write your autobiography:

a. No one will read it anyway.
b. Someone might read it.
c. Nothing has ever happened to you.
d. You don't have the time.
e. English was always your worst subject in school.
f. You can't remember everything.
g. You *can* remember everything, but don't want anyone else to know.
h. No one has told you *how* to write it.
i. Only important people write autobiographies.

But then the other part of you speaks up:

a. Everyone in the (school, church, family) has been asked to write his life history.
b. It would solve the problem of retelling that story the same way each time.
c. Your (children, parents, teacher, etc.) have been pestering you to write your story, and you just haven't taken the time.
d. *You* are an important person.

    e. Life is such a beautiful (or rotten) thing! You have to tell someone about it.

    f. You are going to allow someone else (maybe someone you have never met) to share your life with you.

    g. It's a class assignment, and if you don't write it, you flunk!

    h. Why, here is a book that tells you how to write your story.

The reasons for writing must have won out or you never would have chosen this book to read instead of last year's *Reader's Digest* or your favorite science-fiction paperback.

Two weeks ago my mother showed me the autobiography of my paternal grandmother. As I read the entries tears came to my eyes. My grandmother died when I was very young and I never really knew her, and yet I was sharing her disappointments and her successes through her writing. She told about my father as a youth and how he nearly died as a result of a hunting accident. She also tells of the death of Aleen, her six-year-old daughter. In quiet terms she tells how she dresses the little girl and curls her long blond hair and then waits for the horse-drawn wagon to take the wooden coffin down the bumpy road. In reading her words I felt closer to my grandmother than I ever have. The generations slipped away as I share her grief for a moment. I'm sure my grandmother didn't know that I would read her personal history many years later, but if she had known I think she would have been happy that she could be a part of my life. She allowed me for a few minutes the opportunity to be a part of her thoughts and feelings.

Everyone has one story to tell, his own. And though your immediate reaction might be, "My life isn't interesting," if you would think about it, there are many events in your life that are uniquely yours.

"I have nothing to write about," said one woman who had given a kidney to save her daughter's life. "Who wants to know about me?" asked another who had to flee from Mexico for her life when Pancho Villa was killing whole villages. "Except for one time in my life, I've had a dull existence," said a middle-aged man, and then proceeded to tell a story that would have made Jack London jealous.

Nothing to tell? You have never performed a service for someone? Never taken a trip? Never known an interesting person, or
thought an exciting thought, or faced a challenge? You don't even
believe that nonsense yourself! If you didn't have something to
tell, you would never have picked up this book.

You know there are many reasons you should write about yourself. For one thing, you want it accurate. Right?

If you have golden blond hair, you don't want someone to
write, after you're dead, that you were a dish-water blond.

"Married in 1940, a child bride," a historian writes. But that
makes you five years old.

"Let me tell it the way it was!" you defend. "It was 1950 and I
was fifteen, but I was very mature for my age." Five years old!
Good grief!

"You only live once," a bumper sticker says. "But if you work it
right, once is enough." And as long as you are in life for keeps,
you might as well get it down accurately in writing.

What do you know about Noah's wife's sister and her no-good
husband? Nothing? They must have forgotten to write their autobiographies, along with millions of others. Of course, some of them
didn't know how to read or write, but that's not your excuse. How
valuable it would be to have had the personal stories of now-ex-
tinct civilizations, of the followers of Moses, of the people who
died in the Guatemalan earthquake, of an American Indian
woman in 1492. These stories are lost and so are the identities of
those who lived then, but your story is as interesting and as important as any of these. You are living at a time when more is happening and at a faster rate than ever before. You are an exciting
link between the past and future.

Think of the status symbol of having a book written about you!
You can have it bound and placed in a special place in your
house.

"My autobiography," you mention off-hand to your boss, or the
minister, or the encyclopedia salesman. Anyone can buy a status
symbol, but only you can write your autobiography.

Suppose your neighbor comes over and the beds are unmade
and the breakfast dishes are in the sink. "Come on in," you invite,
"I'm busy writing my autobiography."

"Autobiography!" she says. "Only important people write their autobiographies."

"That's right," you say cheerfully. And if you are in an expansive mood, you can add, "When I'm finished with mine, I'll help you start on yours."

Once you start into the writing, it can be quite enjoyable. It has been fifty years . . . or five . . . since you remembered that cocker spaniel. What was its name? Duchess! Oh, yes. Do you remember how it had a cowlick on top of its head which you tried to smooth down with Grampa's rose hair oil?

You'll find yourself laughing as you remember the scrapes you got into as a kid. (The old school had a circular fire escape built like a winding slippery slide. You would climb up carefully, trying to avoid the custodian who would run you off if he caught you. And then you took the hair-raising ride to the bottom!) You still catch your breath thinking of it. How about the times you rode your bike to school without once grabbing the handlebars, even maneuvering over curbs and around corners.

It's fun to look back and say, "How naïve I was, and how much I've learned since." (When you were little, you thought if there wasn't enough room on the earth, the obvious solution was to build a second layer. So you started by climbing to the top of a junked car and this was the start of a second layer around the earth.)

Sometimes you wonder how you survived this long. (You had a motorcycle which you rode like a demon on a gravel road. You still have gravel embedded in your left hip from one of the thousands of spills you took.)

Enjoyable? Would you give them up? Well, maybe some of them, but most of them are fun to remember now that the pain has gone. Even some of the sad times are brought back with a wry smile as you realize you survived a difficult relative. (An alcoholic father, a senile grandmother, a kissing aunt, a flighty and irresponsible mother, a bully brother—but, hopefully, not all of them.)

There are many games we play. "I have nothing to write about," is only one of the games. Here are others. As long as you know they are only games, then you can get on with the writing.

Game 2: "I only write when I feel the inspiration." And so you wait for inspiration while you trim the roses, change the oil in the car, clean the kitchen, or watch television, and wonder why you aren't more inspired. Writing is 99 per cent hard work and only 1 per cent inspiration. So the trick is to grab a pencil and start writing. Inspiration comes when you have a pencil in your hand and are trying to find a way on your own. Few people have been inspired in the middle of a television show or a golf game. Writing takes time and energy, the same as any other worthwhile endeavor.

Game 3: "I'll start writing as soon as I: (a) get the dishes done; (b) read the morning paper; (c) fertilize the lawn." This list may be expanded to include the spring housecleaning, painting the back fence, putting in a garden, or calling all the friends you have been neglecting for the last two years. By this time there is nothing left to do but go to bed with the promise, "Oh well, I'll start tomorrow."

To win this game, set a definite time every day, if possible, or once a week if that is all the time you have. As long as the time you give yourself for writing is regular, you will accomplish your goal. The shorter time you give yourself, the longer this project is going to take, however. Don't short-change yourself by giving yourself the worst time of the day. You know that your best time is two hours after you wake up, or right after lunch, or at 5:00 A.M. when there is quiet in the house. Whatever time you give yourself, make sure it is a time when you are alert and fresh. After work or just before bed is usually a poor time because you are tired.

You know how much time you have to give to this project. If you have only fifteen minutes, you can get a lot done in that time if you have no distractions and know what you want to write before you start. (Today I'm going to write about the time I took the ski jump the first time I went skiing.) When you sit down with an idea in mind, you'd be surprised how much you can write. Time isn't going to stand around waiting for anyone. If you are going to have time, you have to get out and trap it.

Game 4: "This paper is so nice and white. I must think everything out in my mind first and then put it down. This way I won't make any mistakes."

Forget it. Paper is to scribble and doodle on. So cross out words or write in the margins. Just to prove it, draw a pair of eyes at the top of the paper right now. See? Now you've started. And it doesn't matter how many mistakes you make, you can always start over.

Game 5: "I don't know how to type." Then write it a second time in good penmanship in ink, or talk a friend, daughter, wife/husband, or secretary into doing it for you.

"My hand gets so cramped that it's impossible to write more than a few minutes at a time."

That's all it takes, a few minutes at a time. One writer has arthritis so bad she can type with only one finger, but she writes a book a year. Another has to type flat on her back, but that isn't stopping her from telling her story. An extreme example is Christy Brown of Dublin, who is so crippled he can type only with the little toe of his left foot. Try it. It is very difficult, even with an electric typewriter.

And had you thought of taping your story? Check Chapter 19 of this book for help in that.

Game 6: "I'm a Gemini," you might say. "And a Gemini can't stick to anything." Nonsense. You are sticking to your life, and as long as you do that you can record it.

Games? Excuses? You don't need a crutch. What are you waiting for?

This book is divided into four sections: the first three sections will be step-by-step, how-to-do-it, getting-your-feet-wet sections. Section One covers writing your autobiography; Section Two covers writing your family history; and Section Three covers writing your diary. If you follow instructions and let us help "brainstorm" with you, it will be an enjoyable experience for you. Section Four is composed of specifics in gathering, organizing, and preserving your records.

This book will cover what to include in your autobiography, diary, and family history, how to organize it, how to choose which stories to tell, how to write it, and then how to polish that writing.

And when it is finished, there are suggestions on how to preserve your record.

When I first started writing the autobiography part of this book, I couldn't decide which examples to use. At first I decided to use nothing but stories from my own life with the assumption that "if I could do it, so could you." I was afraid that, if I used excerpts from published autobiographies, you would have the excuse, "Oh, but they're all famous people. I can't write like that."

Then I switched 180 degrees and decided to use only the best published autobiographies for examples because, after all, they were successful in writing their autobiographies, and we would be able to learn from them. So I went through more than a dozen autobiographies and chose only the best stories. When I finished this, I found it was overwhelming. True, I had all the good examples I needed, but that was the problem . . . they were all too good. It would be like handing a paintbrush to a novice artist and telling him to paint another "Whistler's Mother."

I finally compromised by using parts from my own autobiography to show you a "work in progress" with all its mistakes, and by using selections from the autobiographies of Helen Keller, Mark Twain, and Benjamin Franklin to show how the masters work. It is somewhat humbling to place my offerings alongside those fine writers. I hope that, as you read the examples, you will use them for the reason they were offered and not for comparison.

You are ready to start. Who knows—when you finish your autobiography, you might enjoy writing so much, you will start on a second project, such as writing your family history.

Chapter 2

COLLECTING THE BONES

Facts are the bones of your life! On these facts hang all the stories, incidents, and memories. They form the framework on which all else hangs. Every day you are probably giving out facts. You include facts on questionnaires for schools, on job application forms, on the vita for a college degree, on marriage licenses, and ultimately they become the information needed for your obituary.

But your life is more complete than this. A complete form listing most of the facts that you should jot down is found on pages 117–18 and 255–56. If you don't have all this information at hand, start gathering as much as you can. It won't be much of an autobiography without dates, places, and people.

"Oh, I don't worry about that sort thing," you might say. "Uncle Quail and Aunt Ora keep all of our family records."

"You mean every time there is a birth in the family or a graduation you immediately send all your records and certificates to them?"

"No, I don't mean that. I mean, they *keep all the records.*"

"How do they get the information?"

"I don't know, but they have books and books."

"How can they have *your* records, if you haven't sent any information to them?"

"You mean, maybe they don't have *my* information?"

"How could they, if no one told them anything?"

Some families are organized. From the moment little Theresa is born, she is photographed, admired by the paragraph, and even her first wail is tape recorded. All relatives are informed of Theresa's every tooth, step, and new word. One scrapbook isn't enough for all her childish utterances or pictures. When she gets older, she keeps diaries, and by the time she is an adult she could tell you about her entire life (and sometimes she does!).

However, most people haven't been that systematic about their records. By the time Albert is ready for school, Mama is probably frantically trying to find out whether he had his measles shots, and did he have the mumps, or was that his sister?

"I'm sure I kept your immunization records right here in my handkerchief drawer under my last year's Christmas card list! And if it isn't there, I could have slipped it in my recipe box . . . well, I can't find it, so you can just have all your shots over again. Stop your howling! It isn't going to hurt to have a DPT a second time!"

He does have a birth certificate, doesn't he? I mean, he was born! So you have to send in to the Vital Statistics for his birth certificate.

"What do you mean, 'Male Zerkel'? His name is Albert Zerkel!" You must have forgotten to send in his name.

Aunt Joy has a fine old china cupboard in which she keeps her best china. The china is so fine that it is never used. That is, not to eat from. It does get used: all the important papers are stuffed in the bone china teacups, water pitchers, and gravy boats. Cousin Eliel needed his birth certificate to get married, and Aunt Joy hunted for three months before she finally found it tucked behind the meat platter. One teacup held a first-grade report card for twenty-three-year-old Eliel, a guarantee for a transistor radio, which has now been thrown out, a recipe for zucchini bread, and a marriage license.

When Grandma Morgan died, the family sorted out the satin quilts, embroidered pillowcases, and old dresses that were too good to throw out. Underneath it all, they found twenty-seven pictures. No dates, places, or names were included. Hidden even deeper under the lavendar afghan was an old photograph of a young man and the inscription, "All my love, Samuel." Samuel! Who was Samuel? For sure, it wasn't Grandpa Morgan! But Grandma can't tell you now, even if she would.

Collecting the Pieces

But what about your records? And what should you look for anyway? Everything you can find. All legal documents, birth certificates, marriage licenses, wills, newspaper clippings, military records, baptism certificates, family histories, snapshots, passports, naturalization records, school diplomas, funeral programs, and obituaries, etc.

Organize the Facts

The list will grow as you start finding things. If everything is neatly pasted in a scrapbook, then you are one step ahead. But if they are all heaped up in front of you in piles, perhaps you had better start organizing before you throw everything back in a box and give the whole thing up.

If you have manila folders around the house, they will work great. So will large-size envelopes, the 10"×13" size, or even bigger. Decide how you will organize it.

For most people a time-period organization might be the easiest:

   a. Childhood
   b. Elementary School
   c. Junior High School
   d. High School
   e. Post High School (College, Employment, Military, Mission, Peace Corps)
   f. Marriage and/or beginning of career
   g. Raising a family, building a business or career
   h. Settling in (the balding, bifocal period)
   i. Grandchildren or retirement years
   j. Family background

When you finish, you will probably find miscellaneous papers, and you might want to start a file on them. You may have so much material on your career or hobby that it fills an entire folder. Or you might have a pile of clippings or cards on friends or important people in your life. File the material in these folders or envelopes and carefully label each one on the outside, so you can find it easily.

If you moved from one area to another, you might decide to use this as a dividing:

a. Saudi, Arabia
b. Israel
c. England
d. Texas
e. New York
f. Springville

Is everything organized? Before you put everything away, check and see what you have. You look in the family background file. You have a family Bible listing birth, death, and marriage dates, and a newspaper clipping of Mama and Dad's golden anniversary. And that is all?

Well, actually there was a dried corsage which might have been a carnation, but it crumbled all over the floor when you picked it up. Unless you are terribly sentimental, the flower can go.

Do You Really Remember Mama?

Maybe you haven't looked hard enough. Didn't Mama and Dad have school yearbooks? And what about the oodles of snapshots you took every vacation? Mama used to tease you that she would break the camera . . . and one time after you had taken a picture of her, the camera did break. Do you remember Aunt Gen who always wrote those funny letters? Lots of times she told about fun times with Mama before you were born. Mama put those letters somewhere. Maybe the trunk in the attic? Or beneath the seldom-used underwear in the bottom drawer. Did Mama or Dad keep a diary? Not Dad. Not good old Dad. But what was it he put away that time you came into his room unexpectedly?

Mama was PTA president for twelve years from the time your

older sister, Lisa, entered Forrest School until the time your youngest brother, Walt, graduated from sixth grade, and the teachers sighed with relief that the Zerkel family finally graduated. The PTA records tell a lot about Mama and the things she did.

Are you learning a lot about Mama you didn't even know? How about getting together with brothers and sisters for a "Do you remember when?" party? Set out the tape recorder and have each one of them outdo each other on stories each remembers. If Mama and Dad are still alive, type up a copy and give as a Mother's Day present or Father's Day present. You know how difficult it is to find gifts for them. "We don't need anything, just forget us this year," they have told you for so long.

You could spend a few evenings talking with them about their lives, tape recording it if they will let you.

While you are talking with family or friends, why not ask a few questions about your own early years?

"Mama said I wandered away from home when I was three years old, and the police found me by the mill creek. Who knows anything about that?"

Were holidays something special in your home? I remember Grandma coloring the water pink on April Fool's Day, and when I took a big drink I expected pink lemonade. She always pulled some trick on April Fools, but never the same one twice. The next year she served pink lemonade, and I expected colored water.

Childhood is special because of traditions:

"Don't sit on the antique rocker or you'll land on your head."

"No one eats before the blessing on the food, or he gets served last."

"Nobody sits in that chair at the table. That's reserved for Rosie."

"First one up feeds the cat, last one up takes out the garbage."

Jot some of these highlights down on index cards, or if you have five minutes while you are waiting for a daughter to finish her music lesson and all you have is the back of a grocery list, jot these memories down and file it along with the other notes.

List High Points of Each Period

Take a colored paper (to make it stand out from the rest) and put down the things you do remember. Choose one period at a time and concentrate on small time segments. In my file I looked at the information I had about my early childhood. It was almost bare. I had included the following:

1. Birth certificate.
2. Name and blessing certificate.
3. Fragment memory of mother ironing and telling stories.
4. A mental picture of my father's legs.
5. A story my mother told me, but about which I have no memory—the time I wandered away from home when I was about three years old.
6. A collection of pictures of me as a child.
7. A vivid memory of my father's death and the circumstances surrounding that event.

I put the colored paper with this list of seven entries, my certificates and seventeen pictures of me, from diapers through the tricycle stages into the first file. I will probably add to this list and file as I gather more information. For now, it is sufficient.

ELEMENTARY SCHOOL LIFE

Now assemble all the material you have for the next period of your life, say from first grade through sixth grade. If you can list events chronologically, it will impose an order on your life. However, some memories cover the whole period of time and can't be listed chronologically. Here are some questions that might jog your memory. Some will strike a responsive bell, others will not:

Did your family have any difficult times economically?
Did you have any illnesses or accidents?
Did anyone die that you remember?
What good times did you have? Trips? Holidays?
Where did you live?

What family responsibilities did you have?

What do you remember about school and your teachers?

What was your favorite activity?

Did you have a pet? What was its name?

What do you remember about your religious training or belief?

Is there any event in this period that changed your life?

When you finish one period of time, put the colored paper list in the folder and get out another folder. Systematically review your life, a segment at a time. Try to confine yourself to that particular period. Of course you can add to any folder or list when you remember something.

JUNIOR HIGH AND HIGH SCHOOL YEARS

You will probably have two folders for these two periods. Many of the same questions can be asked, but you might get different answers.

What classes, hobbies, activities became interesting to you?

What honors or awards did you receive?

Did you set any goals during these years?

What special friends did you have?

Did you get into any trouble or pull any pranks?

What happened when you learned how to drive a car?

What work experience did you have?

What services did you perform for others?

What sports were you interested in?

Did you attend church? What were your religious beliefs?

Did you receive advancements in your church?

Were you a Boy or Girl Scout?

Do you remember your first date?

What were the fads of the time?

What did you do socially?

This doesn't cover everything. It wasn't meant to. But if it reminds you of some of the activities in your life, then it has value. More than one memory can come from most of the questions.

POST HIGH SCHOOL ACTIVITIES

> *Military Service*
> What was your serial number?
> Where did you receive your basic training?
> Where were you stationed?
> Did you have special friends?
> What did you do on leave?
> Were you in combat? Where?
> What rank and promotions did you receive?
> What experiences off and on base were most important to you?
> What are the benefits you received from military service?
>
> *College Life* (Scholastic or Vocational)
> Why did you choose the particular college that you did?
> What classes or teachers influenced you negatively or positively?
> Did you finish school?
> What social activities did you enjoy?
> How did you finance your schooling?
> Did you become involved in any issues?
> What were your activities apart from school at this time?
> Did you receive any special honors or activities that drew attention to you?
> Did your college experience determine your future career?
> What subject did you specialize in?
> What friends did you make?
>
> *Service* (Mission, Peace Corps, Red Cross, etc.)
> Why did you choose to serve others?
> Where did you go? To what people?
> How were you financially supported?
> What training did you have?
> What friends did you make at this time?
> What was your schedule?
> What did you do?
> How did you help others? How did you feel about it?

What experiences did you have?
How did you affect others?
How did you feel when you finished this part of your life?
How has it changed your life now?

COURTSHIP AND MARRIAGE

How did you meet your future partner?
Did you have special dates?
How long after you knew her/him did you start making marriage plans?
Do you remember the first time you met the in-laws?
How did you ask her to marry you (he ask you to marry him)?
What about wedding plans?
Tell about the wedding day. Who was there? When? Where?
Who officiated? Who was part of the wedding party?
Tell about the honeymoon.
Where was your first home or apartment?
What was the best thing he/she knew how to do? What was the worst?
What happened the first time you went shopping together?

BUILDING A BUSINESS OR CAREER

What was the first job that started you toward your present business or career?
How did you decide to choose this particular work?
What training did you have to prepare you for this work?
What promotions or honors did you have?
What was the biggest problem you had in adjusting to your work?
What successes did you have? Did you have any failures?
How did your work affect your family?
What challenges did you meet and how did you meet them?
Did you have any experiences on the job that are particularly important to you?

RAISING A FAMILY

Give names and birth dates of children.

What are the characteristics, talents, hobbies, personalities of each child. What has each meant to you in your life?

Have these children given any challenges to you?

What did you do as a family? Vacations? Daily routines?

As they have grown, how have you adjusted in your personal life?

What philosophy did you use in raising them? How did you discipline them? How did you praise them?

Would you raise your children the same way if you had a second chance?

SETTLING IN

In what community service are you involved?

How have you expanded or changed in your business or work?

Are you involved in politics? How?

How is your health?

What friends do you have? Are they the same ones with whom you grew up? What new friends have you made? How are they important to you?

Have you had special trips or vacations?

What honors have you had?

Are you living in the same home, or have you moved?

How have you planned for your retirement years?

What is your social life? What activities do you prefer?

RETIREMENT YEARS

What activities interest you most?

Tell about your friends.

Which of your goals have you achieved?

What are your future plans?

What changes do you see in your lifetime that are most significant?

How do you view world events?

What is your philosophy?

What positions do you now hold?

What contributions have you made in your life to making the world a better place?

What is the most important thing a person can strive for?

How many grandchildren do you have? What are their names?

This chapter has been designed to help you assemble all the facts of your life. There are many places that are incomplete, and you will probably want to go back and fill in the holes. But this is a good beginning, and if you have listed the events somewhat chronologically, you can look back and see your life in capsule form. At least this will prove you do have something worthwhile to write.

Chapter 3

THE SKELETON OF YOUR LIFE

"I don't know how to start my third chapter," I told my friend Peg. "Books have been written on plot development and character motivation, but that doesn't apply here. Nothing has been published on how to write a memory."

"How did you write your autobiography?" Peg asked, but I ignored her.

"The techniques of short story and fiction don't apply. And no one has thought it important to tell a beginning writer how to write his memoirs."

"How did you write yours?" insisted my friend.

"Some memories are complete . . . others are fragments. How do I tell them what to include?"

"What did you include on yours?"

It came through. It finally came through.

"You mean I ought to write *my* autobiography?"

"How else?"

Sometimes the simple solutions are the most difficult. I had been fighting writing my own autobiography and had used every excuse. I even came up with a couple that I hadn't mentioned in the first chapter. But it was a good idea, and I realized that I would be able to help better if I went through the same process.

"I'll start with my high school segment," I decided. "I'll be able to give lots of examples, and it will be fun to do."

"Do you always eat the dessert first?" asked my friend.

I got the point. "You mean, if I don't start with the beginning, I might be having so much fun I won't ever go back?"

"Do you eat spinach after you've filled up on cheesecake?"

"But I can't even remember my childhood. Everything that happened before my father's death is blanked out in my mind."

"Everything?"

"Most everything."

"If you can do it with that handicap," Peg argued, "anybody can. I mean, you were born, weren't you?"

Yes, I was born, and that is where to start. So get out your segments on your early childhood, and we'll start our autobiographies together.

I looked at the information I had about my early childhood. It was almost bare. No one can write an autobiography with this scant information . . . or can they?

> I was born May 9, 1932, at the Utah Valley Hospital in Provo, Utah. I was not born twins or blue or caesarean section. In fact, the very commonness of my birth made me wonder for years if I were really an adopted child.

There. It's started. But it is stated so simply. The bare facts written in paragraph form. Have you written this far? Give the date and place of your birth and any important facts about it that you have been told . . . unless you can remember the details yourself. If you know your doctor, your christening date, and person who performed the ordinance, be sure to include that. I questioned my mother about more details and found that I had already made a mistake. I was born at the Cranes Maternity Home on Second South and University Avenue in Provo. Dad had been so delighted to have a daughter that, when I was brought into the room, he had picked me up—an unheard of thing in those days. He hadn't even been sanitized! The nurse tried to reach for me, but Dad managed to stay a couple of steps ahead of her. A small incident, but one that shows my father in a very warm way.

At this point I realized that I needed to read a few autobiographies and see what the trend was and if there was a better way of writing, "I was born."

Mark Twain writes:

> I was born the 30th of November, 1835, in the almost invisible village of Florida, Monroe County, Missouri. My parents removed to Missouri in the early thirties; I do not remember just

when for I was not born then and cared nothing for such things
. . . The home was made in the wee village of Florida, in Mon-
roe County and I was born there in 1835. The village contained
a hundred and I increased the population by one percent.[1]

As you can see, Mark Twain did not go into any detail about
his birth, and included only the date and town. We do not know
whether or not he was born at home or at a hospital, or whether
there was a doctor or midwife in attendance.

Helen Keller writes:

I was born on June 27, 1880, in Tuscumbia, a little town of
northern Alabama.

She then lists her genealogy, starting with her father's family,
her grandfather and father, and then her mother and her mother's
lineage. This takes four paragraphs, briefly summarized:

The family on my father's side is descended from Caspar Keller, a
native of Switzerland, who settled in Maryland. One of my Swiss
ancestors was the first teacher of the deaf in Zurich and wrote a
book on the subject of their education—rather a singular coinci-
dence; though it is true that there is no king who has not had a
slave among his ancestors, and no slave who has not had a king
among his.

My grandfather, Caspar Keller's son, "entered" large tracts of
land in Alabama and finally settled there. I have been told that
once a year he went from Tuscumbia to Philadelphia on horseback to purchase supplies for the plantation, and my aunt has in
her possession many of the letters to his family, which give
charming and vivid accounts of these trips.

My Grandmother Keller was a daughter of one of Lafayette's
aides, Alexander Moore, and granddaughter of Alexander Spots-
wood, an early Colonial Governor of Virginia. She was also second cousin to Robert E. Lee.

My father, Arthur H. Keller, was a captain in the Confederate
Army, and my mother, Kate Adams, was his second wife and
many years younger. Her grandfather, Benjamin Adams, married
Susanna E. Goodhue, and lived in Newbury, Massachusetts, for
many years. Their son, Charles Adams, was born in Newburyport,

[1] Mark Twain, *The Autobiography of Mark Twain*, edited by Charles Neider
(New York: Harper & Brothers, 1959), p. 1.

Massachusetts, and moved to Helena, Arkansas. When the Civil War broke out, he fought on the side of the South and became a brigadier-general. He married Lucy Helen Everett, who belonged to the same family of Everetts as Edward Everett and Dr. Edward Everett Hale. After the war was over the family moved to Memphis, Tennessee.[2]

I included Miss Keller's entire family background because it is covered so concisely. The facts that she considered important are there. She places herself in her family lineage as carefully as Mark Twain places himself in the little village of Florida.

Let me share another example: Benjamin Franklin writes his autobiography as a letter to his son. He spends some time telling of the history of his family. He studied the registers at Ecton and found that he was the youngest son of the youngest son for five generations. He talks about his grandfather who had four sons, and then discusses each one of his uncles in a separate paragraph. His father, being the last son, he lists last:

> Josiah, my father, married young, and carried his wife with three children into New England, about 1682. The conventicles having been forbidden by law, and frequently disturbed, induced some considerable men of his acquaintance to remove to that country, and he was prevailed with to accompany them with freedom. By the same wife he had four children more born there, and by a second wife ten more, in all seventeen; of which I remember thirteen sitting at one time at his table, who all grew up to be men and women, and married; I was the youngest son, and the youngest child but two, and was born in Boston, New England. My mother, the second wife, was Abiah Folger, daughter of Peter Folger, one of the first settlers of New England, of whom honorable mention is made by Cotton Mather in his church history of that country, entitled *Magnalia Christi Americana*, as "a godly, learned Englishman," if I remember the words rightly.[3]

As I read other autobiographies, I found that each statement of birth is different, as yours will be. What you decide to include is your decision.

[2] Helen Keller, *The Story of My Life* (Garden City: Doubleday & Company, Inc., 1954), pp. 23–24.
[3] Benjamin Franklin, *The Autobiography of Benjamin Franklin* (New York: Walter J. Black, 1941), pp. 10, 11.

There are some of you who have learned one language as a child and then adopted English as a second tongue. In this case, write in the language in which you are most comfortable. Few writers feel comfortable in their adopted language. One woman, only two years in the United States, was trying to write her memoirs in English and was having a most difficult time. When she wrote in Dutch she started having problems with her spoken English, and when she wrote in English she couldn't express herself easily. Others might have the same problem, and there is no rigid rule to follow. You may need to try several ways before you find the method that is right for you. You could write in the language you learned as a child and have it translated or translate it yourself later when you have your thoughts down on paper. Another alternative would be to write in English substituting foreign phrases if you don't know the English word. You may find a compromise solution that will work best for you.

Now that you have mentioned your birth and any interesting occurrences that might have happened, the time is right to set the stage or to place yourself firmly into your heritage. Readers feel more comfortable when they know where they are and the atmosphere in which they are placed. Mark Twain did this immediately with his brief description of a tiny peaceful village. He goes on to describe the village and church in more detail. Helen Keller tells how she is located on her family tree. Benjamin Franklin is very explicit in telling of his family history going back three hundred years in Ecton.

If you examine the above autobiographies, you will notice that each person placed himself neatly in a time and place. When a playwright writes a play, he first sets the scene, giving the physical properties with which to work. A movie photographer zooms in on the surroundings. A novelist describes carefully the time and place of his novel. You must do the same.

Let's start with a brief description of your house. Include the location, perhaps landmarks, if an address is unavailable, the size, and anything else that you feel is important about your home.

I lived in several houses, as I have been told, but there is only one house that I can refer to as the "family home." You might want to list all of the homes you have lived in, but a complete description of each one would be not only tedious to yourself, but also to the reader. Writing your autobiography, as in all other kinds of writing, is a matter of selection of the most important facts and details, and only you can make that choice.

You might like to write of the town where you lived, or you might prefer to tell of only one house, or even one room in that house. I have written of my home:

> My family home was located at 365 North First East, Provo, Utah, one block south of the Brigham Young University lower campus. It was a large old house with big rooms and high ceilings. Our front room held a large gas stove with the word "Heatrola" printed on the front. In the winters it was icy cold throughout the house, and it took all the will power I had to throw off the bedcovers and rush to the front of the "Heatrola" to warm myself. It was a moment of great importance and happiness when we got central heating in the house.

Now that I am born and placed in surroundings, I need to bring in the significant people in my life, just as you need to bring in the significant people in your life. This would probably include mother, father, brothers and sisters, and grandparents. But not all of them! Not yet, anyway. Choose one of them at a time and try to remember them, not as they are now, but as they were when you were younger. You have pictures to remind you of their physical appearance.

> The first memories I have of my mother were of all five of us children lined up against a wall with mustard plasters on our chests (we were all coming down with whooping cough) and mother telling us stories as she ironed.

This is only a fragmented memory, but it is a beginning. I suppose most memories include an action or happening. I always remember my mother doing something: checking out books at the library; teaching school; going places; talking to me.

> When I think back, what better way to describe my mother than to have her telling stories, because she was a master storyteller. She loved to read, and her home was always filled with books. She had her own personal collection in addition to the armsful regularly checked out from the library for herself and for us. A

trip to the grocery store included a comic book along with the milk and butter. At one time she was criticized because she allowed us children to read comic books. "The important thing is that they are reading," she answered. "And they'll want something better." She made sure that better books were always available.

A description of my mother—and yet nothing is included of her physical description. I've done it again. I've put the fun things about my mother before the obvious.

My mother is a small woman, 5'4", and slim. She walks quickly and with purpose. She has brown hair and dark brown eyes, but more important, she is always interested in me and what I am doing. Whenever anything important happened in my life, I always told Mother first because I knew she cared.

A physical description should be included, but more important is the attitude and personality of the person you are writing about:

Is she cheerful?
Does she have a strong faith in God?
Is she frugal?
How does she show her love for you?
What are her methods of discipline?
What do you remember best about her?

If this is difficult for you to get started, try writing the physical description first. Once the words start, then it is easier to continue. Try to decide upon one of the most dominant personality traits she has and, if possible, include an anecdote about that trait. In my story of my mother I include the example of her love of books.

You can see that Benjamin Franklin had great admiration and respect for his father. Notice in the following quote the adjectives he uses, "clear, pleasing voice," "sound understanding," "solid judgment" in describing his qualities:

I think you may like to know something of his person and character. He had an excellent constitution of body, was of middle stature, but well set, and very strong; he was ingenious, could draw prettily, was skilled a little in music, and had a clear pleasing voice, so that when he played psalm tunes on his violin and sung withal, as he sometimes did in an evening after the business of the day was over, it was extremely agreeable to hear. He had a mechanical genius too, and, on occasion, was very handy in the use of other tradesmen's tools; but his great excellence lay in a sound understanding and solid judgment in prudential matters, both in private and publick affairs . . . At his table he liked to have, as often as he could, some sensible friend or neighbor to converse with, and always took care to start some ingenious or useful topic for discourse, which might tend to improve the minds of his children. By this means he turned our attention to what was good, just and prudent in the conduct of life; and little or no notice was ever taken of what related to the victuals on the table, whether it was well or ill dressed, in or out of season, of good or bad flavor, preferable or inferior to this or that other thing of the kind, so that I was bro't up in such a perfect inattention to those matters as to be quite indifferent what kind of food was set before me, and so unobservant of it, that to this day if I am asked I can scarce tell a few hours after dinner what I dined upon.[4]

Mark Twain gives only a brief description of his mother:

She had a slender, small body but a large heart . . . a heart so large that everybody's grief and everybody's joys found welcome in it and hospitable accommodation . . .[5]

Actually Mark Twain describes his mother many times in different ways, none at any great length. He gives stories about her, but not a physical description. I like the following story because it tells in specific detail how his mother felt and thought:

We had a little slave boy whom we had hired from someone, there in Hannibal. He was from the eastern shore of Maryland and had been brought away from his family and his friends half-way across the American continent and sold. He was a cheery spirit, innocent and gentle, and the noisiest creature that ever was, perhaps. All day long he was singing, whistling, yelling, whooping, laughing . . . it was maddening, devastating, unen-

[4] Ibid., pp. 14, 15.
[5] Twain, op. cit., p. 25.

durable. At last, one day, I lost all my temper and went raging to my mother and said Sandy had been singing for an hour without a single break and I couldn't stand it and wouldn't she please shut him up. The tears came into her eyes and her lip trembled and she said something like this:

"Poor thing, when he sings it shows that he is not remembering and that comforts me; but when he is still I am afraid he is thinking and I cannot bear it. He will never see his mother again; if he can sing I must not hinder it, but be thankful for it. If you were older you would understand me; then that friendless child's noise would make you glad."

It was a simple speech and made up of small words, but it went home, and Sandy's noise was not a trouble to me any more. She never used large words but she had a natural gift for making small ones do effective work. She lived to reach the neighborhood of ninety years and was capable with her tongue to the last . . . especially when a meanness or an injustice roused her spirit.[6]

There are other important people in your childhood: a strong-willed grandmother, an aunt with a pantry of cookies, a cousin who listened to you when you needed to talk, a younger brother whom you alternately resented and confided in. Your list is growing, but be particular whom you choose or you will have a book filled with nothing but character sketches. I would include only two or three at first and then, when incidents occur involving a brother, sister, or friend, you can briefly describe him.

Helen Keller writes about her father:

My earliest distinct recollection of my father is making my way through great drifts of newspapers to his side and finding him alone, holding a sheet of paper before his face. I was greatly puzzled to know what he was doing. I imitated this action, even wearing his spectacles, thinking they might help solve the mystery. But I did not find out the secret for several years. Then I learned what those papers were, and that my father edited one of them.

My father was most loving and indulgent, devoted to his home, seldom leaving us, except in the hunting season. He was a great hunter, I have been told, and a celebrated shot. Next to his family he loved his dogs and gun. His hospitality was great, almost to

[6] Ibid., pp. 5–6.

a fault, and he seldom came home without bringing a guest. His special pride was the big garden where, it was said, he raised the finest watermelons and strawberries in the county; and to me he brought the first ripe grapes and the choicest berries. I remember his caressing touch as he led me from tree to tree, from vine to vine, and his eager delight in whatever pleased me.[7]

Have you noticed how each one describes the person in relationship to himself. Benjamin Franklin discusses the way his father taught him about the values of life and stimulated him in public affairs; Mark Twain tells about his mother and how her words touched him and made him more tolerant; and Helen Keller tells about her close relationship with her father and how he gave her special favors.

Actually this section has not been difficult to write. I have only three brief stories to use in addition to what I have already written. But how many more memories everyone else must have! As I look ahead to my school years, I realize how many stories and memories need to be included. What I really need is an outline. The list written on colored paper has not been put in order. There are no restrictions on what I have remembered, but I can see now that if I gave a complete accounting of every memory, and all the stories in my life, my autobiography could become a many-volumed book. At the moment it is a wondrous kaleidoscope of the past.

In every other writing that I have done, I have had to choose the best examples. I didn't allow every image and description. I very carefully selected the best examples and details. Too many descriptions distorted what I wanted to say. Wasn't it the same with my own story? How could I select and organize my story best?

"It's easy," said my neighbor, who wrote her autobiography in three typewritten pages. "Just write everything chronologically." But I couldn't remember for sure what I did at any specific age and even if it were very important.

I needed something to organize my outline, something more than chronological events, although I don't dismiss chronological events as being unnecessary, only as being inadequate.

[7] Keller, op. cit., pp. 30–31.

Helen Keller was aware of this problem, along with others, and she was of some help to me at this point. She said:

> It is with a kind of fear that I begin to write the history of my life. I have, as it were, a superstitious hesitation in lifting the veil that clings about my childhood like a golden mist. The task of writing an autobiography is a difficult one. When I try to classify my earliest impressions, I find that fact and fancy look alike across the years that link the past with the present. The woman paints the child's experiences in her own fantasy. A few impressions stand out vividly from the first years of my life; but "the shadows of the prison-house are on the rest." Besides, many of the joys and sorrows of childhood have lost their poignancy; and many incidents of vital importance in my early education have been forgotten, in the excitement of great discoveries. In order, therefore, not to be tedious I shall try to present in a series of sketches only the *episodes that seem to me to be the most interesting and important.*[8]

I studied the autobiography of Mark Twain and discovered that he didn't know how to organize his autobiography. He tried to write it many different ways. He seemed overwhelmed by the immensity of the task of writing and mentioned several times that it would be many volumes. Charles Neider wrote of him in the introduction to the *Autobiography* that "Perhaps if he had lived a few years longer, he would have found a sufficient perspective to organize the Autobiography and edit out of it all the irrelevant materials which his odd methods of composition had allowed to sneak in."[9]

Mark Twain writes his philosophy several different ways, but this theory seems to be one of the guiding forces:

> . . . I told him the whole scheme of this autobiography and its apparently systemless system . . . only apparently systemless, for it is not that. It is a system which follows no chartered course and is not going to follow any such course. It is a system which is a complete and purposed jumble . . . a course which begins nowhere, follows no specified route, and can never reach an end while I am alive . . .[10]

[8] Ibid., p. 23. (Author's italics.)
[9] Twain, op. cit., p. xv.
[10] Ibid., p. xii.

I suppose Mark Twain understood his scheme, but it seemed aimless and haphazard to me. I needed something with more direction.

Benjamin Franklin came closer to giving a writing plan. When he was sixty-five years old, in 1771, he took a short vacation at the country home of Bishop Jonathon Shipley. It was during this time that he penned eighty-six closely written pages of his autobiography covering the first twenty-four years of his life.

Before he started, however, he wrote an outline of his projected autobiography. It was what he felt would be the highlights of his life. It was systematically thought out and probably carefully followed because a line is drawn through the middle of the first page to the words, "Library erected . . . manner of conducting the project . . . its plan and utility." This ends the first section of his autobiography. It probably means that he followed his outline and marked his notes where he would next begin.

His outline is simple, usually written in nouns or subject matter, although occasionally he writes in complete sentences. It was written as a reminder to him and he decided in advance what would be included. Following is a sample of how his outline appears:

> My writing. Mrs. Dogood's letters. Differences arise between my Brother and me (his temper and mine); their cause in general. His Newspaper. The Prosecution he suffered. My Examination. Vote of Assembly. His manner of evading it. Whereby I became free. My attempt to get employ with other Printers. He prevents me. Our frequent pleadings before our Father. The final breach. My Inducements to quit Boston. Manner of coming to a Resolution . . .[11]

Benjamin Franklin never finished his autobiography. He died completing only two thirds of his outline and covering his life to the age of fifty-one. He never completes the important time in his life in which he served as one of the political leaders of our country. Nor does he tell us his part of the writing of the Declaration of Independence. Many of the notations in his outline lead us to wonder what he would have said, such as, "King of Denmark in-

[11] Franklin, Benjamin, *Autobiography of Benjamin Franklin* (New York: Everymans Library, Dutton, 1948), p. 1.

vites me to dinner. Recollect my Father's Proverb. Stamp Act. My opposition to it." These were important times in his life, perhaps turning points.

That's it! The answer. Turning points!

What are turning points? I thought back in my life. There was a pattern. Everything went along smoothly for long periods of time, and then, when I was lulled into complacency, something came along and forced a change. One of the following may have been a turning point for you:

> I lived in one house all my life and suddenly the family moves. A sudden change! I don't walk the same way to the grocery store; I must seek out new friends; I have new teachers. Everything is different. It is a turning point!
>
> I am on the school ground on the teeter-totter. The school bell rings, and I jump off suddenly. My friend bumps to the ground and becomes angry. He takes after me and I run. A turning point. I must live the rest of my school days with the title "coward." And every bully has to prove my title.
>
> I run into the street and am hit by a car. My running days are stopped . . . at least for a time. In my cast and bandages I discover books and a land of my own imagination. My life has changed.
>
> I lose a quarter which I need to buy a birthday present. I decide to test God and see if He answers prayers.
>
> My mother objects to the crowd I'm going with. Whichever way I choose is a turning point . . . away from my mother, or from my friends.
>
> Death in a family, financial reverses or successes, school failures or successes, finding or losing a friend . . . all these are turning points.

Not all turning points are positive. But they aren't all negative either. Because of the choices you have made or which have been forced upon you, this is where you are today.

There are many turning points in each person's life. Some are big and dramatic and others may not seem as big, but they still change your life. I started talking about turning points in the lives of my friends and family and discovered the excitement they felt as they remembered back.

"I remember when I was three," said one person. "We moved from a mining town to the city. It was a big change in my life."

"When I was in first grade I hated my teacher," recalls another. "I was failing first grade because I refused to do anything for her. My father had to go to the superintendent of schools to get me transferred."

"When I entered junior high, all the popular girls banded together. They decided to exclude me from their group, and I was forced to find new friends. It was a traumatic moment to be told I wasn't good enough. I have spent my life trying to prove that I wasn't worthless."

By choosing the turning points in your life, you are giving direction to your autobiography and selecting the most important, decision-making times. You may want to add other events in your life, a few of the plateaus or quiet times, but each plateau is thrust forward by the changes and choices you make.

Usually there are not as many turning points in your early childhood years as there are later on. Most of the turning points during these years are forced upon you in the form of a move, an illness, or a death.

In my life the first turning point that I remember was the murder of my father, a traveling salesman, who was killed by a hitchhiker when I was eight years old. It meant not only the loss of one of my parents, but moving to a new home in a new city, new friends, my mother leaving the home to work, my grandmother stepping into my mother's role, and the hours and days that I spent at the murder trial. It was such a dramatic and sudden change that I forgot almost everything that happened before that time.

How do you go about writing about your turning points? How much do you say? Of course, a lot depends on how much you remember and how old you were. If you were three years old and you moved from one city to another, there isn't too much you can say about it. Ideally, your story would include:

1. A summary of conditions. How things look in the plateau state.
2. Events as they lead up to the change.
3. What actually happens.
4. How it affects your life.

The four basic areas are only a suggestion to help organize your story. The turning point in my life, as I have mentioned, was the death of my father. To show you the various steps it takes, I'll outline my story for you.

I. Background
    1. My father was a traveling salesman in southern Utah.
    2. He had a wife and five children living in Salt Lake City. I was the oldest of the children.
    3. This was to be his last trip selling. He was going to start his own business.

II. Rising Action
    4. In March 1940, police tried to stop a car which ran a red light in Salt Lake, but the man panicked and a high-speed chase followed.
    5. Police discovered the car belonged to my father, but the man who was driving the car was Donald Condit.
    6. There was blood in the car.
    7. Donald Condit confessed to the murder of my father.

III. The Event
    8. The police informed my mother, and our lives were changed.
    9. Mother moved from Salt Lake to Provo and took a job at the Provo City Library.
    10. Mother took all of the children to the trial, which turned out to be a long, drawn-out affair.

IV. Analysis
    11. The change in each one of our lives was affected by the death of my father.
    12. How I feel about the turning point as seen now.

If you have written one of your turning points, ask yourself the following questions:

1. Do you have all the facts?
2. Are they accurate?
3. Do they follow in order?
4. Why is this a turning point in your life?

There will be many turning points in your life. By writing the first one, you are learning the basic form, and you are time-removed from the event, which makes it easier to be objective. Emotional events that have occurred within the last year or two, such as death or divorce, are more difficult to handle.

Although at times areas overlap, I believe it is quite easy to fit Helen Keller's story into an outline. I have numbered the paragraphs for clarity. You may want to look at the outline first and then read the excerpt from Helen Keller. Compare the two. Notice how she writes about the turning point in her life.

I. Summary or background material
   #1 paragraph: Telling about the day Anne Sullivan came.
   #2 paragraph: Feeling that a change was about to take place.
   #3 paragraph: Feeling footsteps. Anne Sullivan holding her close.
II. Events leading to change
   #4 paragraph: Anne Sullivan writes in Helen's hand. Introduction of doll.
   #5 paragraph: Words "doll," "mug," and "water." Helen's frustration.
   #6 paragraph: Helen's frustration is shown by the breaking of the doll.
III. What actually happens? The Event
   #7 paragraph: Water runs over her hand and Helen realizes that water has a name.
IV. How it affects your life
   #8 paragraph: Realization that everything has a name. The beginning of repentance and feeling for others.

The problem with giving examples from published writers is that you see only the finished work. You don't see the first draft with its fragmented sentences, crossed-out words, and added paragraphs. And so you write your words and realize how amateurish yours sounds. First writing never sounds as good as material that has been polished, but you need a first draft before you even worry about anything more.

You will not want to write each story the same way, but as you write each one, you will discover that when you add details, the outline will flesh out and each story will be as different as people are different.

Helen Keller writes about the turning point in her life:

1. The most important day I remember in all my life is the one on which my teacher, Anne Mansfield Sullivan, came to me. I am filled with wonder when I consider the immeasurable contrasts between the two lives which it connects. It was the third of March, 1887, three months before I was seven years old.

2. On the afternoon of that eventful day, I stood on the porch, dumb, expectant. I guessed vaguely from my mother's signs and from the hurrying to and fro in the house that something unusual was about to happen, so I went to the door and waited on the steps . . .

3. . . . I felt approaching footsteps. I stretched out my hand as I supposed to my mother. Someone took it, and I was caught up and held close in the arms of her who had come to reveal all things to me, and, more than all things else, to love me.

4. The morning after my teacher came she led me into her room and gave me a doll. The little blind children at the Perkins Institution had sent it and Laura Birdgman had dressed; but I did not know this until afterward. When I had played with it a little while, Miss Sullivan slowly spelled into my hand the word "d-o-l-l." I was at once interested in this finger play and tried to imitate it. When I finally succeeded in making the letters correctly I was flushed with childish pleasure and pride. Running downstairs to my mother I held up my hand and made the letters for doll. I did not know that I was spelling a word or even that words existed; I was simply making my fingers go in monkey-like imitation. In the days that followed I learned to spell in this uncomprehending way a great many words, among them pin, hat, cup and a few verbs like sit, stand and walk. But my teacher had been with me several weeks before I understood that everything has a name.

5. One day, while I was playing with my new doll, Miss Sullivan put my big rag doll into my lap also, spelled "doll" and tried to make me understand that "doll" applied to both. Earlier in the day we had had a tussle over the words "mug" and "water." Miss Sullivan had tried to impress it upon me that

"mug" is mug and that "water" is water, but I persisted in confounding the two. In despair she had dropped the subject for the time, only to renew it at the first opportunity. I became impatient at her repeated attempts and, seizing the new doll, I dashed it upon the floor. I was keenly delighted when I felt the fragments of the broken doll at my feet. Neither sorrow nor regret followed my passionate outburst. I had not loved the doll. In the still, dark world in which I lived there was no strong sentiment or tenderness. I felt my teacher sweep the fragments to one side of the hearth, and I had a sense of satisfaction that the cause of my discomfort was removed. She brought me my hat, and I knew I was going out into the warm sunshine. This thought, if a wordless sensation may be called a thought, made me hop and skip with pleasure.

7. We walked down the path to the well-house, attracted by the fragrance of the honeysuckle with which it was covered. Someone was drawing water and my teacher placed my hand under the spout. As the cool stream gushed over one hand she spelled into the other the word water, first slowly, then rapidly. I stood still, my whole attention fixed upon the motions of her fingers. Suddenly I felt a misty consciousness as of something forgotten . . . a thrill of returning thought; and somehow the mystery of language was revealed to me. I knew then that "w-a-t-e-r" meant that wonderful cool something that was flowing over my hand. That living word awakened my soul, gave it light, hope, joy, set it free! There were barriers still, it is true, but barriers that could in time be swept away.

8. I left the well-house eager to learn. Everything had a name and each name gave birth to a new thought. As we returned to the house every object which I touched seemed to quiver with life. That was because I saw everything with the strange, new sight that had come to me. On entering the door I remembered the doll I had broken. I felt my way to the hearth and picked up the pieces. I tried vainly to put them together. Then my eyes filled with tears; for I realized what I had done, and for the first time I felt repentance and sorrow.[12]

Decide on a turning point in your life, preferably your first. Gather the material you have. If it is possible, organize it into the four basic areas:

[12] Keller, op. cit., pp. 35-37.

1. Background
2. Rising action
3. The event
4. Analysis

Sometimes the areas will overlap; other times you may not be able to include them all. You have to decide where the most emphasis should be.

Benjamin Franklin tells a story of his youth when he was ten years old:

1. I disliked the trade [of candlemaking] and had a strong inclination for the sea, but my father declared against it; however, living near the water, I was much in and about it, learnt early to swim well, and to manage boats; and when in a boat or canoe with other boys, I was commonly allowed to govern, especially in any case of difficulty; and upon other occasions I was generally a leader among the boys, and sometimes led them into scrapes, of which I will mention one instance, as it shows an early projecting public spirit, tho' not then justly conducted.

2. There was a salt-marsh that bounded part of the millpond, on the edge of which, at high water, we used to stand to fish for minnows. By much tramping, we had made it a mere quagmire. My proposal was to build a wharff there fit for us to stand upon, and I showed my comrades a large heap of stones, which were intended for a new house near the marsh, and which would very well suit our purpose.

3. Accordingly, in the evening, when the workmen were gone, I assembled a number of my play-fellows, and working with them diligently like so many emmets, sometimes two or three to a stone, we brought them all away and built our little wharff.

4. The next morning the workmen were surprised at missing the stones, which were found in our wharff. Inquiry was made after the removers; we were discovered and complained of; several of us were corrected by our fathers; and, though I pleaded the usefulness of the work, mine convinced me that nothing was useful which was not honest.[13]

13 Franklin (Walter J. Black, ed.), pp. 13–14.

The following section from Mark Twain is quite humorous, but still is written using the suggested outline. As you can see, each writer has his own style, which hides the practical outline. Generally speaking, each paragraph fits one section of the outline:

In the autumn my sister gave a party and invited all the marriageable young people of the village. I was too young for this society and was too bashful to mingle with young ladies, anyway, therefore I was not invited . . . at least not for the whole evening. Ten minutes of it was to be my whole share. I was to do the part of a bear in a small fairy play. I was to be disguised all over in a close-fitting brown hairy stuff proper for a bear. About half past ten I was told to go to my room and put on this disguise and be ready in half an hour. I started but changed my mind, for I wanted to practice a little and that room was very small. I crossed over to the large unoccupied house on the corner of Main Street, unaware that a dozen of the young people were also going there to dress for their parts. I took the little black boy, Sandy, with me and we selected a roomy and empty chamber on the second floor. We entered it talking and this gave a couple of half-dressed young ladies an opportunity to take refuge behind a screen undiscovered. Their gowns and things were hanging on hooks behind the door but I did not see them; it was Sandy that shut the door but all his heart was in the theatricals and he was unlikely to notice them as I was myself.

There was a rickety screen with many holes in it but as I did not know there were girls behind it I was not disturbed by that detail. If I had known, I could not have undressed in the flood of cruel moonlight that was pouring in at the curtainless windows; I should have died of shame. Untroubled by apprehensions, I stripped to the skin and began my practicing. I was full of ambition, I was determined to make a hit, I was burning to establish a reputation as a bear and get further engagements; so I threw myself into my work with an abandon that promised great things. I capered back and forth from one end of the room to the other on all fours, Sandy applauding with enthusiasm; I walked upright and growled and snapped and snarled, I stood on my head, I flung handsprings, I danced a lubberly dance with my paws bent and my imaginary snout sniffing from side to side, I did everything a bear could do and many things which no bear could ever do and no bear with any dignity would want to do, anyway; and of course I never suspected that I was making a spectacle of myself to anyone but Sandy. At last, standing on my head, I paused in that attitude to take a minute's rest. There was a moment's silence, then Sandy spoke up with excited interest and said:

"Mars Sam, has you ever seed a dried herring?"

"No. What is that?"

"It's a fish."

"Well, what of it? Anything peculiar about it?"

"Yes, suh, you bet you dey is. Dey eats 'em innards and all!"

There was a smothered burst of feminine snickers from behind the screen! All the strength went out of me and I toppled forward like an undermined tower and brought the screen down with my weight, burying the young ladies under it. In their fright they discharged a couple of piercing screams . . . and possibly others . . . but I did not wait to count. I snatched my clothes and fled to the dark hall below, Sandy following. I was dressed in half a minute and out the back way. I swore Sandy to eternal silence, then we went away and could not have faced that giddy company after my adventure, for there would be two performers there who knew my secret and would be privately laughing at me all the time. I was searched for but not found, and the bear had to be played by a young gentleman in his civilized clothes. The house was still and everybody asleep when I finally ventured home. I was very heavy-hearted and full of a bitter sense of disgrace. Pinned to my pillow I found a slip of paper which bore a line which did not lighten my heart but only made my face burn. It was written in a laboriously disguised hand and these were its mocking terms:

You probably couldn't have played bear but you played bare very well . . . oh, very very well!

. . . I suffered miserably over that episode. I expected that the facts would be all over the village in the morning but it was not so. The secret remained confined to the two girls and Sandy and me. That was some appeasement of my pain but it was far from sufficient . . . the main trouble remained: I was under four mocking eyes and it might as well have been a thousand, for I suspected all girls' eyes of being the ones I so dreaded. During several weeks I could not look any young lady in the face; I dropped my eyes in confusion when any one of them smiled upon me and gave me greeting: I said to myself, "That is one of them" and got quickly away. Of course I was meeting the right girls everywhere but if they ever let slip any betraying sign I was not bright enough to catch it. When I left Hannibal four years later the secret was still a secret; I had never guessed those girls out and was no longer hoping or expecting to do it.[14]

Basic Structure of Your Autobiography

At this point it sounds as if there is only one way you can write your autobiography and that is by starting with your birth and proceeding systematically from one turning point to the next in chronological order until you reach the now of your life.

Although this is the easiest and most common structure it is by no means the only way to proceed. It is not a set rule to start at the beginning. Many authors have chosen a turning point in their lives and filled in their backgrounds as flashbacks. Most of them have included their birth, parents and background as instructed in this chapter, but this information may come at any spot in the book. Doris Schwerin uses this technique in her *Diary of a Pigeon Watcher*. She chooses to start her book at the present turning point as she is recovering from an operation for breast cancer. As she is trying to put her life into perspective she uses flashbacks into her past.

Each individual flashback is a complete episode in her life structured with a beginning, middle and ending as outlined in this chapter, but the episodes don't necessarily follow in their natural sequence. Ms. Schwerin always returns to the present to remind the reader that her stories are memories of the past being used to help her find herself in the present.

[14] Twain, op. cit., pp. 38–39.

Chapter 4

ADDING THE DETAILS

The facts are down. The bones are gathered. The turning points in your life have been listed chronologically. You are ready now to flesh out your material.

In the book, *The Writer's Guide and Index to English,* the author says:

> The principal weakness of amateur writing is in not presenting enough details, failure to bring forth enough particulars to make the subject clear, convincing, and interesting. A little time spent in consideration before writing to bring into mind people, things, incidents, anything specific that belongs to the subject will make the writing easier and will do more than anything else to bring the reader to an understanding of the subject.[1]

Concrete details are word pictures of things that can be seen and touched. The more specific you can get, the closer your reader can see as you do. "Lemonade" is more specific than "drink"; "Uncle Charles" is more specific than "man" or even "uncle"; "weeping willow" is more specific than "tree."

The image of an old flower is not as specific as a dried carnation. You can get even more specific if you use the phrase, "There was a dried corsage that might have been a carnation, but it crumbled all over the floor when I picked it up." This is a concrete detail. "Dried corsage," "carnation," "crumbled on the floor" are all images that can be seen and felt. The implied image is there too, a memory from the past, a special occasion, celebrated with a corsage.

Many children had a dog when they were young. The word "dog" doesn't evoke any visual images. The terms "cocker span-

[1] Porter G. Perrin (New York: Scott, Foresman and Company, 1950), p. 174.

iel," "poodle," "German shepherd," or "mutt" give more. When you start to give the details of the dog, then you are able to give a better visual image.

> Most people would not say "Uncle" was a beautiful dog. He was a mutt of many varieties, mostly cocker. He held his long plumed tail high in the air like a skunk when he ran, and one eye was blind as a result of his chasing one too many cars. Whenever any member of the family came home he went into an act; he howled in a treble voice and ran around the yard, his tail waving a flag of truce and we knew that he was happy we were home. We always thought he was a most handsome animal.

Add the details up and you will have a visual image of one dog: a halfbreed mutt with a blind eye, a tail that is raised in the air like a skunk, and a treble-voiced bark—a beautiful dog only to a very biased owner.

In Chapter 3 my family home is described: "It was a large old house with big rooms and high ceilings . . ." This sentence is generalized. No pictures come to mind. It could be any old house . . . a castle, a barn, a modern home with open beams. It gives no picture at all. There are many questions that need to be answered. Check the description of your family home and see if you are specific or generalized.

1. How old is the house?
2. What are the building materials and color?
3. What is the style?
4. What made it different from the house next door?

It may not be important to you to include this in your writing, but as a practice in using concrete details, it could be valuable.

"My family home was built in about 1900, a large brick house, painted white."

This gives a better idea of its outward appearance, and in word length isn't much longer than the original.

The second part of the description says: ". . . big rooms and high ceilings." How big are the rooms? You could give dimensions, but unless you think in yards and feet, you still don't have a visual image. You could describe the size of the room by showing things that were done in the room, and you have not only given size, but purpose.

The rooms were so big that every Christmas Eve we would set up four card tables and matching chairs and not have to move any furniture out. In the kitchen we could serve a sit-down dinner for thirty people.

Now for the ceilings. How high are they?

The ceilings were so high we had to climb to the fourth rung of the ladder once a year to clean them with pink wallpaper cleaner that crumbled in our hands.

The secret in writing detail is to become more observant. Look at your shoes. They are not merely shoes; they are dirty tennis sneakers, pumps, clods, oxfords, sandals, or galoshes. The ring on your finger is a diamond, a turquoise, a gold wedding band, or a five-and-dime special that turns your finger green. As you remember back, try to remember specifics instead of general terms.

It is interesting in the story from Helen Keller that Anne Sullivan teaches the generalized word first. In the selection used earlier we see that the general words "doll" and "water" are the first ones understood by Helen Keller.

But she is aware of differences and specifics long before she knew there were names for them. She mentions specifically:

Even in the days before my teacher came, I used to feel along the square stiff boxwood hedges and, guided by the sense of smell, would find the first violets and lilies. There, too, after a fit of temper, I went to find comfort and to hide my hot face in the cool leaves and grass. What joy it was to lose myself in that garden of flowers, to wander happily from spot to spot, until, coming suddenly upon a beautiful vine, I recognized it by its leaves and blossoms, and knew it was the vine which covered the tumble-down summer-house at the farther end of the garden![2]

Using All Our Senses

One time I attended the lecture of a noted poet. After the lecture I watched him as he walked across the campus. He stopped by a tree and touched a leaf. He rubbed the leaf between his fingers and smelled it. He touched the bark, stood in the shade of

[2] Keller, *The Story of My Life*, p. 24.

the tree and looked up through the branches. It was the first time
I was aware of someone enjoying and using the sense of touch and
smell and sight. We take them for granted.

Helen Keller uses the sense of touch and smell in describing the
garden. She is more aware, perhaps, than most people, of the importance of using all of the senses:

> People who think that all sensations reach us through the eye and
> the ear have expressed surprise that I should notice any
> difference, except possibly the absence of pavements, between
> walking in city streets and in country roads. They forget that my
> whole body is alive to the conditions about me. The rumble and
> roar of the city smite the nerves of my face, and I feel the cease-
> less tramp of an unseen multitude, and the dissonant tumult frets
> my spirit. The grinding of heavy wagons on hard pavements and
> the monotonous clamour of machines are all the more torturing
> to the nerves if one's attention is not diverted by the panorama
> that is always present in the noisy streets to people who can see.[3]

We need to use the five senses in our writing. It makes our
writing vivid and real. We want our readers to feel the same way
we did when we experienced it. But we must do it with words.
The secret is to use sensory words, which are only details as experienced through one or more of the senses. Too many writers use
only one of the senses . . . that of sight. And although sight is important, you must not forget the senses of sound, smell, taste, and
touch. Without at least one of these five senses, no human or ani-
mal could survive.

You need to get into the habit of using all of your senses more.
Go back over what you have written and see if you are using only
one of the senses. Make a conscious effort to incorporate all of the
senses into your writing.

In the description of the dog, "Uncle," I use the sense of sight
(long-plumed tail, blind eye) and sound (his treble bark). If I
were to include all the senses I could have mentioned how he
licked our hands, leaving an odor of liver dog food, and the touch
of his coarse golden coat, but I doubt I could use the sense of
taste without stretching my imagination. You don't have to use

[3] Keller, op. cit., p. 103.

all the senses in every writing, only be aware of them and what
they can do for you.

Mark Twain uses the sense of sound in his story of the slave
boy in Chapter 3. He uses the words "cheery spirit, noisiest creature, singing, whistling, yelling, whooping, laughing, lost his
temper, raging."

Let's go back to the story of the turning point in my life, my father's death, and start putting details in the story. By using details
and as many of the senses as I can, I will try to show instead of
tell the story. As it is written in Chapter 3, it is no more than an
outline. I could leave it as it is, but my story is not complete. By
adding details, I am completing the picture, as I remember it. I
must keep it from ending until I have included all the significant
details. If I leave too many details out, or if I include too many,
then my picture will be distorted.

First of all, I need to set the scene, let you know what the situation was, the plateau, peaceful condition of our life before the
event happened:

> This was to be my father's last trip! He was going to have his
> own business and never have to travel again. I knew that made
> Mother happy, because she smiled all the time now. I looked up
> at him, past the long legs, and wondered if he would be able to
> play with me more if he were home longer.
>
> Six-year-old Joyce and five-year-old Mary Lou played hide-and-
> go-seek around his legs, but I was too old for that. Daddy sold
> jams and jellies to stores in southern Utah. We had more straw-
> berry jam than anyone in all of Salt Lake, I thought.
>
> The year before Joyce and I went with Daddy on one of his
> trips. I remember that it was so hot my crayons had melted to-
> gether in the back window. Daddy had been cross, because the
> crayons had made a drippy mess in his brand new car. I also
> remember the Indians sitting in the shade by the old stores. I had
> jumped the rope for one old Indian, and he had laughed and it
> sounded like a drum rumbling in his fat belly. I think Daddy
> knew everyone we saw and they knew him.
>
> Daddy sat down and picked up three-year-old Jimmy and two-
> year-old Sally and bounced them on his knee. I sat quietly by him
> and held onto Sally, so she wouldn't fall. I was eight years old

and figured I knew more about baby-sitting than Daddy did. Through the blue serge suit pants, I felt his strong legs. I didn't know it then, but I would remember his legs longer than his face, or his smile, or his voice. My friend Dale, from next door, and I had had arguments several times on the subject of "dads." I had conceded that maybe his father was probably stronger, but mine could run faster.

Dad stood up. All I could see were his legs. "I'll call you from Cedar City," he said and hugged us all. "It's the last time I'll be going away." And he was gone.

Check back and see if everything that was in the outline is included. Actually I had forgotten to mention that he was going into business for himself and had to go back and add it. Have I used all the senses?

Sound—The Indian laughing, my father's voice
Taste—strawberry jam
Touch—feeling his legs, holding onto Sally
Sight—Crayons, Mother smiling, hide-and-go-seek
Smell—I goofed. I could have added that the sagebrush smell tickled my nose, or the dust of the desert made me scrunch down and wish I could smell rain or grass instead.

Specifics or Generalities

There are other questions you can ask yourself. Have you written in specifics or used generalities? As I go back over my writing, I see that I have used the word "car." Inasmuch as the car is very important to the entire story, I should be more specific: "dark blue four-door Dodge with light gray upholstery," should have been used instead of simply "car." As I was describing my trip to southern Utah the year earlier, I could have also mentioned how lonely it was on the road and how few cars we saw on the desert. These are clues that I should give early in the story.

It is easy for generalities to slip through, and sometimes it is better to use the general term. Try to be more aware of which you are using, and why.

Benjamin Franklin often makes a general statement and then illustrates it with detail:

> *general statement:* We have an English proverb that says, "He that would thrive, must ask his wife." It was lucky for me that I had one as much dispos'd to industry and frugality as myself. She assisted me cheerfully in my business, folding and stitching pamphlets, tending shop, purchasing old linen rags for the papermakers, etc., etc. We kept no idle servants, our table was plain and simple, our furniture of the cheapest.
>
> *specific example:* For instance, my breakfast was a long time bread and milk (no tea), and I ate it out of a twopenny earthen porringer, with a pewter spoon. But mark how luxury will enter families, and make a progress, in spite of principle: being call'd one morning to breakfast, I found it in a China bowl, with a spoon of silver! They had been bought for me without my knowledge by my wife, and had cost her the enormous sum of three-and-twenty shillings, for which she had no other excuse or apology to make, but that she thought her husband deserv'd a silver spoon and China bowl as well as any of his neighbors. This was the first appearance of plate and China in our house, which afterward, in a course of years, as our wealth increas'd, augmented gradually to several hundred pounds in value.[4]

Word Details Lead to Example Details

Mark Twain describes his village and church in specific detail. Note the two ways he uses detail:

> The village had two streets, each a couple of hundred yards long; the rest of the avenues mere lanes, with rail-fences and cornfields on either side. Both the streets and the lanes were paved with the same material . . . tough black mud in wet times, deep dust in dry.
>
> Most of the houses were of logs . . . all of them, indeed, except three or four; these latter were frame ones. There were none of brick and none of stone. There was a log church with a puncheon floor and slab benches. A puncheon floor is made of logs whose upper surfaces have been chipped flat with the adz.

[4] Franklin, *Autobiography*, pp. 125, 126.

The cracks between the logs were not filled; there was no carpet; consequently, if you dropped anything smaller than a peach it was likely to go through. The church was perched upon short sections of logs, which elevated it two or three feet from the ground. Hogs slept under there, and whenever the dogs got after them during services the minister had to wait till the disturbance was over. In winter there was always a refreshing breeze up through the puncheon floor; in summer there were fleas enough for all.[5]

Mark Twain uses two types of details: those that show specific words, and those that give examples. He usually uses them one after another. He describes the floor, how it was made, and how it looked and then he gives an example of what happened if you dropped anything smaller than a peach. He explains that the church was built of logs, which elevated it two or three feet off the ground, and then he gives the example of the hogs sleeping underneath and the dogs getting after them.

In Chapter 3 I talk about a large gas heater: "Our front room held a large gas heater with the words 'Heatrola' printed on the front. In the winters it was icy cold throughout the house, and it took all the will power I had to throw off the bedcovers and rush to the front of the 'Heatrola' to warm myself . . ." If I were to add an example the way Mark Twain does, I would add:

One morning when the thermometer hit zero outside, I stood closer to the old stove than usual. I smelled something burning and quickly moved away. Too late. I discovered the word "Heatrola" branded on the back of my flannel nightgown.

You can add detail through concrete words or by using an example.

Time Controls

In writing your story, time controls many of the details you will use. As events happen, or as you remember them happening, you add detail upon detail in a chronological way.

I cheated in my story of my father, by using a brief flashback to the year earlier in the previous trip with him. I did it this way for

[5] Twain, *Autobiography*, p. 1.

two reasons: (1) the memory of the previous trip was so short it wouldn't stand on its own as a complete story; (2) it reinforced the type of work my father did, and the desolation of the country my father traveled.

If you were to take out the third paragraph, then the story would be chronologically correct, but not as rich in background detail.

Usually the best way of writing is to use the past-tense verb. "Said," "went," "was," "wondered," "sold" are all verbs from my story of my father.

Although the motion of your story must move forward to a climax or conclusion, you may want to flash back briefly to a background bit of information, such as I did. If your flashback is too long, the reader will become confused. Make sure the flashback is appropriate and applicable at that point. Too many flashbacks in any particular story should warn you to go back and check your outline. Perhaps you should begin the story at a different point.

Time Remembered or Time Re-created

You can write your autobiography as time remembered or as time re-created. Usually, time remembered is summarized memories and time re-created is dramatized memories.

The description of the house is remembered memories. Helen Keller's description of her father and Mark Twain's description of his mother are also time remembered.

In the story of my father, I use both methods. I start out writing as if I were there at that time. This is time re-created. Then, when I use the flashback paragraph about the trip I had taken the year earlier with my father, I use the time-remembered technique. Helen Keller uses time remembered in her story about the realization of words. Mark Twain uses a combination of both techniques in his bear story.

It is not difficult to do. Actually, it is only another way of giving a detail and then making it live through example. You try to "show" the story, instead of telling about it. Instead of summarizing what you want to say, you present it dramatically, trying to show it as it happened. The next section, in writing of my father, is the story of his actual death. Inasmuch as no one was there to witness this except my father and his murderer, Donald Condit, it is more honest to merely summarize it as it unfolded for us at his trial. If the story were being written for a cheap detective magazine or for one of the endless police TV shows, this section would be dramatized to the point of soap-opera explicitness. However, for my purpose, it is better to summarize the events rather than present them dramatically.

> Three days later, on March 21, 1940, at 3:00 A.M., a dark blue four-door Dodge ran a red light in Salt Lake City, and police signaled it to a stop. The driver panicked, and a high-speed chase followed.
> The driver was a young man, Donald Condit, a twenty-five-year-old, paroled convict from San Quentin. He was driving my father's car. Blood stains on the light gray upholstery caused the police to investigate and question Condit. Condit confessed to the murder of my father the next day, and he led the police back to the shallow grave in the southern Utah desert.

Some of the details had been used earlier in the story, the color and style of the car (remember, I had to go back and add it in), and the color of the upholstery. I use them again to establish Condit's guilt. Except for a description of Condit, my details are sparse. I am mostly concerned with the facts at this point.

Miser or Spendthrift

Have you used too many details? Some writers go off on a tangent giving thoughts that distract rather than those that add to the main thought. I could have used more detail. I could have given the physical description of Condit, a more complete history of Condit's confession, details of the murder. I chose to leave this out, at least for now. Earlier in the story I could have given a description of my brother and my sisters, but I chose to wait. Another tangent is my discussion with my friend Dale about the qualities of fathers. I used it as an irony because, no matter how fast my father could run, he wasn't able to outrun a bullet.

The following excerpt from Mark Twain shows how he went on a tangent in his writing:

It was a heavenly place for a boy, that farm of my Uncle John's. The house was a double log one, with a spacious floor (roofed in) connecting it with the kitchen. In the summer the table was set in the middle of the shady and breezy floor, and the sumptuous meals . . . well, it makes me cry to think of them. Fried chicken, roast pig; wild and tame turkeys, ducks and geese; venison just killed; squirrels, rabbits, pheasants, partridges, prairie-chicken; biscuits, hot batter cakes, hot buckwheat cakes, hot "wheat bread," hot rolls, hot corn pone; fresh corn boiled on the ear, succotash, butter-beans, string beans, tomatoes, peas, Irish potatoes, sweet potatoes; buttermilk, sweet milk, "clabber," watermelons, muskmelons, cantaloupes . . . all fresh from the garden; apple pie, peach pie, pumpkin pie, apple dumplings, peach cobbler . . . I can't remember the rest. [At this point Mark Twain starts to wander.] The way that the things were cooked was perhaps the main splendor . . . particularly a certain few of the dishes. For instance, the corn bread, the hot biscuits and wheat bread, and the fried chicken. These things have never been properly cooked in the North . . . in fact, no one there is able to learn the art, so far as my experience goes. The North thinks it knows how to make corn bread, but this is mere superstition. Perhaps no bread in the world is quite so good as Southern corn bread, and perhaps no bread in the world is quite so bad as the Northern imitation of it. The North seldom tries to fry chicken, and this is well; the art cannot be learned north of the Mason and Dixon, nor anywhere in Europe. This is not hearsay; it is experience that is speaking. In Europe it is imagined that the custom of serving various kinds of bread blazing hot is "American," but that is too broad a spread; it is custom in the South, but is much less than in the North. In the North and in Europe hot bread is considered unhealthy. This is probably another fussy superstition, like the European superstition that ice-water is unhealthy. Europe does not need ice-water and does not drink it; and yet, notwithstanding this, its word for it is better than ours, because it describes it, whereas ours doesn't. Europe called it "iced" water. Our word describes water made from melted ice . . . a drink which has a characterless taste and which we have but little acquaintance with.[6]

6 Ibid., p. 4.

Mark Twain goofed! Doesn't it make you feel better to think that he wrote all that material about fried chicken, hot bread, and ice water?

How do you choose which details to use? Decide, first of all, the most important point you want to make. In the story of my father, I first wrote a general outline of what I wanted to say. This way I have focused in on my story, and most of the tangents have been brought under control (if I follow my outline, that is). Then I try to bring in as many of the vital details as will serve a purpose to my story. I chose details and examples to describe the people involved, the setting, and atmosphere.

After you have finished writing your story, go back over it and see if each detail is meaningful. Does it add to the story, or does it take away from it? Have you used too many or too few details? Have you let general terms slip in where specific words are better? In other words, does each detail serve a purpose?

In the final writing, no one can tell you which details to use any more than I can tell you which incidents and turning points are vital to your life. You have to ask yourself, "Does this detail add to my story?" and "Is there a reason for using it?" If you have a question as whether or not to use a detail, then leave it in. It is much easier to cut it out later than it is to add.

Chapter 5

HIT A NERVE

Now that you have the facts and details written down, you have a good start, but something is missing. Attitudes, emotions, feelings —these are the elements that make your autobiography uniquely yours. John Ruskin wrote: "The ennobling difference between one man and another is that one feels more than another."

Many people think that if we show our emotions, it makes us appear weak or foolish or vulnerable. It is also very human. In the Bible it says that "Jesus wept." He was not afraid to show his feelings.

The May 1976 issue of the *Reader's Digest*, carried an excellent article on this subject by John Kord Lagemann. His concluding paragraphs summarize better than I could why we should share our feelings:

> Through feeling we gain self-insight, tap our creative powers, deepen and enrich our relationships with others.
>
> Why, then, do we so often deny our feelings? Why do we cultivate a defensive, withdrawn quality, a deadpan emotional unresponsiveness? "It's the new untouchability," a college dean told me. "The idea is never to be shocked, surprised or deeply moved . . . or at least not to show it."
>
> Feelings commit us one to another, and thus involve the risk of disappointment. They make us take sides, blurt out awkward truths, form personal preferences. "Playing it cool," on the other hand, means being "with it" until the going gets rough, then turning without regret to something else . . . another mate, another job, another cause. It may spare us a lot of heartache, self-searching and struggle. But when you subtract feelings from marriage, friendship or work, what is left? You can share money, food

or sex with another and still remain complete strangers. In the
end, the only way you can mean anything to another human
being is to share his feelings.[1]

To paraphrase his last sentence. The only way you can mean
anything to another human being is to share *your* feelings. It is
not enough to write facts and details. We need to know how you
feel about them. A newspaper article includes facts and details,
but lacks personal feelings or emotion. The story of my father is
written two ways. The first section shows my feelings, the second
section does not. The reason it is written this way, is that the first
section is my own personal memories of my father, and are naturally colored by how I felt. The second part of the story is reported like a newspaper account. I wasn't there when the police
caught Condit, or when Condit killed my father. And so I wrote
it without emotion or comment. Compare the two styles.

Although Mark Twain's story of his Uncle John's farm rambles
and goes off on a tangent, you are very much aware of his personal
feelings about food. Who would dare fry chicken for Mark
Twain, knowing his high chicken standards?

As you remember the stories and people in your life, try to fill
yourself with the feelings you once had for them.

I have included previously the story of Mark Twain's dancing
bear (bare), but how did he feel about it?

> We think boys are rude, insensitive animals but it is not so in
> all cases. Each boy has one or two sensitive spots and if you can
> find out where they are located you have only to touch them and
> you can scorch him as with fire. I suffered miserably over that
> episode.[2]

How much closer we feel to Mark Twain because he shares his
embarrassment with us. We are then able to admit, "Yes, I've
been embarrassed plenty of times." And then we become thoughtful as we remember. We could go through the other emotions
and find a story to illustrate each one.

We feel emotion about places and things. Why not share those

---

[1] Lagemann, "Don't Be Afraid to Let Your Feelings Show," p. 210.
[2] Twain, *Autobiography*, p. 39.

feelings? A tract home, built like three hundred others in the same area suddenly becomes a special place because someone writes how he feels about it. Our kitchen was no different from others, and yet I'm happy when I remember the family gathered at mealtimes, for treats, to do our lessons, or just to talk:

> Meal time in the kitchen was a time of warmth and learning in our family. I still remember how Mary Lou would spill her milk nearly every meal and how Grandma would get so angry at President Roosevelt and the New Deal. Even in college history classes, I found my papers on this subject colored by Grandma's intense dislike of the man. And she never failed to give us her personal opinion of anything and everything. We talked about school, boys, "Our Gal Sunday," and whose turn it was to do the dishes. But under the teasing and laughing, we felt the love and togetherness of a family who cared about each other.

This is a story about a kitchen, a family, and a feeling.

If you are a carpenter, let us know how you feel about the wood you touch, your tools, and what it means to you to build a bookcase. If you worked your way up to the top of your profession or business, what was your motivation? Tell how you enjoyed solving difficult problems, how you met challenges. If you are a salesman, talk about the people you meet and how you feel about them. If you are a housewife, tell how you feel about raising your family, or baking an apple pie, or how you feel as a woman. When you are telling incidents in your life include your feelings. When you talk about your family and friends, a description isn't enough.

It is difficult to describe someone without displaying your personal feelings about that person. Helen Keller uses the terms "loving," "indulgent," "caressing touch" in describing her father. It is not difficult to guess how she felt about him. Whenever Mark Twain talks about his mother, it is with loving pride. He can hardly praise her enough. His personal feelings show through his writing. The technique he uses most of the time is to show one of his mother's qualities and then to give an example or story illustrating that quality.

You are going to remember people and places if you had strong emotions about them. Love, hate, pity, fear, embarrassment, are all going to play strong points in your memory. If you knew a person but didn't care much about him, he was only incidental to your life. This is the person you will forget. The same is true of places and events. Emotion sorts out the memories you have and leaves you with the happy, sad, or fearful at the same time as it dulls the tedious, repetitious, apathetic times.

When you write, how do you reveal your feelings?

Tell How You Feel

The easiest method is to merely tell how you feel. "I was embarrassed," "I was afraid," "I hated," "I loved" are simple statements of feeling. Mark Twain says, "I suffered miserably." When Anne Sullivan spells the word "water" into Helen Keller's hand, Miss Keller relates: "I stood still, my whole attention fixed upon the motions of her fingers. Suddenly I felt a misty consciousness as of something forgotten . . . a thrill of returning thought." She also says:

> It would have been difficult to find a happier child than I was as I lay in my crib at the close of that eventful day and lived over the joys it had brought me, and for the first time longed for a new day to come.[3]

Give an Example

Illustrate your emotion by giving us an example or a story you remember. Don't say, "I was happy when I was a child." Show us how you were happy.

> Every night the kids of the neighborhood got together and played, "Piggy Wants a Wiggle," a version of kick-the-can. Once I was hiding on the hood of our car and slipped on the license plate gashing my knee. I tried to ignore it as long as I could, but when the blood wouldn't stop spurting, I finally had to give myself up in order to go inside for a bandage. Mother looked in horror at my knee and rushed me to the hospital despite my plea, "Let me finish one more game." The doctor took fifteen stitches

[3] Keller, *Story of My Life*, p. 37.

and put me on crutches for a month. The attention the crutches brought was almost, but not quite as good as playing with the gang.

A happy time? So happy I didn't want to stop my playing even for an accident. The general terms "happy," "sad," "lonely," "frustrated," "successful" are better understood when you *show* us in addition to telling us how you feel.

Go back over your material and find the places where you write such statements as:

"My father was always good to me."

"I'll never forget the happy times we had on the farm."

"My grandmother was a character, but I loved her anyway."

"My first-grade teacher was an inspiration to me."

"My mother taught me many things by the example she set for me."

We could go on, but I hope from these statements you get the idea that something is unfinished. You want to ask, "What happened at the farm to make you happy?" or "What did your mother teach you and what examples did she set?" General statements are easy to make and slip in anywhere. Go back now and ask the questions in your own writing, "Why?" or "What happened?" In other words, *show* us why or how your father was good to you, or how your first-grade teacher was an inspiration. What did she do to merit this respect?

Use of the Senses in Our Feelings

One way to communicate our feelings is to be aware of everything around us and to use all of our senses in writing. When we feel emotion, it affects us physically. When we are happy, we see objects in colors and brightness, but when we are unhappy, blacks and whites are predominant. Our faces flush or are drained of color, depending on our emotion. We hear birds or thunder; our skin gets goose bumps; our hair stands on end; we sing; we walk on air; we vomit; our mouth is dry. Use the senses in writing, and you will be showing us your feelings.

In your writing, be selective about your words and details. Try

to create the same mood you felt when you were actually experiencing the situation.

Re-experience the Emotion

To re-experience an event is to recapture the emotion. Since our
birth, we have been storing our thoughts, emotions, and experiences inside of us. When we are ready to use these memories, we
may find that they have undergone a change.

Think back to your high school days and the importance you
gave to winning a basketball game. At the time it might have
been the most important thing in your life. If you won, it meant a
state championship. Important? Of course! As you remember back,
the original feeling has been replaced by a different emotion.
Time has given perspective to your thinking. You have gone
through other experiences. Perhaps you have experienced failure
in your work, or success. You have had your share of death, set-
backs, joys, honors. Whatever the experiences, you have changed
and you can smile, wryly perhaps, at things you once thought you
would never live through.

You can write about these experiences now, even though you
might not have been able to write about them at the time.

The embarrassment Mark Twain felt when he realized he had
been seen performing bare was traumatic. But he wrote about it
later with amusement and with emotion. Forty-seven years later
he met with an old friend and the embarrassment was almost
erased from his mind.

> We sat down and talked. We steeped our thirsty souls in the
> reviving wine of the past, the pathetic past, the beautiful past,
> the dear and lamented past; we uttered the names that had been
> silent upon our lips for fifty years and it was as if they were made
> of music; with reverent hands we unburied our dead, the mates of
> our youth, and caressed them with our speech; we searched the
> dusty chambers of our memories and dragged forth incident after
> incident, episode after episode, folly after folly, and laughed such
> good laughs over them, with the tears running down; and finally
> Mary said, suddenly, and without any leading up:
> "Tell me! What is the special peculiarity of dried herrings?"

It seemed a strange question at such a hallowed time as this. And so inconsequential too. I was a little shocked. And yet I was aware of a stir of some kind away back in the deeps of my memory somewhere. It set me to musing . . . thinking . . . searching. Dried herrings? Dried herrings? The peculiarity of drie . . . I glanced up. Her face was grave, but there was a dim and shadowy twinkle in her eye which I . . . all of a sudden I knew and far away down in the hoary past I heard a remembered voice murmur, "Dey eats 'em innards and all!"[4]

Although Mark Twain still remembers the event, it no longer has the same impact that it did forty-seven years earlier.

One way of re-experiencing an event is to find a quiet place and close your eyes. Try to put everything else out of your mind. One particular impression will recur. Hold onto it as long as you can. It will come back again each time stronger if you don't try to force it. When you feel you have reached the point of saturation, and the impression is now fully developed in your thoughts, this is the time to start writing. Don't worry about form, grammar, or punctuation. Concentrate only on getting the writing down on paper. Don't stop until you are finished or you will lose the emotional quality. When you have finished, put it aside and make no changes. Let it rest for a day or more without looking at it, so that when you do go back to it, you can see it more objectively. When you go back to it, you will find that some parts are better than others. The parts in which you actually were able to include the feelings will be more unified and vivid. Some parts are going to be easier for you to write than others, but do go back and try to rewrite those places that are unfinished. It will give you deep satisfaction when you find that you are able not only to put words onto paper, but also emotions and feelings.

Just as you are able to talk about an emotional time after the experience, so are you able to write about it.

"Wait a minute!" you might say. "I don't want to relive some of my life. I mean, it was bad enough the first time! I can't go through that again. I don't even want to remember it, let alone re-experience it!"

But these traumatic times stay in the background of your mind

[4] Twain, *Autobiography*, p. 40.

and slip out unexpectedly when something reminds you. If you are able to write this experience as clearly as you can, helping us experience how you felt, you will feel much better. If you can express your feelings rather than keep them bottled inside you, you will be able to see the situation in a new light. In time you might even be able to analyze it and perhaps understand a part of it, and finally accept it in your own way.

"All right," you might say, "maybe it is good for me to get it off my chest, but I sure don't want anyone else to know about it. I was embarrassed [or hurt or ashamed]."

Of course, what you write is entirely up to you, but isn't it possible that your experience might help someone else? Sharing your mistakes or embarrassment or hurt may prevent someone else from making the same mistake. Your assessment of it, or your acceptance, may open the door for someone who is at this very time going through a similar experience.

However, there may be a time in your life that is of such a nature that you cannot write of it without pain. If this is your situation, wait until you can be more objective before writing about it. Finish your autobiography without it, and perhaps later—even years—you may be able to complete your story.

"I don't mind being honest and frank about the things I have done," said a thoughtful woman, "but how do I write about a close family member who has saddened my life?"

I knew the woman and her circumstances. Her rebellious teenage daughter had experimented with drugs and was now living at home with an illegitimate baby. She had given her mother several years of heartache, and yet the mother stood by her. Now the girl was trying to straighten out and the mother didn't want to write anything that would stop that progress.

In other words, "Are there some things that are better not said?"

You could pass over certain times and pretend they never existed, but wouldn't it be obvious to those who know you that you have deleted something? Those you are trying to protect could misinterpret by thinking, "I didn't matter in her life," or "What I did was too painful: she can't forgive me." Either thought would be a distortion of what you meant. Ignoring a major event is not the answer.

Try to get perspective on the entire situation. Even though the actions of others have affected your life, it is still *their* story and not yours. Try to summarize in generalized terms what has happened to them. Rather than detail all their misdeeds or sins, put the emphasis on what you did and how you felt.

Use restraint, common sense, and the wisdom of hindsight in writing about the situation. If you can allow the bitterness and unhappiness to mellow into an honest appraisal of your successful and unsuccessful reactions, you could not only help others who are going through a similar problem, but will allow that family member to understand you better and realize that he/she isn't hated, outcast, or alone.

By now you have probably noticed that I have not finished the story of my father's death. It is easy for me to tell you to write about your difficult times. It is not as easy to tell about mine. It took me all morning to write the following account. The mailman and a neighbor interrupted my writing, and I'm sure they wondered if I always spent the day with tears streaming down my face. But at least now I can say to you that I understand how difficult it is to write about emotional times.

Strange, I can't even remember being told of my father's death, or of his funeral which I attended.

But I do remember my mother's tears. Mama put her arms around all of us and held us until Jim squirmed away and Sally squealed. Mama cried, a low moaning sound as though it hurt her inside, and I didn't know what to do.

"What have I done that's bad?" I thought. "Must be me." I tried to make it up to her, and so I picked one of the first daffodils of the spring from next door and placed it carefully in an empty strawberry jam jar. But it was dwarfed by the baskets of roses and lilies that began to fill the house. Some of the vases of flowers were bigger than Sally, and they smelled so sweet I wanted to open all the windows.

Everyone came to see Mama now . . . neighbors who lived down the block came to see us, even though they never had before . . . and Mama's friends . . . and those who said they knew my daddy. But he wasn't here any more and I didn't know why they came. They all made Mama cry more, and I wished they would all go away so we could be as before.

Something had changed. Something was different and I wasn't sure exactly what. We clustered close to Mama whenever we could, to give her strength or maybe to draw from her.

"Your daddy's dead," Dale said. "So my daddy can run faster."

"He was old anyway," I answered. Dad was thirty-two years old.

I didn't see Dale much after that. We moved to Provo and lived with Grandma. The moving was overshadowed by Condit's trial. It seemed to last such a long time. The trial took place in Parowan, the county seat where the murder had taken place. We stayed with a relative.

"Why is it taking so long?" I asked Mama.

"Because they can't find enough people to make up a jury," Mama sighed.

It seemed to me there were plenty of people around. They all would pat our heads and murmur in low, sad voices, "And these are the children!"

The trial lasted into the summer, and it was hot and dry. The fine red dust covered my Sonja Heinie paper dolls and scattered into swirls as I jumped the rope.

When Condit came into the court the first time, I knew him from the newspaper pictures. Jim's clear voice was heard throughout the court, "There's the man who killed my daddy." He had clear speech for a four-year-old. Condit had vacant blue eyes, so light the blue was almost white, and I stared at his eyes each time I saw him. He looked at us all during the trial, but I didn't know if he ever saw us because he never changed expression. I wondered if eyes without color could really see.

I helped Mama with the younger children so she could hear the trial. She cried some then, but I watched her swallow hard and make the tears stop. She kept the tears inside until night, and then she'd bring them back in gulping sobs when she thought everyone was asleep.

After three weeks, Condit was pronounced guilty and was given the death sentence, and one year later he was shot by a firing squad.

During the days after the trial, Mama seemed happy and she told us stories and taught us how to ride a bike and rollerskate and fold paper to make boats that sailed down the gutter. But for months after, in the night I heard her cry from behind closed doors, and I didn't know what I could do to make her stop.

Becoming older, I've known myself the grief she felt and I understand. As a child I felt inadequate in meeting grief. But instinctively we clustered close to her, and that was the only thing we could do. With all the wisdom I've gained now, the only thing that really helps is to open up my arms and say "I love" and "I understand," and even now it seems inadequate.

Overwriting

With all the emotions and feelings flooding onto the pages, there is a tendency to overwrite. A few suggestions that might help are:

a. Don't explain your story after you have finished. Let it stand by itself. If you have written it with the facts and significant details including your feelings within the story, it will stand by itself without explanation or apology.

b. Don't explain the jokes. A joke is never funny when explained. If you have ever tried to explain a Charlie Chaplin movie, you will know what I mean.

c. Cut out anything that is tangent to the mood, story, or character you are writing. Usually adjectives and adverbs go first. Make your verbs work for you.

d. Many people use the first few paragraphs of a story to get warmed up and the last couple of paragraphs to summarize. Check back on your stories and see if this is your practice. You may want to cut the first and last paragraphs.

e. After you have made the point of your story, stop.

Chapter 6

THE VITAL ORGANS,
OR THE HEART OF THE MATTER

If you have systematically reviewed your life and written all of the turning points, you probably have a good basic story—or at least an outline of your life—and it might even be possible to conclude your personal history. Before you lay your pencil down, there is one question you might ask yourself. What is missing in your autobiography that is present in your life?

Think about the quiet times, the fun stories, the people who are a part of you. These are not turning points in your life, and yet they are important. Your life, after all, is not one dramatic conflict after another.

The story I gave about playing "Piggy Wants a Wiggle" was not one of the turning points in my life. It was one of the happy times. My grandmother was an important person in my life and I have hardly mentioned her.

Need for Humorous Stories and Fun Times

I have had many funny times, and they are as vital in their way as the turning points because they prepare me for difficult times. I may reach a point where I think I can't go on, and then I remember back:

> I remember how proud and scared I was when I got my driver's license. I was a whole two years older than most kids because, when I first started to drive, Mother had taken me out for a practice drive on the river-bottom road, an isolated area where I had little chance to run into anybody else. As we were driving along, someone shot a .22 at the car, and the bullet passed, kitty-corner,

through an open back window, between our heads and shattered the corner left front window. We were both so upset that I didn't try driving for a year and a half after that.

I was a senior at Provo High School, and the car was a 1940 blue Plymouth with a floor stick shift. I had talked my mother into letting me take the car back to school to pick up a book I had conveniently forgotten. My best friend, Marilyn, climbed in beside me. She was a better driver than I was, and proved it by giving plenty of back-seat help, which I probably needed but resented at the time.

"You forgot to signal," she said.

I had a hard time managing the hand signal, the shifting, and the steering wheel at the same time. When I reached the old Provo High School on Center Street, I was slightly unnerved anyway, but when I saw the entire football squad sitting on the front lawn, I came unglued.

"What am I going to do?" I whispered frantically.

"Stop the car and get out." Marilyn was so practical.

I stopped the car, and we both climbed out of the car. I was sauntering nonchalantly up the front steps, when I noticed a 1940 blue Plymouth, vaguely looking like our car, slowly moving on down the street, driverless.

"Didn't you put on the handbrake?" Marilyn asked.

I dashed for the car, and upon reaching it, threw myself in front, stopping it with both hands like a female Superman.

As I stood there, I realized how foolish I looked. It didn't help the situation. I didn't dare let go. I looked around. Where was Marilyn? She had collapsed on the front seat in a siege of giggles, and I could hear the guffaws of the football squad. Finally Marilyn recovered from her giggles long enough to pull on the handbrake, and I was able to relinquish my embarrassing position.

Although I was teased about this incident several times I was able to laugh about it with my friends, and even now when I begin to think myself high and mighty, I remember this event and ask myself, "Who do you think you are anyway . . . Superman?"

In every person's life there are fun and sad, difficult and easy times. If we were to use a musical term, we might say that our lives are orchestrated, a blend of many moods, tunes, and intensities.

In writing, we use the same techniques. Very few books progress from one crisis to another. You need to give the reader a chance to rest, to assimilate all the material you have presented. Just as you need time to prepare yourself for your next crisis, your reader needs time to prepare himself. I am one of those optimists who believe that for every difficult, unhappy, or dramatic crisis in your life, you probably have a thousand happy moments. It would be impossible and tedious to include all the happy times, but a few representative times are needed. In both Mark Twain's book and Helen Keller's autobiography, the pleasant times far exceed the difficult.

Balance Your Material

Go back through your autobiography and add some of the quiet and fun times. I have included in the rest of this chapter some of the other material which should be in your autobiography to help round it out. Fit this material chronologically in your story. Try to place them between each of the turning points if possible.

Take out the envelope that you assembled when you first started your autobiography for each time period (see Chapter 2). Go over this information. It will give direction, facts, and details that you could use.

Need for Stories

I have talked about stories and incidents. Almost everything you have written have been stories up to this point. Perhaps by now you are wondering why the word "story" is used instead of "memories" or "recollections." First of all, what is a story?

Basically a story has three parts, a beginning, a middle, and an ending. In fiction writing, it can be compared to getting the hero up into the tree, throwing rocks at him, and getting him down. Translated into autobiographical stories, it means "something happened to you, how you handled it, and what it meant to you."

A story is a complete thought put in perspective, whereas a memory is incomplete. When you have thought through an incident and are able to give it meaning, it becomes more than a memory.

A day at the beach is only a memory. If something happened at the beach, it became an incident. If you are able to realize that because of that incident you have changed, then the incident becomes a story. Perhaps you weren't even aware of its significance at the time. Following this idea through might bring this result:

You were at the beach. This is a memory. As you sat, you saw swarms of birds flying overhead and schools of fish in the water. The waves tossed the fish onto the sand in front of you. Because something happened, it has become an incident. You don't recognize what is going on, and you throw the fish back into the water, trying to save their lives, only to have them washed ashore again and again. Finally you give up, and the birds eat their fill and fly away.

If this incident has a meaning to you, then it becomes a story in your life. Perhaps you finally realize that the fish are trying to lay their eggs in the sand. They have to give their lives in order to perpetuate their own, but they give willingly. The birds see their vulnerability and swarm over the fish, frustrating their attempts. You look again at the remaining dying fish as they lay their eggs and flop miserably each time the salt water covers their drying bodies. And you wonder about your own life and your sacrifice for your own. You see life and death together in the sand. You might even ask yourself, "Could I do that for someone else?"

An incident? Not after you started making it a part of your thoughts. Then it became part of you.

Perhaps it was only a memory for a long time, but your mind kept going back to it, trying to find meaning. As you go back into your mind, go farther than asking, "What happened then?" to "What did it mean?" Try writing it down. More memories and more meanings will come. When the full story comes to you, you will find joy in realizing you have found a truth.

Why do you think you carry some memories and incidents around all your life and forget others? There must be a reason. It might be that it was very significant in your life, and you haven't taken the time to really think about it.

Subconsciously, all your life, you have been sorting out the significant from the insignificant. Now you are putting pieces together. When you get the facts, details, and personal feelings honestly written down, you will begin to understand yourself better than you ever have before.

Stories are significant. They are incidents that you have taken the time to piece together.

Need for Memories

Each memory isn't a story. Perhaps some day it will be, but for now you can remember games you played, or places or scenes that have no meaning. You have time to slip in memories that stand on their own without being analyzed.

> I remember the wonderful summers filled with nothing more than exploring. We explored the area in which we lived for tree shoots to make swords and whips. We would strip off the bark and uncover their ivory whiteness. We would make up stories of bravery in which we vanquished all evil with our mighty weapons. We searched for mint on the ditch banks and yellow buttercups in the creek. We hid under overgrown lilac bushes and planned our lives.
>
> We explored our own inventiveness and made shoes out of discarded tires. We even tried to wear them until they made blisters on our feet or fell off when we walked. One summer we tied our own tennis net, knot by knot. It took all summer.
>
> Sometimes we took summer school classes in crafts or drama, but most of the time we tried our own projects, and it didn't matter much if they succeeded or failed.

This memory covers several summers and is quite generalized. I have tried to bring in some specific details by listing a few of the things I did—making shoes out of tires, tying tennis nets out of string, and hunting for flowers and mint. None of this is earth shattering, but it gives a different picture of me than the confused child of eight you saw at the time of my father's death. Both pictures are necessary.

Need for Memory of Places

In another chapter you wrote the description of your home and
the feelings you have about your home, or even rooms in the
home. As an example, I wrote a description of our kitchen and
the memories I have of it.

There are going to be other places that you have lived or vaca-
tioned or visited that need to be included. It is difficult to write
about a trip without making it sound like a travelogue. If you
went many places, choose the most significant part of the trip and
be specific about that, and generalize about the rest.

> Somewhere in Oregon we searched for an overnight camping
> spot to spend the night. It was getting dark, and we were tired.
> Steven had been sick the entire trip with a throat infection and
> was grumpy, and he set all the others off.
>
> At 8:00 we saw a sign which read: "Garbage dump and camp-
> ing site . . . three miles."
>
> "I'm not sleeping on any garbage dump," Steven grumped. But
> it was getting late, and we turned off the side road and started off
> on a one-lane road, winding off into the mountains.
>
> By the time we had set up the tent and fixed a hot meal, it was
> too dark to explore the area. But the next morning as we looked
> around, we discovered we had camped in a most beautiful camp-
> ing site. A short hike led us to a natural swimming hole with a
> diving rock. We spent the day relaxing and swimming. Shade
> trees and grass lined the river area.
>
> "Let's stay here the whole vacation," Steven begged. Douglass
> found a tree just right for climbing, and Dan and Charles ex-
> plored some trails close by. We never did find the garbage dump.
>
> We hadn't planned on spending the time in this quiet place.
> We had Disneyland to see and the California beaches. We were
> going to Fisherman's Wharf and the Golden Gate Bridge, and
> then to Los Angeles and Universal City. We would stop by
> Grand Canyon and Bryce and Zion's on the way home. It was to
> be a cram-packed vacation. Our days were planned. How could
> we explain to waiting relatives that we had found a waterhole in
> Oregon!
>
> After two days, the children were sunburned and scratched up
> and still begging to stay longer, but we moved on. We promised

ourselves that some day we would go back. I doubt now if we could even find the place again, especially if they have taken down the sign: "Garbage dump and camping site . . . three miles."

Need for People

As mentioned before, in writing about people include a brief physical description, but more than that include how you feel about them, what you did with them, and examples or stories about them.

Be sure to make them believable. That means that you include their faults along with their virtues.

"I don't want to say anything bad about my family," a friend said. "I only remember the good things. My grandparents were noble, honorable people."

Noble and honorable. Both are fine traits. But I remember my grandmother as being opinionated, yet willing—eager—to defend me against anything. She was tidy and clean, except on Mondays, and then she hung the washing all over the house, during winter months, to dry. That was before clothes dryers. She criticized women who wore slacks when they were pregnant . . . and defended me when I wore them, saying that "pants were more modest." She was outraged at gambling, but spent every Saturday night with her friends playing Pinochle. My grandmother was noble and honorable too . . . and very human.

The humanness comes when you present the person honestly and with specific personal information. If it is someone close to you, one who will be included in several stories, you might want to include a brief background.

If you remember favorite expressions, use them.

> After my father's death, we moved in with Grandma Markham, my mother's mother. We called her "Grams," or "Grandma," and as our own children came, she became "Grandma Mary."
>
> When we moved in, friends predicted it would "kill Grandma." Three years earlier Grandma had fallen down the stairs, a flight of eighteen steps. Her beautiful auburn hair had turned gray overnight, I'm told. She was not well. But when we

moved in, she had something to live for, and I can't remember her ever complaining about her health. She worked harder in her seventies than I did as a teen-ager, and she was active in mind and body until shortly before her death at age ninety-six.

Her parents, Frederick Lewis and Agnes Reid Ferguson, were Mormon pioneers who cleared a farm in Leland near Spanish Fork, Utah. Grandma spanned the century and progressed from horse and buggy to jet travel.

"Can't you drive any faster?" she would ask, as I carefully stayed within the speed limit. "You're not going to let that car stay ahead of you," she would persist. "You know I don't like any car ahead of me." I stopped at a busy intersection and waited for a break in traffic. "What's the matter with you?" she demanded. "You could have crossed that street at least four times!"

When she was ninety-two years old Mama took her to California. Mama was like most visitors, unused to California freeways, trying to find the right roads, adapting to the fast traffic. But Grandma was delighted. "Isn't this delightful!" she said, as Mama approached a clover-leaf intersection. "I don't know why everyone makes such a fuss about freeways."

Later they got caught in traffic and were creeping along at five miles an hour. "Isn't this fun!" Grandma exclaimed. "Why, we could reach over and shake hands with everyone."

Because of Grandma's attitude of adaptability, she was able to bridge the generation gap. Her attitude was young, and because of that, she always had fun. Mama took her to Disneyland and Grandma had a wonderful day. She was resting for a moment in the shade of a bougainvillea bush, and an older woman was sitting close by.

"Isn't this terrible?" the woman complained. "They shouldn't bring old people to a place like this. I'm seventy-five years old, you know."

"I'm having a perfectly wonderful time," Grandma replied, "and I'm ninety-two."

Grandma dated boys who called for her in a horse and buggy; later on she drove a Model A Ford; and at ninety flew East in a jet to visit a grandchild. Whenever I'm inclined to complain or criticize, I remember Grandma's ability to adapt, and I decide that if I'm going to stay young in spirit, I'm going to have to make the most of every minute. Then I'll be able to say, as Grandma did, "I'm having a perfectly wonderful time, and I'm ninety-two."

Need for Dialogue or Conversation

Conversation or direct quotes from a person, such as I have used in the preceding paragraphs, are useful for many reasons. It breaks up a long paragraph; it pushes your story forward; it is useful for transitions; it shows characterization; and it shows more than one point of view.

People like to see many short paragraphs and few long paragraphs. In fact, when they are choosing books from a bookstore or a library, they will pick a book up and flip through it. If a book has long paragraphs and lots of writing, most people will put it down. "Give me a book with lots of white spots," instructed one child to the librarian.

Dialogue may be used to push your story forward. "Let's go," takes a story from a static situation to one of action. Dialogue gives the feeling of action or something happening. Even though the story might have taken place thirty years before, by using dialogue, you give the impression of immediacy. The memories I have of my grandmother occurred at least fifteen years ago, and some of them as long as thirty years ago. And yet, through the use of dialogue, it could have been only a few minutes ago.

Dialogue can also be used for transition. If you make a general statement about a person, place, or event, you can use dialogue to start the example.

> My grandmother spanned the century and progressed from horse and buggy to jet travel.
> "Can't you drive any faster?" she would ask . . .

As you can see, I used a general statement and then slipped in the dialogue to go into the specific example.

An obvious use for dialogue is in showing the people in your life. When a person speaks, you get a more complete impression of him. In Chapter 3 I gave a story by Mark Twain. He says of his mother, "She never used large words, but she had a natural gift for making small ones do effective work." But his mother becomes more real when he includes her words concerning the noisy slave boy, "Poor thing, when he sings, it shows that he is not remembering, and that comforts me; but when he is still I am afraid he is thinking, and I cannot bear it." Through her own speech, we can see into her thinking. Through dialogue, we slip into the minds of others. Be careful, though, that you don't give thoughts of other people. "He thought" is a phrase to beware of.

If you would like to give more than one point of view, dialogue is a useful tool. A conversation or argument can be effectively written, using nothing but dialogue.

Use of Dialect

Perhaps someone in your family or one of your friends came from another country, or their speech was distinctively theirs. You may want to capture their language in your writing. Sometimes this is done in the word order you use. For example, instead of saying, "You are not a good father," by rearranging the word order, you could say, "You are not good the father." Sometimes dialect is used, which is the substitution of some letters for others. When you use dialect, the secret is to use it sparingly. An entire page of dialect is very difficult to read. A few words or a sentence now and then are enough to give color and flavor, but not so much as to be difficult reading. Use it like salt or seasonings. A little bit in the right places is great, but too much spoils.

Mark Twain uses dialect effectively in his book:

> "Mars Sam, has you ever seed a dried herring?"
> "No, what is that?"
> "It's a fish."
> "Well, what of it? Anything peculiar about it?"
> "Yes, suh, you bet dey is. Dey eats 'em, inards and all!"

Mark Twain uses just enough dialect to give a flavor and a feeling about the boy, and yet not enough to make it difficult to read.

As with dialect, the same is true of dialogue or conversation—a little bit is fun, but a lot is tedious. Use it carefully, like spice, and it can add variety and interest to your writing.

Need for Poetry or Other Writings

Poetry is sometimes the most autobiographical part of you. It gives a hint into that part of you that may be hidden otherwise. Of course, if you have a lot of poetry, it would be better to use it at the end of your book. But a representative poem interspersed occasionally to forward an idea or a special time in your life might add greatly.

If you have written other material which is concise enough to fit in without slowing the forward movement in your book, it may also be used. Benjamin Franklin wrote his epitaph which no one took seriously. It reads:

> The Body of
> B Franklin,
> Printer;
> Like the Cover of an old Book,
> Its Contents torn out,
> And Stript of its Lettering and Gilding,
> Lies here, Food for Worms.
> But the Work shall not be wholly lost:
> For it will, as he believ'd, appear once more,
> In a new & more perfect Edition,
> Corrected and amended
> By the Author[1]

Need for Traditions

Every family has traditions or customs. These can be included in your personal history. The obvious traditions are observed at holidays. What family doesn't celebrate Christmas in its own special way? Or New Year's or birthdays? But what about the little traditions?

> Every April 1, Grandma would pull some trick. It usually started with her announcement that Smokey had a new batch of kittens. Inasmuch as Smokey always had new kittens, we fell for

[1] Franklin, *Autobiography*, p. 300.

it every year. We were always suspicious of the food Grandma
served. What appeared to be pink lemonade was usually colored
water . . . and vice versa.

Need for Philosophy

Why not? Every day you are making judgments. You have lived
through many experiences and should have learned from it. Why
not share these ideas with others? You might say, "But other people know that." That may be so, but when you tell your reasons
why you believe as you do, you are adding your evidence of truth
to that of the wisdom of the ages. Tell your philosophy and add
to it the reasons why you have come to believe and accept it as
your philosophy. Back it up with your experiences. It is not
enough to throw out fragments of truth without your reasons.
Maybe it is a tiny bit of philosophy like Mark Twain used about
his views on practical joking, or it might be your philosophy on
service to others, service to your country, or even your beliefs on
the hereafter or God. The important thing is that if you have
learned from it, someone else also might learn from you.

Philosophy is better accepted if you include an example, either
preceding or following the advice. Mark Twain demonstrates this
very well:

> In those extremely youthful days I was not aware that practical
> joking was a thing which, aside from being as a rule witless, is a
> base pastime and disreputable. In those early days I gave the mat-
> ter no thought but indulged freely in practical joking without
> stopping to consider its moral aspects. During three-fourths of my
> life I have held the practical joker in limitless contempt and de-
> testation. I have despised him as I have despised no other crimi-
> nal, and when I am delivering my opinion about him the reflec-
> tion that I have been a practical joker myself seems to increase
> my bitterness rather than to modify it.
>
> One afternoon I found the upper part of the window in Jim's
> bedroom thickly cushioned with wasps. Jim always slept on the
> side of his bed that was against the window. I had what seemed
> to me a happy inspiration: I turned back the bedclothes and, at
> the cost of one or two stings, brushed the wasps down and

collected a few hundred of them on the sheet on that side of the bed, then turned the covers over them and made prisoners of them. I made a deep crease down the center of the bed to protect the front side from invasion by them and then at night I offered to sleep with Jim. He was willing.

He goes on to tell how Jim climbs into bed and is covered with wasps who proceed to sting him all over his body. He goes into detail about the incident but concludes with this statement:

I played many practical jokes upon him but they were all cruel and all barren of wit. Any brainless swindler could have invented them. When a person of mature age perpetrates a practical joke, it is fair evidence, I think, that he is weak in the head and hasn't enough heart to signify.[2]

Benjamin Franklin shows us how he attempts to achieve moral perfection. As is his practice he decides what needs to be changed, conceives a plan, practices the plan, and reports its success or failure:

My list of virtues contain'd at first but twelve; but a Quaker friend having kindly informed me that I was generally thought proud; that my pride show'd itself frequently in conversation; that I was not content with being in the right when discussing any point, but was overbearing, and rather insolent, of which he convinc'd me by mentioning several instances; I determined endeavoring to cure myself, if I could of this vice or folly among the rest, and I added Humility to my list, giving an extensive meaning to the word.

I cannot boast of much success in acquiring the reality of this virtue, but I had a good deal with regard to the appearance of it. I made it a rule to forbear all direct contradiction to the sentiments of others, and all positive assertion of my own. I even forbid myself, agreeably to the old laws of our Junto, the use of every word or expression in the language that imported a fix'd opinion, such as certainly, undoubtedly, etc., and I adopted, instead of them, I conceive, I apprehend, or I imagine a thing to be so or so; or it so appears to me at present. When another asserted something that I thought an error, I deny'd myself the pleasure of contradicting him abruptly, and of showing immediately some

[2] Twain, *Autobiography*, p. 49.

absurdity in his proposition; and in answering I began by observing that in certain cases or circumstances his opinion would be right, but in the present case there appear'd or seem'd to me some difference, etc. I soon found the advantage of this change in my manner; the conversations I engag'd in went on more pleasantly. The modest way in which I propos'd my opinions procur'd them a readier reception and less contradiction; I had less mortification when I was found to be in the wrong, and I more easily prevail'd with others to give up their mistakes and join with me when I happened to be in the right.

And this mode, which I at first put on with some violence to natural inclination, became at length so easy, and so habitual to me, that perhaps for these fifty years past no one has ever heard a dogmatical expression escape me. And to this habit (after my character of integrity) I think it principally owing that I had early so much weight with my fellow-citizens when I proposed new institutions, or alterations in the old, and so much influence in public councils when I became a member; for I was but a bad speaker, never eloquent, subject to much hesitation in my choice of words, hardly correct in language, and yet I generally carried my points.

In reality, there is, perhaps, no one of our natural passions so hard to subdue as pride. Disguise it, struggle with it, beat it down, stifle it, mortify it as much as one pleases, it is still alive, and will every now and then peep out and show itself; you will see it, perhaps, often in this history; for, even if I could conceive that I had completely overcome it, I should probably be proud of my humility.[3]

Emerging Patterns

As you look back over your written material, perhaps you will find that the philosophy of your life has emerged without your even being aware of it. As you recall the incidents and people in your life, you might find that you have tested them according to what you believe. Sometimes your beliefs weren't strong, and you failed in something because of it. Maybe you had to earn this belief the hard way, searching one thing and then another before you came to be what you are today. Perhaps you have spent your

[3] Franklin, op. cit., pp. 143–44.

life searching for something to be a guiding force in your life. Try analyzing the decisions you have made. If your book does nothing else, it should allow you to see yourself better than you ever have.

You may find that your autobiography has become a soapbox for some cause and you have spent your time (and perhaps your life) defending your actions or beliefs. This is especially true of religion, race, or sex. For example, the entire theme of a personal history could be based on the sentence, "All blacks/Catholics/women are discriminated against." Instead of honesty you have substituted explanations, rationalizations, or anger. Or you may look at it from a more positive approach. You may decide that your most important contribution to the world was your involvement in a cause, and you admit that everything is filtered through that one perspective.

You may ask, "Have I tried to present a rounded picture of myself, or have I emphasized only one part of me?" To answer this, look back at your writing. How much space has been allotted to each issue? In one published autobiography, the author spent the same amount of time talking about one grievance that had lasted about five minutes as he did in reporting his marriage, difficult pregnancy of his wife, and birth of his first child. His grievance was his soapbox which permeated the book. If you spend most of your autobiography talking about your career, then rightly so this is where your greatest interest lies. Or it may be your family, your ideas, or your activities. If you look at your autobiography carefully, you may see yourself as others see you.

Ending Your Autobiography

Here you are writing along, adding anecdotes, telling of your travels, talking about traditions and favorite sayings, and all of a sudden you realize that you have nothing more to say. Could it mean that you have come to the end of your autobiography?

I suppose that, logically speaking, an autobiography ends with your life, but that isn't the way it generally works. You could continue writing your book all of your days, of course, but you need to come to a conclusion or a rounding out of your book.

SUMMARY ENDING

There are many ways to conclude your autobiography. You might go back over the writing you have done and summarize what you have accomplished and what you have learned. This could be very much like ending with your philosophies, or if you have discovered an overriding theme in your life, the discovery and discussion might make a very good ending.

PREDICTION ENDING

Lincoln Steffens, in his autobiography, went one step further than summarizing his beliefs. He predicted what he saw in the future for the world if they continued the way they were going. He had visited many people in many lands and had seen war and the results of war first-hand. His predictions are valuable, as yours could be. If you have learned from "cause and effect" and can see what might happen to others, it is your obligation to share and help others. You see life differently from anyone else, and your evaluations are valid.

TRIBUTE TO FRIENDS

Helen Keller concludes her autobiography with a tribute to her friends. She spends a paragraph or more on each person in her life who has meant something to her. She tells what each has done and how she appreciates them. These are people who are not included in the forward motion of her autobiography. The last three paragraphs conclude her autobiography:

> I shall mention only two other friends. One is Mrs. William Thaw, of Pittsburgh, whom I have often visited in her home, Lyndhurst. She is always doing something to make some one happy, and her generosity and wise counsel have never failed my teacher and me in all the years we have known her.
>
> To the other friend I am also deeply indebted. He is well known for the powerful hand with which he guides vast enterprises, and his wonderful abilities have gained for him the respect of all. Kind to every one, he goes about doing good, silent and unseen. Again I touch upon the circle of honoured names I must not mention; but I would fain acknowledge his generosity and

affectionate interest which make it possible for me to go to college.

Thus it is that my friends have made the story of my life. In a thousand ways they have turned my limitations into beautiful privileges, and enabled me to walk serene and happy in the shadow cast by my deprivation.[4]

HIGH POINT OR FINAL TURNING POINT

The death of his daughter Jean is a major turning point in the life of Mark Twain. He ends his autobiography with the discovery and report of her body, her funeral, and his sense of loss at her death. Evidently she was his secretary, and he didn't write anything significant after this event.

Christmas Night.—This afternoon they took her away from her room. As soon as I might, I went down to the library and there she lay in her coffin, dressed in exactly the same clothes she wore when she stood at the other end of the same room on the sixth of October last, as Clara's chief bridesmaid. Her face was radiant with happy excitement then; it was the same face now, with the dignity of death and the peace of God upon it.

They told me the first mourner to come was the dog. He came uninvited and stood up on his hind legs and rested his fore paws upon the trestle and took a last long look at the face that was dear to him, then went his way as silently as he had come. He knows.

At mid-afternoon it began to snow. The pity of it . . . that Jean could not see it! She so loved the snow.

. . . When Clara went away two weeks ago to live in Europe, it was hard but I could bear it, for I had Jean left. I said we would be a family. We said we would be close comrades and happy . . . just we two. That fair dream was in my mind when Jean met me at the steamer last Monday; it was in my mind when she received me at the door last Tuesday Evening. We were together; we were a family! The dream had come true . . . oh, preciously true, contentedly true, satisfyingly true! and remained true two whole days.

And now? Now Jean is in her grave!

In the grave . . . if I can believe it. God rest her sweet spirit![5]

4 Keller, *Story of My Life*, pp. 114–15.
5 Twain, op. cit., pp. 379–80.

HOPES OR GOALS FOR THE FUTURE

When Olive Burt, a writer in her eighties, was interviewed by a high school student, she was asked, "What are your goals for the future?" Mrs. Burt was delighted with the question. At eighty years of age, most young people would have supposed that her goals had been achieved. "I still have a lot of life left in me!" she said.

Whether you are eighteen or eighty, it can be valuable to list your goals, just to make sure you still have them. In writing them down, you are more likely to make them definite and commit yourself to them, and to reassess your life in terms of what you want.

AN EXPRESSION OF APPRECIATION

Paramhansa Yogananda concludes his autobiography with an expression of appreciation of life. He says, "Lord, Thou has given this monk a large family."[6]

It is never remiss to thank those who have given so much to you, and especially to God who has given life.

QUESTIONS ABOUT AND HOPES FOR AN ETERNAL LIFE

Both Cecil B. DeMille and William Allen White, in their autobiographies, express a hope for an eternal life in the hereafter and a questioning of their own worthiness.

Cecil B. DeMille says:

> The Lord giveth and the Lord taketh away. Blessed be the name of the Lord. It can only be a short time . . . until those words, the first in the Episcopal funeral service, are spoken over me . . . After those words are spoken, what am I? . . . I am only what I have accomplished. How much good have I spread? How much evil have I spread? For whatever I am a moment after death . . . a spirit, a soul, a bodiless mind . . . I shall have to look back and forward, for I have to take with me both.[7]

[6] *Autobiography of a Yogi* (Los Angeles: Self-Realization Fellowship Publishers, 1956).
[7] *The Autobiography of Cecil B. DeMille*, edited by Donald Hayne (Englewood Cliffs: New Jersey, Prentice-Hall, Inc., 1959).

William Allen White concludes:

> And now they are dust, and all the visions they saw that day have dissolved. Their hopes, like shifting clouds, have blown away before the winds of circumstance. And I wonder if it did not matter much. Or is there somewhere, in the stuff that holds humanity together, some force, some conservation of spiritual energy, that saves the core of every noble hope, and gathers all men's visions some day, some way, into the reality of progress?
>
> I do not know. But I have seen the world move under some, maybe mystic, influence, far enough to have the right to ask that question.[8]

There are as many ways to conclude your autobiography as there are people. And I might add, there are as many ways to write your autobiography. That is what makes your autobiography uniquely yours.

Your autobiography is finished, but your life continues. You may want to continue your daily activities by writing in a diary or personal journal. Section Three tells you how you can write your diary. You may even want to add to your autobiography later on. To do this, it is very helpful to keep a record. Chapter 14, "Portraits in Miniature"; Chapter 22, "Preserving Current Family Happenings"; and Chapter 23, "Recording Children's Beginnings" will be of help.

[8] *The Autobiography of William Allen White* (New York: The Macmillan Company, 1946).

Chapter 7

THE POLISHING TOUCHES

This chapter is to be read only after you have written every story, memory, tribute, philosophy, and humorous anecdote. Finish everything you want to include in your memoirs first. You cannot polish or correct until you have the words on paper. The purpose of this chapter is to help you polish your manuscript so that it will look its best.

If your manuscript is out of your sight, be sure you have an extra copy. You have worked hard on this material, and it cannot be replaced if lost or destroyed. No one knows how much work has gone into your writing except you.

Most people, when typing, use a carbon for a second copy. If you have neglected to do this, or have written it all by hand, it is usually fairly inexpensive to have it photocopied. It might cost a few dollars depending on the size of your manuscript and cost of duplication, but when you consider the time you have spent on it, it isn't that expensive to have that extra copy.

Check for Inaccuracies

It is easy to make mistakes. When you are working with words, it is so easy to think one thing and write another. Before you do anything else, go back over your material and make sure your facts are correct. If you have a family member close, let him read it for accuracy (this is one of the times you should have that extra copy). It is surprising how many simple mistakes can be found by allowing another family member or close friend to check it over. Usually these mistakes are dates, names, and spellings of names. When I had my mother check my manuscript, I found that I said we had an oil stove, when in reality it was gas, and that my father's car was the wrong color. I could name several other mistakes, but the point has been made.

How to Correct Mistakes

I don't know any good writer who hasn't had to correct, revise, and retype his manuscript at least once (some of them do it seven or eight times). The physical act of typing is tedious, and if you have someone else type it for you, it can become expensive. The following suggestions are given to save you time, money, and extra typing in correcting your first copy. Of course, your final copy should be free from mistakes:

1. Do not start retyping until you have made all the necessary changes.
2. If you use a bright yellow felt-tip pen, you can cross out any words you wish and still see the original. It is not as painful to eliminate words if you know it is not irreversible.
3. Add words or phrases right on the copy. Use arrows or any other familiar code to add sentences, phrases, or to rearrange word, sentence, or paragraph order.
4. If you want to add an extra paragraph, don't retype the entire page. Use a pair of scissors and cellophane tape and splice in the paragraph where you need it. (And be sure it's the type of tape on which you can write.)
5. If you need to add an extra page, add letters to the page numbers, that is 5, 5a, 5b, 6. This will keep your pages in order without having to redo the page numbers every time you make an addition. The paging will be corrected anyway with the final typing.

Fill In the Holes

Sometimes you don't need very much rewriting, but it is always a good idea to go back with a checklist and see if you have included all that you thought you did. You know your material better than anyone else and subconsciously fill in the background. When you were writing it the first time, you probably took it for granted that "everyone knows that!" when in reality, it was common knowledge only to you. Try to imagine yourself an outsider to your material. In other words, try to be as objective as you can in evaluating your writing.

Try reading it aloud. Many times you can pick up errors, just by hearing it. If it sounds awkward, change it. The read-aloud test is a good way to check rhythm, awkward phrases, bad grammar, punctuation, and spelling.

The mechanics of writing include spelling, punctuation, and grammar. The important part of writing your autobiography is in getting it down. However, sometimes if you haven't paid close attention to the small matters, others will notice the mistakes, and it will detract from the basically good job you have done on your material.

A good basic English text is a worthwhile investment for quick reference.

Before you type up your final copy, go over the manuscript and check for the following:

1. If you aren't sure of the spelling, check the dictionary.
2. A sentence is one thought or idea. Make sure it has a subject and a verb.
3. Punctuate each sentence correctly.
4. Make sure the subject and verb agree.
5. Take out unnecessary words, phrases, or sentences. Most people have a favorite expression. You may use it, but in moderation. If you use that same expression on every page, try to eliminate some of them. "For example," "of course," "just," "okay," are some overworked expressions.

If you are brave enough, read your manuscript to someone. Don't listen while they say, "That's great! You're the most talented person!" or else the opposite with, "Who said you could write? It isn't worth finishing!" There will always be both kinds of critics. Usually they are people who have never written and are either jealous or in awe. Occasionally you can find someone who says, "It's good because . . ." or "I don't understand that part

. . ." Maybe they are right and maybe not, but at least they are thinking constructively. After the immediate comments, listen for the questions, "How come you did . . . ?" or "Why did you . . . ?" Don't defend your piece of work. Listen. Make notes. Then look back and see if you have really put into writing what you intended. Maybe you thought you put it in, but didn't.

When your manuscript has been checked for accuracy in facts and mechanics, you are ready to make that final copy. Choose a good bond paper. Leave at least one-inch margins top, bottom, and right side, and one and a half inches on the left side in case you decide to bind your manuscript. The binding will reduce the left margin. Make sure your typewriter characters are clean.

Typewritten material should be double-spaced and on one side of the paper only. If multiple copies are to be made, each additional page means expense. Therefore, you may have to single space. Keep in mind that this slows down the reader. Double-spaced copy is much easier to read. If you don't know how to type and cannot afford to have it typed, then recopy your manuscript in pen as legibly as you can. You can make a carbon if you use a ball-point pen. Indent your paragraphs about one inch for long-hand and five to eight spaces on the typewriter.

Make carbon copies, using lightweight good-quality carbon. For multiple copies, refer to Chapters 20 and 21. If you are planning to make multiple copies, it is better to correct typographical errors with Liquid Paper correction fluid rather than an eraser.

Pages should be numbered and arranged in order.

Now that You Are Finished

Your autobiography is finished. Your life continues. I hope you have been gentle as well as thorough with yourself. You have been probing into your past, into your emotions, like an analyst and have found areas of tenderness. You have looked at yourself as a child, as a young person, and each succeeding year.

What a marvelous thing it is, this life, which allows you to grow physically, morally, intellectually, and spiritually. You are allowed experiences to help you grow. These "turning points" test you, and you are strengthened or weakened, depending on your reactions. You have reflected back on these experiences and understand, in perspective, things that at one time were incomprehensible.

> There is nothing a man can do to improve himself so much as writing his memoirs.[1]

Your life continues, perhaps now with greater self-love and self-knowledge. You are the child, the young person, the adult, and you take each part of yourself and hold it closer with love, insight, tolerance, and understanding. When you completely accept yourself, then you can accept others.

Set your goals a little higher, realizing that no matter what your age, you still have turning points to meet. It would be nice to add an epilogue to your autobiography by saying:

"Where I once was weak, now I am strong . . . because I know myself."

[1] *Reader's Digest,* April 1976, p. 91.

Section Two

WRITING
YOUR FAMILY HISTORY

The farther back we extend our knowledge of mankind's existence on this planet, the stronger grows the conviction that even to prehistoric man the desire to preserve a record of himself was only second to the desire to preserve himself.

Marston Balch
Modern Short Biographies and Autobiographies

Chapter 8

FOCUSING THE LENS

Some years ago, when my sisters and I were first starting our homes and families, a friendly debate occurred centering around personal taste. Joyce, whose home was filled with lovely abstract paintings (which her mother-in-law had painted) was challenging Mary about her realistic Norwegian scenic paintings (Mary's in-laws and husband having come from Norway). Both sisters had momentarily forgotten that it wasn't art about which they were really arguing, but the entire family tradition of their newly acquired in-laws.

"Which is better?" they asked me.

Facetiously, I answered, "What I really like on my walls are photographs!"

It was true then and even more so now. A regular rogues' gallery of photos covers one entire wall, and each one of them holds a memory for me. A living wall, I call it, because the influence of each one is alive in me.

There, in a small gold frame, is my Grandma Mary. Her jaw is set, a matriarch if I ever saw one, but I love her most of all. Sometimes when I open up my mouth her voice comes out ordering others in that no-nonsense tone.

My father, ever young, smiles out as I pass each day. He loved his friends and family and was torn between the two. His need for companionship caused his early death when he picked up a hitchhiker one lonely trip.

My Grandmother Thorne sits relaxed in a polished oak frame. She seldom relaxed, however, except when she posed for this photo. She was a woman with super-drive who worked as a newspaper reporter and postmistress in the days when women didn't usually work outside the home. She had so much energy she wasn't content to remain at home. We're part of each other, even though she died of cancer when I was six.

My husband at the age of six months is flanked by our own children at the same age in similar poses. They all look alike. In fact, there are smudge marks on the glass where the children have pointed to their friends which one is which.

My children are found in family portraits, all of us together, reminding us that we are a close unit.

My Great-Grandmother Lewis back in the mid-1880s was chosen to represent the women of Utah in women's suffrage. She poses proudly on my wall daring anyone to put her down. The attitudes she held have carried down from her through Grandma Mary and my mother down to me and on to my own daughter, Lucy. I have always considered myself an individual thinker, and yet I reflect attitudes dating nearly one hundred years.

I am a part of my past just as you are part of yours.

As we search back into our records we discover that we are more like our ancestors than we are unlike them. They have given us values, traditions, and habits which we carry through our lives. If those values are distorted or disrupted by divorce, death, or other disaster, then the tie from the past is disturbed creating confusion and disorientation.

But it is not always a calamity that severs the past from the present. More often than a breaking away is a drifting away. Sometimes this drifting starts with the death of a mother, father, or grandparent. Grandma may have been a clearing house for the family. Everyone wrote or phoned her with all the news and expected a recounting of news about other family members. On special occasions, such as birthdays, Christmas, Thanksgiving, or summer vacations, the family was expected to and looked forward to family gatherings. With the death of Grandma the organizing tie is severed and gradually family members find excuses why they can't return.

Other times, family members move so often or so far away that it is physically and/or financially impossible to return. "Where is home?" cry many who are uprooted often. Home used to be the family home, but houses are often sold and replaced by an apartment or condominium. Home sometimes meant the locale or neighborhood, but now there is so much mobility that neighborhoods too often become houses filled with strangers.

When the children are still living at home, the family drifts in even subtler ways. The family meal is disrupted by television shows, which destroy communication between members. Individual interests draw members away from family interests. Dad may need to work late or pursue a sport or hobby away from the home; Mom might be involved in community or social activities; Doug has swim team workouts; Lucy has ballet; Dan has track. Family unity is being replaced by individual needs.

Of course, each one of us needs to develop our own talents and interests, but a special time needs to be set aside for family interests too. Growing up doesn't necessarily mean growing apart. In any organization each member must actively work to make it a vital unit, and the family is no exception. Working, playing, learning, and praying together unifies a family. The sharing of family history can be the beginning of a long-term family interest.

What Then Is Family History?

A family history is the story of a family's heritage. It is not simply a collection of names, dates, and facts, but the story of a person's ancestors written in such a way as to re-create a glimpse of humanness from the past. It touches on the areas of history, sociology, biography, psychology, genealogy, and creative writing. It is a part of each field and yet distinctly different because specialists aren't the ones who are writing these histories. We are. All over the country we are searching for family Bibles, long-forgotten diaries, letters, scrapbooks, the remembering of family stories and traditions, and the quizzing of all those who remember the past.

Our children need to know our parents and grandparents and beyond, as we know them, not as names and places and unsmiling photographs, but as warm, real people.

When you gather mementos or spend an evening with a brother, daughter, or aunt enjoying and sharing memories, this is a part of family history, but when you take the time to write down those family stories you have something far more lasting, something tangible, like a photo, that you can remember. This is a beginning of family history.

When a neighbor boy was suddenly killed in an accident last month, instead of sending flowers or a card, a neighbor wrote a letter to the parents telling them of the boy coming to her home early one Saturday morning and mowing her lawn and trimming some bushes without ever being asked. She tells about inviting him inside and talking with him about school. The neighbor liked the boy and told the parents why she liked him. The parents treasure this letter because it holds a moment in the life of their son that they might not have known otherwise. I know that my neighbor has written other letters, and in a small way she is writing segments of many family histories. A memory then. But much more.

No longer is the practice of tracing families limited to the elite few whose parents founded the country or those who were trying to trace their families to royalty. Each one of us is uncommon or unique in his own way. As we write we discover that special quality.

What Is the Value of a Family History?

A young child, whose parents both work, has been going around the neighborhood telling anyone who listens that she is adopted, which she isn't. The parents have been so busy working that they have only provided her with beautiful clothes, the latest toys, and a competent baby-sitter. There has been no time for unposed photos of her at the zoo with daddy or with mama going shopping, or with her first birthday party. Her photographs are formal, taken alone. And that is how she pictures herself—alone. There are no scrapbooks she can look at, and no stories she can remember. Essentially, she is an orphan even though she isn't adopted. She has no touchstone with her own identity.

It seems a simple enough thing to tell this child about what she did when she was a baby, but evidently these parents have not realized its importance. My own five-year-old Billy never gets tired of watching home movies of himself as a baby. I tell him simple stories of his first words, how he ate everything on the floor, and how he pulled the cat's ear. A few minutes later I hear him telling a friend the same stories. He is delighted in things he did even as short a time ago as yesterday.

Billy's daddy tells him stories of a pet lamb that he raised, and I tell him about wandering away from home when I was his age and getting lost. Grandma can hold Billy captive for as long as a five-year-old is able to sit with stories of mine shafts, rattlesnakes sleeping on railroad tracks, and lizard pets named Jack and Jill, all stories from Grandma's past.

These are more than stories. They are part of a heritage which helps establish our identity. As we search our past we discover special qualities that reinforce our own individuality.

In his book, Alex Haley searches for his identity which has almost been destroyed. He sees the Rosetta Stone which is the key to the writings of ancient times and this sparks his own imagination:

> The key that had unlocked a door into the past fascinated me. I seemed to feel it had some special personal significance, but I couldn't imagine what . . . Using language chiseled into stone, the French scholar had deciphered a historic unknown by matching it with that which was known. That presented me a rough analogy: In the oral history that Grandma, Aunt Liz, Aunt Plus, Cousin Georgia, and the others had always told on the boyhood Henning front porch, I had an unknown quotient in those strange words or sounds passed on by the African . . . What specific African tongue was it? Was there any way in the world that maybe I could find out? . . . I flew to Kansas City again, to see Cousin Georgia.
>
> I think that I will never quite get over her instant response when I raised the subject of the family story. Wrinkled and ailing, she jerked upright in her bed, her excitement like boyhood front-porch echoes:
>
> "Yeah, boy, dat African say his name was 'Kin-tay'! . . . He say de guitar a 'ko,' de river 'Kamby Bolongo,' an' he was choppin' wood to make hisself a drum when dey cotched 'em!"
>
> Cousin Georgia became so emotionally full of the old family story that Floyd, Bea, and I had a time trying to calm her down. I explained to her that I wanted to try to see if there was any way

that I could possibly find where our 'Kin-tay' had come from . . .
which could reveal our ancestral tribe.

"You go 'head, boy!" exclaimed Cousin Georgia. "Yo' sweet
grandma an' all of 'em—dey up dere watchin' you!"

The thought made me feel like something like . . . My God![1]

There is a searching out, not only by Alex Haley, but by many
others who feel the need of finding their roots. Mr. Haley didn't
write in so many words exactly why it was so necessary for him to
trace his ancestry, but he did have a compelling drive, as do many
others, to search out truth. This search can provide an identity for
the young, a sense of meaning and continuity in the hectic middle
years and a strength in your mature years. Once you understand
your need for this truth, you will discover an added bonus that
Catherine Drinker Bowen talks about when she remembers her
family:

> Now in the years of my age the sound of their names gives me
> strength.[2]

Your family can become closer and more unified when you
search out your family stories by asking family members what
they remember, when you share the information you gather, and
when you gain strength from establishing your own ties with your
ancestors.

[1] *Roots* (Garden City: Doubleday & Company, Inc., 1976), pp. 570–71.
[2] *Family Portrait* (Boston: Little, Brown and Company, 1970), p. 298.

Chapter 9

GATHERING THE CLAN

When I was newly married, we lived with my husband's grand-mother who had suffered a stroke and needed someone in the home to help her. She was eighty-three years old and in poor health and her family came often to visit her. I should have kept a record of the stories they told in reminiscing with her, but I didn't. My year wasn't completely lost. I started copying all Grandmother's family records and stories as a Christmas present for my mother-in-law. It was the best gift we ever gave her. When Grandmother died family members came and each took that por-tion of the family scrapbook and records he wanted. It was scat-tered. My mother-in-law's copy and its carbon are the only com-plete records we have. We did sort it into somewhat of an order, but it was not organized into one complete record. It was so valu-able even in this disorganized state, that we Xeroxed copies and gave to close family members as wedding presents.

Here in the United States and in Europe, we have not realized how vital it is to remember our own family stories and traditions. Other nations such as Hawaii, New Zealand, and Africa have cap-tured their histories in chants, songs, artwork, and stories. Alex Haley in searching out his heritage, discovered that in Africa some men, called griots, are specifically trained from childhood to remember the history of families or tribes.

We have many ways of gathering and storing information, but we may not even be aware of it. In my own files and drawers I have documents and information not only about myself and my children, but also about parents and grandparents. They are all jumbled together, like families.

We all live with our parents for twenty years, more or less, and during that time the lives of each are separate, but still meshed with those of the others. Brothers and sisters become a part of that pattern—grandparents, aunts, uncles, and cousins fill out the design—each one separate and yet fitting together like a picture puzzle. Each fragment is separate and yet incomplete without the others. A family is like that puzzle.

When you open up a puzzle box and see the many pieces, you might sigh and wonder where to start. As you begin, you find it intriguing and return time after time to fit a section together or fit in another piece. Some pieces of the puzzle are recognizable and you quickly grab the easy ones. With family histories it is much the same. Some of your family members you know well, such as your own parents. Like a puzzle you start with one piece at a time.

Even though you may not consider yourself history, your life is a part of your family history, just as those of your parents. If you have already completed your autobiography, then you are a step ahead of everyone else and one entire section is already complete. Start with your own life first and then work backward in time.

Now choose one other family member you would most like to write about. Make it easy on yourself by choosing someone who can supply the necessary information about himself, preferably someone close. If you have a family member who is in poor health or advanced age, you may have to start with that member first. Common sense will dictate which direction you will go.

Beginning Your Search

Pull out everything you can find around your own home that might have information about the various members of your family. Look for letters, pictures, diaries, documents, and family stories and analyze just what information you already have. Chapter 15 goes into detail about home sources.

As you begin your search, you may wonder what you are looking for. At first you may feel unsure of what you do need. A checklist for each person, such as the following, may prove useful.

You may not be able to fill in all the facts, but some should not be overlooked. Certainly the birth, death, and marriage dates along with locations are most important.

Individual History Outline

NAME IN FULL:

BIRTH: Day, month, year, house or hospital where born, town, county, state or country, and surrounding circumstances.

PARENTAGE AND FAMILY BACKGROUND: Names, birthdates, birthplaces, marriage date and place. If married more than once, include name of other spouses, and which spouse you are descended from.

RELIGIOUS INFORMATION: Include day, month, year, place, and by whom the ordinance was performed. Blessings, Christenings, Baptisms, Confirmations, Bar Mitzvah, Priesthood might be included.

HOMES: Give as full an address as possible. If addresses aren't available, give landmarks. At least give city and state. List as many of the homes and places the individual has lived as possible.

BROTHERS AND SISTERS: Give names and birthdates. If they are married, give married name, spouse's name, and addresses of each.

MARRIAGE INFORMATION: Give name of spouse in full, spouse's parents, place, and date of marriage. If married more than once, include all names, dates, and places. Include death, divorce, annulment information as needed.

SCHOOL INFORMATION: Include names, places, and dates of schools attended.

VOCATION AND BUSINESS ACTIVITIES: Include Social Security Number, positions, employment, by whom, tasks, wages, etc.

CIVIC AND PROFESSIONAL POSITIONS: Give positions, dates, and explain duties.

PUBLIC AND POLITICAL POSITIONS: Give positions, dates, and activities.

MILITARY SERVICE: Give dates, title, activities, serial number.

CHILDREN: Give names, dates of birth, marriages, deaths.

DEATH INFORMATION: Day, month, year, place, circumstances surrounding death.

Transfer the information you already have to the Individual
History Outline. Be sure that all the information you have is accurate as you will refer back to this outline often in checking your
material.

Filling in the information on this sheet may be the most
difficult and distasteful part of your family history; at least it is for
me. If you can get through this simple survey, the rest is fun.
Many people love to fill in statistics, but I would much rather be
listening to family anecdotes.

When you have finished filling in the information on the Individual History Outline, you will probably find that you can't answer some of the questions. Perhaps someone else in your family
would have those answers, so make a visit or write a letter. You
may even have to go to public or church records for your information (see chapters 15–17 for help).

Now that the basic facts are gathered and carefully recorded,
we can start remembering stories, retell family anecdotes, and talk
to friends and family.

There is only one thing more devastating than saying, "Tell me
about yourself," and that is, "tell me about your family." The subject is overwhelming unless you can break it down into segments
and ask specific questions. After you have chosen which family
member you want to write about, take out a sheet of paper for
each of three sections:

   a. Childhood
   b. Middle age
   c. Retirement years

Try to remember the stories you have heard and facts you already know about that one person.

After you have put down the stories you remember, it is time to
visit with that family member. Call or write and tell him you are
coming and why, so that he can be looking for his diary, scrapbook, documents, etc. Take a tape recorder with you, if possible,

so you can check back on those stories and facts, and won't be slowed down by taking down all those stories by hand (see Chapter 19, "Interviewing").

When you start your interview remember that time is the organizing factor in all of our lives. Start with his childhood period and try to discover the highlights of that person's life. In the Autobiography Section these were called "turning points." As he tells you his stories, ask how old he was at the time of that event. Try to follow his life chronologically. Stories told at random, one highlight after another will be confusing without this time tag. Nearly everyone likes to talk about himself, and before you know it you will have a wealth of stories on your tape recorder. Follow his life through the middle and retirement years. It may take you more than one interview to cover this information. A couple of hours at a time is a good length of time to talk. More than that and you both become tired.

Take the tape home and listen to it. If you have questions, make a note. There will be many stories, more than you could possibly use. In fact, your problem will be in choosing which stories are the best. At this point don't try to edit or choose, however. Your principal task now is in searching and gathering information.

After you have talked to that family member about himself, find out how much he knows about others. You may want to spend another time talking about his parents and grandparents. Be sure to ask who else could supply you with the information you need. Perhaps there are family records, letters, autobiographies, diaries, or other written material available. Ask who has that material.

You may not be a trained interviewer and you could make all the mistakes in the book, but if you are genuinely interested and considerate you will find a wealth of stories, anecdotes, and personal feelings that become a part of your heritage.

As you can see you are working backward in time from yourself to your parents to your grandparents. Discover each preceding generation, not only facts and dates, but the richness of character and color of personality that give pictures value and worth. Stories, traditions, and personalities fill in missing segments to make your history as interesting to a teen-age son as it is to you, the researcher-writer.

Organize Your Research

In order to keep your information straight, organize your research. A loose-leaf notebook with a section for each member of your family is a convenient method. This notebook is your traveling family history to be taken with you when you talk to family members, so don't stuff it full of pictures, newspaper clippings or rare documents. Leave those at home in file folders or labeled boxes.

The first page of your notebook should contain your name and address. This is only a precaution in case you should lose it or leave it someplace.

One of the best organizing devices is a Pedigree Chart that shows relationships and gives vital statistics. A quick look will refresh your memory and give direction to your research. Additional charts may be found in Chapter 18.

Look through this chart and prepare a section for each family member. Dividing sections can be purchased in any stationery and in most variety and grocery stores. Starting with your parents, label each section for each individual member. The first sheet after the dividing section will be that person's Individual History Chart giving the dates, places, and factual information. If the Individual History Outline is accurate then you can cross-check all the other information you receive against this.

As you interview family members, write the anecdotes and facts on separate sheets. You may decide to shuffle those sheets or transfer them to your home file and it is easier to do if each story is separate. You may find your material in different places, so be sure to give the source of your material on each sheet. As you interview your family members individually they may give you information about another family member. If you write your information down on separate sheets, you can slip it into the appropriate file.

If you decide to tape your interviews, label the tapes and file

PEDIGREE CHART

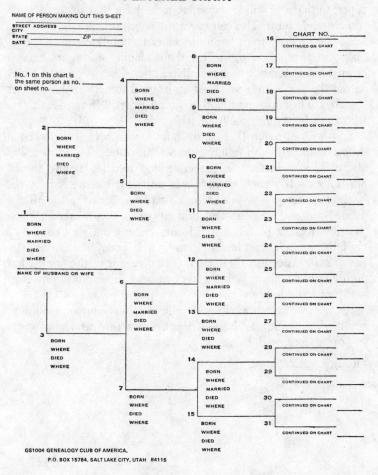

NAME OF PERSON MAKING OUT THIS SHEET _____

STREET ADDRESS _____
CITY
STATE _____ ZIP _____
DATE _____

No. 1 on this chart is
the same person as no. _____
on sheet no. _____

CHART NO. _____

GS1004 GENEALOGY CLUB OF AMERICA,
P.O. BOX 15784, SALT LAKE CITY, UTAH 84115

1

them so you can find them easily. An identifying sentence at the beginning of each tape will identify the person speaking, date, and subject. You could also slip the tape into an envelope giving the same information and perhaps a summary of the type of information contained in that particular tape. At this point, don't try to transcribe these tapes, but jot down a key to the information on paper, so that you will know where to look for that material when you are ready for it. This can go on the envelope.

As you proceed from family member to family member gathering your information you will find that family stories are handed down from generation to generation. The ancestors of Alex Haley passed the stories over and over again until sometimes his mother objected. Then his grandmother would retort, "If *you* don't care who and where you come from, well, I does!"[1]

You will discover that some family members have taken a deeper interest in the family stories than others. My mother has always had an interest in gathering and retelling family stories. She tells of the time when newly married, she helped in the kitchen in her new in-law's home preparing for a party. All the women mingled together and told stories as they worked. When the time for the party came, Mother knew more about some of my father's family and history than he did. Today she can tell stories of many ancestors on not only her own side of the family, but on my father's side as well. In her own way she is our family griot —a special and honored member.

It's time we search for those family members who are willing to admit, like Grandma Haley, "If *you* don't care who and where you came from, well, I does!"

[1] *Roots*, p. 566.

Chapter 10

SETTING THE SCENE

"The past is a foreign country," said C. P. Hartley. "They do things differently there."

When you started your family history you probably had no idea how far into the past you were going. Perhaps you were only going into your parents' lives, or maybe you were going to record the lives of your grandparents. Now that you have searched out your information you have a better idea just how far back you really are going. The question now is, "How well are you going to know this foreign country of the past?"

Travel tour companies take travelers to most of the countries of the world. They might stay a day or so in selected metropolitan cities flying between stops. When the travelers return they brag that they have seen the world . . . and they have, from 35,000 feet. A friend sails on freighters and spends six months traveling. At each port she stays two or three weeks and takes the time to explore the country at her leisure. Other people spend a year or more in a different country, living with the people, knowing their customs, and facing the same problems they face.

In order to write about the past you have to do more than fly 35,000 feet above. You need to know about conditions that existed at the time your ancestors lived in order to understand why they lived as they did and what prompted their decisions. Your visit to the past will not cost money, but it will take time for research.

Remembering your own childhood days is a beginning. When you look into yearbooks and discover old letters, it will all come back quite vividly. If you have already finished your autobiography, you will have an idea how to start. You must do the same for each family member. First you need to establish the dates you will be working with. Birth and death dates are the most logical. For example, if a grandmother was born in 1875 and died in 1934, then you are interested in the period of time within those dates.

What are you looking for? I have listed some information that would be helpful to know. You may not be able to find out everything, but what you do learn will give you a better feeling about the era and the area.

Politics: Which President most affected the nation during those years? What policies affected your family? Were there racial problems? Which war or wars were being fought? What involvement did family members have in the military service?

Economics: What were your family's finances? During this time was the country in a period of inflation or depression? What was your family's business or vocation? Were there any natural disasters and did they affect your family (droughts, hurricanes, earthquakes, fires, floods, disease)?

Religion: What was the general religious climate? Were there any religious problems or harassments? What were the specific family beliefs?

Homes: What was the location? City or farm? How were the homes heated? Plumbing? Electricity? How was the cooking done? Stove? Ovens? Did your family have hired help? Were children born at home?

Transportation: How did the family travel (bicycle, walk, horse and buggy, car, bus, trolley)? For long distances did the transportation change (bus, train, covered wagon, horse)?

Clothes: Were clothes and shoes homemade or store-bought? What material was used? What was the style . . . men and women's?

Food: Was the food simple or fancy? Scarce or plentiful? Did your family prefer food originating in a specific country (Norwegian, Mexican, Chinese)?

Culture: In the art fields of music, theater, dancing, art, and literature, can you find out what type of art was popular or appreciated, how much it affected your family, and famous artists of the day in each of the fields especially as it influenced your family members?

Schools: Were the schools private or public? Were they large schools or one-room school buildings? What subjects were taught? What were the educational theories of the day?

It would be impossible to fill out all the categories listed and you probably wouldn't want to either. Take notes about anything that might have affected their lives. For example, your parents were married December 4, 1941. It's just a date until you realize Europe was at war, Hitler was on the march, and three days later Pearl Harbor was attacked. Some honeymoon!

For those family members who are still alive, ask them about their memories of home and town as a youth, but don't expect them to remember everything. Go to a library and ask for help from the librarian. They have been trained to help and can save you hours if not days of work by finding the right books. Look in general books first, encyclopedias, yearbooks, or magazines of the day. Other sources are listed in the Appendix. Use the encyclopedias or yearbooks as a reference as you write your stories. When I write my family histories I try to keep a reference book close by, because I am always wanting to recheck different points.

If your family moved from one country to another, you would want to compare and research both countries. It will give you a much better background into their lives and decisions.

Remember that each person lives through a period of time and they are constantly meeting new changes. My grandmother, who lived to be ninety-six years old, lived her youth in horse-and-buggy times. During her middle years she watched the development and streamlining of the automobile, and in her ninetieth year she flew across the country in a jet. She was constantly adjusting and changing with the times, as we all are.

There are several sets of books out that cover several time spans. *This Fabulous Century*, put out by Time-Life Books, gives the history of America with lots of pictures and is enjoyable to read. It starts with 1870–1900 and proceeds in ten-year time spans to the present. The *Album of American History* is another encyclopedia covering the material chronologically with lots of pictures and starts with the colonial period.

The more you know about the time and place, the more accurate you become. Without this awareness of the past you become like the *Connecticut Yankee in King Arthur's Court*, an intruder into the past. In order that you see Grandma in her youth, with her beaux calling for her in horse and buggy, you have to move to the country of her youth. Unless you do some background searching you place your ancestor in a vacuum. She will exist without the politics, economics, or geography of their own time.

In my husband's family history we have the story of his grandfather, the first Charles Dixon about eight generations back, who lived from 1730–1817. In no way would I be able to reconstruct his history without additional reading. If I were to start to fill in the background material for him (for simplicity, rather than call him great, great, great, great, great grandfather, I'll call him Grandfather) I would first look at the basics. Grandfather wrote a six-page autobiography and this forms the basis of my research. Without this I wouldn't have the particulars. In addition to this record, I have a ten-page family history written by his grandson and also the information taken from the family Bible.

From these records we find that at the age of forty-two he and his wife and four children leave England and sail to Nova Scotia in March 1772. I will quote about two paragraphs from this autobiography in which he describes his arrival in Nova Scotia so that you will have the same information as I. Then we will proceed to fill in additional background from there:

> We had a rough passage, none of us having been at sea before; much sea sickness prevailed. After six weeks and four days, we arrived at Halifax, the capital of the Province, and were received with much joy by the gentlemen in general, but were much discouraged by others, and the account we heard of Cumberland (the place of our destination) was enough to make the stoutest heart give way . . . Through many discouragements we arrived and landed at Fort Cumberland on the 21st day of May, and went into the Barracks with my family until we could find a resting place. At first glance things wore a very gloomy aspect. There were few of the inhabitants but wanted to sell their lands and go hence. I thought there must be some cause for this universal discontent. The spring was very late. I began to walk about the country, and went over to Sackville. After a few days investigation, finding the cause of discontent to be largely due to indo-

lence and lack of knowledge, I purchased a tract of land at Sackville of Daniel Hawkins, containing 2500 acres, for the sum of
260 pounds. To which I removed my family on the 8th of June.[1]

If we take each move in these two paragraphs and fill in the
necessary details our organization might be as follows:

1. The family: ages, how many involved, names.
2. The sailing vessel: name, type, conditions.
3. Halifax: What reports could cause "the stoutest hearts to
   give way"? (possibly give the political background)
4. Fort Cumberland: description of barracks, conditions, location.
5. Charles' trip to Sackville:
     a. geographic description
     b. possible economic description
     c. roads
     d. climate
6. Family moves to Sackville:
     a. existing homes
     b. neighbors
     c. dangers for children
     d. schools
     e. culture

First of all, let's look at the family. According to birth dates, all
the children are young. Mary would not yet be eight years old;
Charles was six; Susannah would be five in July; and Elizabeth
wouldn't be two years old until August. In addition, Susannah,
Charles' wife, was five months pregnant when they arrive in
Halifax. These figures were easy to calculate from the dates given
in the family Bible and included in the short family history.

Charles had sold all his property and was bringing a pregnant
wife and four children under the age of eight to an unsettled land.
Even today with our luxury accommodations and the fastest jets,
this would be a major move.

Now, what can we find out about the sailing vessel? The family
history tells us that the name of the ship was the *Duke of York.*

[1] *History of Charles Dixon,* compiled by James D. Dixon (Rockford, Ill.:
Forest City Publishing Co., 1891), pp. 3–4, limited edition. Copy in hands
of Willard Dixon, 4806 Quail Point Road, Salt Lake City, Utah (1976).

What were ships like in 1772? I haven't found a description of
this particular ship, but research tells me that the ships of that
day were large sailing vessels with square sails, raised forecastle,
and quarterdeck. Most of them were imposing ships on the exterior, but highly uncomfortable inside.

Using the basics from the autobiography and the background,
let's construct a first draft for the family history on this small section:

> Charles Dixon and his family sailed from Liverpool on March 16,
> 1772, on board the *Duke of York*. They had sold their property,
> said good-bye to friends and family. There would be no return-
> ing. His wife, Susannah, was pregnant with a fifth child, and their
> four children were young: Mary, the oldest child, was not yet
> eight years old; Charles was six; Susannah would be five in July;
> and Elizabeth wouldn't be two years old until August. How much
> they were allowed to examine the raised forecastle, quarterdeck,
> and cockpit is unknown, but the interior of the ship with its
> musty and bilge-water odors would probably have added to their
> discomfort and queasy stomachs. Charles writes, "We had a
> rough passage, none of us having been at sea before, and much
> seasickness prevailed." The ship was typical of English ships of
> the day, and after they got some "sea legs" the children probably
> played quietly under the shade of the large square sails and the
> close scrutiny of anxious parents. They sailed for six weeks and
> four days before they sighted land and anchored at the harbor.
>
> They went ashore at Halifax, the capital of the Province, while
> the crew made ready for the rest of the journey.

Basically, all I did with the first section was to figure out ages
and give names to the family. Then I placed them aboard ship. I
could have been more complete in the description of the ship. I
made one mistake, and that was to say that the children might
have played in the shade of the large square sails. Actually I had
forgotten that they sailed in March, and the weather was probably
very cold with winter winds filling those sails. If they went above
at all, it would be to seek the sun, not the shade. This mistake
shows how necessary it is to place yourself imaginatively in their
situation. I would at this time write a note to myself to search out
more particulars on ships of that day, particularly the interiors of
the ships.

Let's go on to the next section which concerns the arrival of the family at Halifax. We would first ask the question, "What did Halifax look like at this time?" An engraving made ten years earlier gives us an idea of the population, types of homes, variety of shipping vessels, and the harbor. When they arrive in Halifax they were "received with much joy by the gentlemen in general, but were much discouraged by others . . ." What is the reason for this discouragement? I found several books in the library among them *Acadia* by Andrew Clark and *Nova Scotia's Massachusetts* by George Rawlyk and they gave a number of answers.

1. In 1755 the British Navy forced the French Acadians to leave their lands and settle in other areas. Later the Acadians started their migration back to their homes, the biggest group arriving in about 1772. But by this time their lands had been taken over by English settlers.

2. The Acadians were deported and sent to various ports and cities mostly in Massachusetts. Governor Charles Lawrence then issued a charter to the colonies promising grants of land to any who would settle there, plus protection from the Indians. Many farmers and fishermen relocated. One Baptist Church moved en masse to the area near Sackville. This was in 1763. The settlers from the New England areas had strong political views and demanded freedom from Great Britain.

3. Lieutenant-Governor Franklyn gave similar promises to Great Britain citizens, and as a result Ulstermen, Yorkshiremen, Scottish Highlanders, and Irish Roman Catholics migrated to Nova Scotia. Their views were different from those of the colonists. They wanted some freedom from Great Britain also, but felt they could get better terms by negotiations than from demands.

4. The Revolutionary War would erupt in four years and already tempers were getting high. Loyalists from the colonies were fleeing to Nova Scotia, battles were fought at Fort Cumberland, and peaceful inhabitants were looted.

This is the political situation in Nova Scotia at the time Charles Dixon and his wife and family arrived in 1772, and these were some of the problems being discussed. Some background is needed to know how the people felt, what the problems were, and the situation in which they would soon be involved. This material needs to be summarized and organized, but most of the information does need to be included in the family history.

> In 1772 Nova Scotia was a scene of political upheaval. England and France had been warring for many years, and in about 1755 England forced the French Acadians from the area and burned their homes and lands. Then in 1759 Governor Charles Lawrence issued a charter to the colonies promising grants of lands to any colonist who would settle the now-vacant lands. An entire Baptist Church moved en masse to Sackville in 1763, along with farmers who had been promised rich lands and fishermen who envisioned great fishing ports and fisheries. Some found what they were seeking, but others were disappointed and wanted to return to the colonies. Later Lieutenant-Governor Franklyn gave similar promises to English citizens in Great Britain, and many responded.
>
> The English immigrants and colonists took the lands vacated by the Acadians. When the Acadians started to return to their lands in about 1772, the English-speaking inhabitants refused to let them stay. In addition, those settlers from the colonies and those fresh from Great Britain had differing views about the motherland. Loyalists, fleeing from the colonies, added their own opinions. There was an estimated total population of 17,000 to 20,000 in Nova Scotia, and they were about equally divided in their political views.
>
> It is no wonder that Charles Dixon was received with "much joy by some and discouraged by others." It was not a peaceful time to be arriving in a new land.

Most of the work done in the above section was in organizing and cutting my research material. It is longer than most background material, but essential to know. As a person moves from one land to another, politics, geography, and economics change. We have to know those changes. Later on in the family history, with the political background already etched in, we would show the problems of the Revolutionary War, the battles at Fort Cumberland, the looting of the peaceful inhabitants. In other words, try to keep current with major events of that day as it affects your ancestor.

Following the outline, I would continue to fill out the background information needed. The process is the same, but the information is different. Sift out the significant points, and include anything applicable to your ancestor. For example, I found a book on the geography of Nova Scotia which historically traced the development and changes of the land. I used this data in describing Sackville.

A map of the area was helpful because it showed the ports and cities at that time and also gave the scale of miles which made it easier to get an overall idea of the location. It was much easier to show a map than to describe everything on it, so I included a map in my family history.

Nova Scotia's Massachusetts, George A. Rawlyk, page xi.

2

This is a beginning, certainly not a finished history. As I go into the history of the country at this time, both the history and the life of Charles Dixon becomes more interesting. I'm sure that as you go into the backgrounds of your ancestors you will discover the same excitement.

The past is there, waiting for you to discover it. Each venture is a new experience and an exciting one. As you start filling in the puzzle pieces of your ancestors you discover the mystery of the past. That mist which has surrounded them is dispelled and you find people with problems, with decisions to be made, and with emotions and character.

Chapter 11

EVERYONE LINK ARMS

While you are discovering that, indeed, the past is a different country, what you are really trying to find is that sameness that has carried through from generation to generation, that allows you to relate to the past and to your family for as many generations as you can recall.

Marbles, jump-the-rope, hide-and-seek, dressing up in old clothes are all activities that can be traced a long time. My own fifteen-year-old daughter loves to dress up in her grandmother's clothes. Grandma rewards her with stories of her own youth when she wore those same dresses for special occasions. Grandmother and granddaughter are pulled closer together as Grandma tells about her dates and dances and Lucy looks forward to that time when she can have the same privileges.

Most people have at one time or another fished for catfish, trout, minnow, or smelt. It doesn't matter what kind of fish, the experience is similar. We are able to relate to this story by Abigail Adams Homans because of its universal appeal.

There is a story of Father in his mature years when he had acquired a reputation and was, presumably, a responsible lawyer. One of his more important clients, finding that his case was coming up in court very shortly, tried in vain to find Mr. Adams whom he had engaged to defend him. After a long chase, my father was finally discovered placidly fishing for smelts in one of the isolated salt creeks of the Quincy shore. When hailed with the summons he refused to leave his sport but volunteered to write a note to the judge satisfactorily explaining his absence. Judge Horace Gray, who was later to be an Associate Justice of the Supreme Court, was certainly a sport himself, for on reading the hastily scribbled note he merely instructed the clerk to continue Mr. Adams' case "as he had been detained on important business." The note, on later inspection, read: "Dear Judge, for the sake of old Isaac Walton please put my case over,—the smelts are biting and I can't leave."[1]

The whole idea is to bring the past closer through familiarity with the time and area and to find that material from the past that will relate with the present.

By placing your ancestors in a historical background you have added another dimension to them and have also given the reader a second link with which they can relate. There are other ties as well.

Ties to the Country's History

Many families proudly trace their ancestors through actions and deeds performed in the building of this country. Sometimes this becomes a link from generation to generation. Many families carry on a tradition of being political leaders with fathers, sons, and brothers serving their country as senators, governors, ambassadors, or representatives at either a national or local level. Several of our Presidents have been related, most notably John and John Quincy Adams.

These ties have carried on in many cases for several generations. But what happens when that link is broken? The very fact that it is broken can sometimes be a link in itself. In the Adams family, the sons and grandsons continued to be statesmen, but not Presidents, and this seemed to give them a feeling of inferiority, even though by anyone else's standards they were successful men. The link is still there with a negative emphasis rather than a positive one.

There are other families serving the country through the military. These families move from base to base but they have a common link in the service. Sons and now daughters are raised knowing they will enter the army, navy, or air force and continue in family tradition.

[1] *Education by Uncles* (Boston: Houghton Mifflin Company, 1966), p. 27.

If your family has served the country in political, military, or other service, these links strengthen the family as well as our country and can be used in writing your family history.

Ties to Business, Career, or Vocation

In nearly every city, town, or spot in the road you will see signs proudly displayed on top of buildings announcing the name of the establishment and then the term "and son." It has been a common practice for families to follow in the tradition of their fathers. This practice, however, is not as common today as it was a generation or more back, and it is causing sadness and a breakdown in families as a result.

Families have carried on the business for generations, and customers have traded there because they "know the name and what it stands for." Farmers have worked their lands, with their sons working beside them. Children inherit the lands and their own children follow in the same tradition. Families are close-knit because they have worked together in a common cause.

These traditions have, in most cases, tied families together and can add continuity to your history.

Your family might not have owned a business, but might have had professional or skilled trades in common. You might note that many of your progenitors were doctors, lawyers, policemen, or teachers. There are many families who can boast of generations of sheet metal workers, carpenters, or other skilled trades.

This probably stems back to the apprentice programs in which a young boy was apprenticed and learned the trade from his father or other close relative. In the early days the father had the shop close by and taught his children the trade. Now the father works away from home, and often the children have no idea what their father really does. This is another breakdown in the family unit. But some traditions carry on, especially if the father loves his job and transfers that enthusiasm to his children. These vocational ties can make you feel closer to your ancestors if, for example, your profession is that of a teacher and you can look back and recognize that your grandmother and great grandfather were also teachers.

Religious Ties

Families often take on the same religious attitudes of their parents. If a parent is devout, attends church, and has a strong belief in God, then usually the children develop those same attitudes.

We can find this link with the first Charles Dixon who tells of several religious experiences. He feels that he has not worked in the service of God and repents and prays for an entire year for the spirit of forgiveness. He then tells us:

> At length on Wednesday, September the 21st, 1759, while seeking and striving upon my knees, the Lord proclaimed his name merciful and gracious to forgive my iniquities, healed all my diseases, and set my soul at liberty.[2]

In the history of our family we can find many men and women who have devoted their lives to the same kind of dedication as did this ancestor. This is another unifying link in our family history. You will find that you can bring the past and present closer by showing these reappearing links. In them is a key and a guide to the future.

Catholics, Protestants, and Jews each have religious traditions tracing back for as long as anyone can remember. The Jewish pilgrimage back to the Holy Land is an excellent example of religious unity for a cause they believe in. These beliefs tie families together. In the Mormon religion, members return to Salt Lake City twice a year for church conferences. The tie is not with Salt Lake City as a city, but because the Church has its headquarters there.

If you are able to say, "My ancestors were searching for the truth even as I am today," it would strengthen your ties with the past.

Geographical Ties

My brother-in-law complains each year, "Why do we have to come home *every* year!" After a day of visiting family he is ready to hike the mountains, boat the lakes, and explore the wastelands.

[2] Dixon, *History*, p. 2.

But my sister is content to visit and re-establish family relationships.

Even though some people establish themselves in another community they still consider the place in which they were raised as home. As families become more mobile the family ties with a specific place are broken. If you do have one home where the family celebrates births and marriages, compares children and lets cousins become acquainted, where deaths are mourned together, then this home is a link with the past.

My grandmother, in her ninety-sixth year, often wanted to go home. She didn't mean the home she had lived in for sixty or more years, but the home of her childhood.

Sometimes a city, town, or state can be that link with the past. Sometimes ancestors have built the community or have been leading members from the beginning. In the West, a few families sometimes colonized an area which became a town.

One writer I know left her home and community because it was too "regional." She traveled far and lived in the great metropolitan areas all over the world. At first she wrote well, and then she reached a slump and couldn't write at all. Finally she realized that she had lost her identity and had to return home. Now she returns every year or so "to find my roots" as she puts it.

Many naturalized Americans have a need to make a pilgrimage back to their homeland. They spend many years saving for the trip even though they may be perfectly happy where they are.

The traditions of celebrating Christmas, Easter, and other holidays have often come to us from other lands. These traditions are another tie to our past and should be included in our histories.

Ties of Recurring Talents or Interests

Certain talents seem to run in families. If one person has a musical ability, often you find that several in the same family have that same ability as demonstrated by the musical ability of the famous Osmond and King families. The same is true with art, writing, dancing, and drama.

Interest and appreciation in the home has much to do with the development of that talent. Mothers or fathers who love music will teach their children the piano or other musical instruments. Perhaps your ancestors weren't famous, but the fact that they enjoyed singing, painting, writing, or any of the arts can be a link that has been traditional in your family. Catherine Drinker Bowen tells us about her own feelings for music and those of her brother, Harry:

> But with me as with Harry music became a passion, almost a way of life, though as performers we never, for all our practicing, were to achieve more than respectable amateurism . . . And there was a family story of Harry practicing in summer beside the open window with his friends outside batting balls and shouting until he put his hands over his face in misery. "Oh, Ma!" he moaned, "I wish I didn't love music so much!"[3]

As you research your family, keep an eye on your ancestral chart. If you find any of the mentioned links appearing in your family, make a note. You might even prepare a separate chart with names and links which have carried down through the generations. These links should not be forced. You are not forging links, only trying to uncover them.

These links of family similarities run through families tying generations together because the past is part of us and so is the future.

Catherine Drinker Bowen reviews her past and present and asks:

> What had my generation gained from them all, what had we lost and where lay their mark upon us? Does fate lie in the seed, or does one's future depend upon the ground where the seed falls? There is no answer to the questions. "Americans don't talk about their ancestors." Yet to remember them is partial answer.[4]

Americans are beginning to talk about their ancestors and to write about them and to gather their stories and their strength. We are discovering that we are unique, and special. We know where we're going because we see where we've been.

[3] *Family Portrait*, p. 52.
[4] Ibid., p. 298.

Chapter 12

POSING THE PORTRAIT

One well-known biographer studies for several years about the life of each person he writes about and then doesn't start writing until, as he puts it, "I hear him speak to me." All the time that you are researching the background of your ancestor you are getting to know him better because you are understanding his problems. By now you are getting to know your ancestor better and before long perhaps he will "speak to you." You have the advantage of knowing many of your family members personally, and you are probably still learning about others.

One of the first things to do is to place a photograph of the person about whom you are writing in a prominent place where you will see it often. If you have more than one picture, that is even better. Try to obtain a picture of the person in the three main periods of his life—youth, middle age, and old age. This will remind you that the person didn't remain static, but changed and grew. The more you see those photographs the better acquainted you will become with him. The farther back you go in time, the more difficult it will be to find photographs or paintings.

You can include in your family history selected pictures of your ancestors as you tell of their lives. It is expensive to print these pictures, however, so if you do include them, try to put the pictures together on a few pages rather than scatter them throughout the history. Be sure to date and identify each photo. You may know which photo is which, but others may not. An ancestral photo chart is fun to study (see Chapter 18).

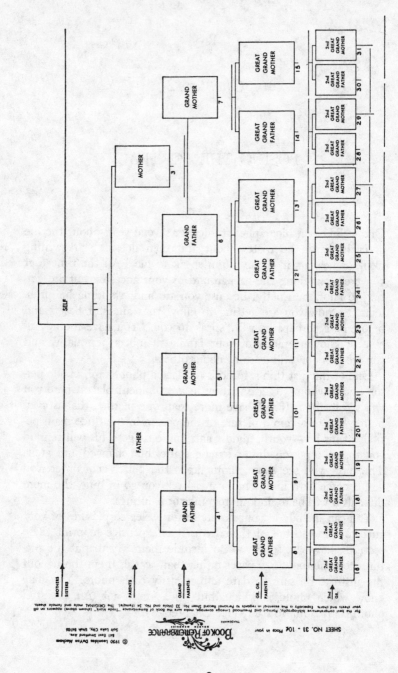

SHEET NO. 31 - 104 Place in your BOOK OF REMEMBRANCE

3

Physical Description

Without a photograph or painting we have to rely on a written physical description. If you are writing about a close family member, such as a parent or grandparent, try to give a description of him in his prime as well as his old age. For earlier ancestors the problem becomes more difficult, especially if no likeness has been preserved. In this case you will be searching the written record for any information and be happy for anything that you find. The sketch of Grandmother and Grandfather Dixon does include their description:

> Mrs. Dixon was blessed with a strong and vigorous constitution, and also in a marked degree possessed the ornament of a meek and quiet spirit. She cheerfully and patiently endured the discomforts and privations incident to pioneer life, while diligently discharging her duties as wife and mother. She was somewhat low in stature, though capable of an unusual amount of physical endurance. She was some nine years younger than her husband, but survived him as many years.
>
> Mr. Dixon was a man of medium height, strongly built, and well proportioned, possessing an excellent constitution, capable of great physical exertion, and lived to ripe age. His death occurred August 21st, 1817. Mrs. Dixon died June 13, 1826. Each of them in the 88th year of their age.[1]

I feel very fortunate to have this description of the first Charles Dixon and his wife. However, I can find no description of his son, Charles, who is also an ancestor.

Another great-grandfather on my mother's side was very shy. Although he was a leader in many ways, he never wanted to be praised or noticed, and refused to have photographs taken of him. In fact, every time a family portrait was to be taken, he disappeared, and as a result, his physical likeness is unknown except for chance remarks, such as "Grandpa looked a lot like Frederick, only his face was thinner," or "He was tall and slender, like his son, Joseph." This year an artistically inclined uncle took all the photographs of Great-Grandfather's brothers and sons and constructed a composite portrait based on comparative descriptions.

[1] Dixon, *History*, pp. 15–16.

Inasmuch as there is a close family resemblance among family members, the portrait is probably close to his likeness. Composites are useful, but often inaccurate. Use them only as a suggestion, not as an identical likeness.

Abigail Adams Homans doesn't ever give the physical description of her father except by comparing him to his brother:

> Between my father and his brother Charles, a short two years his junior, there was always a very close and affectionate relationship. They even looked alike . . . short, stocky, broad-shouldered and in later years, of course, completely bald.[2]

Describe the Inner Man

It is difficult to catch all the qualities of a person and set them down on paper. Catherine Drinker Bowen, a biographer, gives some helpful suggestions:

> There are many ways to describe a man; the biographer seldom succeeds at first try. Where, for instance, shall a description begin . . . with the face, the eyes, the manner of walking? With some concealed idiosyncrasy of the subject or with his most noticeable trait, such as a limp, or extraordinary height? "President Johnson is a big man and speaks with a Texas accent." Should one slide into it more subtly, by hint and suggestion? . . . On a printed page the description of a person should conjure up not only the person's appearance, it should suggest the inner man and make good reading.[3]

A physical description or photo of a person is extremely useful to have, but the inner quality of that person is more important than the outward appearance. Mrs. Homans tells about her father, and we don't learn his height, weight, or color of his eyes. However, we do discover something far more important, his personality.

> His brother Charles, only a year his junior, spoke of him while they were in college as essentially a good fellow with a very charming and endearing personality and cordial manners, and his

[2] *Education by Uncles*, p. 17.
[3] *Biography, the Craft and the Calling* (Boston: Little, Brown and Company, 1968), p. 80.

brother Henry described him as "one of the best talkers in Boston society and perhaps the most popular man in the State though apt to be on the unpopular side [of an issue]." Henry also wrote later to a friend who was coming to Boston: "I hope that you will meet my brother John . . . he is the best and ablest of the lot, the sort of fellow who could make you laugh when the ship was sinking." Uncle Brooks often told me how jealous he had always been of my father for possessing those social qualities of charm and conviviality which he himself painfully lacked, adding in the same breath that John was far too lazy ever to make effective use of them.[4]

In telling your story put the emphasis on the human qualities of that person, and the accomplishment will speak for itself without overwhelming either the subject or the reader.

Abigail Homans says of her father:

> Under a brusque exterior he did his best to hide a warm heart, but at times even his abrupt manner could not entirely conceal it. A distressed barber who had rented a shop from my father for many years called on him to pay some money on his back rent which was badly in arrears. Much disturbed he stated his case. "Well," said Mr. Adams, "What are you kicking about? Don't you kick till I do." Later when the new Adams block was built in Quincy my father showed his friend the barber up to a nice front room and said, "How will this suit you?" That was typical of him . . .[5]

"That was typical of him." This is a vital clue for you in deciding which stories to choose.

In Chapter 9 I suggested that you list the highlights of each ancestor's life. Now take a good look at those highlights. Have you listed only his accomplishments? Although it is impossible to divorce what a person *does* from what he *is*, it is also important to realize that there is a difference.

Several years ago, I was asked to be president of an organization. I hesitated, knowing how much time it would take. They pressed me further, adding the bait, "Think how it will look in your obituary!" After a good laugh I accepted the position in spite of the bait and not because of it. Accomplishments are inescapable and do become part of our biography and eventually our

4 Homans, op. cit., p. 26.
5 Ibid., p. 37.

obituary. There are many dimensions to every person, and what a person accomplishes is only one small part. Too many times a list of accomplishments, such as "My father was president of the Junior Chamber of Commerce, a successful businessman and a member of the Board of Education" is substituted for your father's real qualities. It is much easier to summarize a person with long lists of accomplishments than to give examples of his personality traits.

"But that is what he did!" you might object. And you're right, of course. We can't dismiss his accomplishments that easily. So let's take that list of accomplishments and do something with it. Fact without the human element is mighty cold and impersonal.

Abigail Homans discusses this aspect of her own father:

> A word about my father . . . and it may be quite a long word . . . for I cannot dismiss him as just an unsuccessful politician, amateur farmer and indifferent businessman. The adjectives may describe his career but they do not in the least describe the man himself. He was a very unusual and delightful person with great natural abilities, enormous personal charm, a lovely sense of humor, and a completely vigorous, balanced, independent and courageous mind.[6]

On one side of your paper make a list of the accomplishments of your ancestor in chronological order. In the above quote Mrs. Homans lists her father's vocations:

Lawyer
Farmer
Politician
Businessman

Beside that list, can you remember any stories that might be typical? Use a few words to recall it to your mind. The more stories you can remember, the better, even though you may decide to delete some of them later on. Try to find contrasting stories.

1. Lawyer   Success story.
                   Story of going fishing instead of going to
                   court.

[6] Ibid., p. 25.

2. Farmer	Determination of running a farm in his father's absence.
	Difficulty of raising salt hay with a war around him.
3. Politician	Saying what should be said instead of politically safe speeches.
	Always belonging to the minority party.
4. Businessman	Success story.
	Giving free rent to tenant, receipting bills in advance.

In writing up the list I had difficulty in finding the successful examples, and only listed "success story" until I could find the right one. Mrs. Homans tends to give the human side of her father rather than the successful one. Most families tend to do the opposite. It is up to you to find both. In your writing remember that your subject is or was very human. The minute he starts becoming perfect, your readers will start doubting your story.

In one of our family histories, I read the life of one of my grandfathers. He was a good man, almost perfect, if I am to believe the comments about him. "A dear sweet husband" writes Grandmother; "A loving father," write the children; "A generous friend," writes a neighbor. But it wasn't until I heard the story of Grandfather getting so angry at one of his teen-age sons that he kicked the son in the rear-end and broke his own toe that I truly believed that Grandfather was a real person.

Trying to keep the human part of an ancestor is even more difficult to do when you go back many years. No one wanted to say anything bad about the dead and so they tended to enlarge the virtuous. In the autobiography and family history of the first Charles Dixon, I find that only the stories of his virtue are preserved. Several stories are given that show his generosity and kindly nature. There is nothing wrong with telling these stories because they are part of the man. But they tend to give a one-sided picture of him. Mrs. Dixon escapes this one-sided view somewhat because of one story that is told. During the Revolutionary War some of the colonists besieged Fort Cumberland. Later on they found it more profitable to raid the homes of the inhabitants and took whatever they needed carrying off valuables and guns.

> On one occasion when some of these people were approaching the house, Mrs. Dixon hastily gathered up her silverware and other valuables and deposited them in a barrel of pig feed, where they quite escaped the notice of the visitors.[7]

Relationship with Others

Very seldom is a person seen alone. Each of us interacts with family members, friends, business associates, and even enemies. As you are telling your stories you are including those relationships with other people. In doing so, you are showing other dimensions. Mrs. Homans tells stories of her father as a younger man taking over the responsibilities of the home and his relationship with his father and brothers and sisters; we hear about her own childhood association with her father when she goes fishing with him for smelt; we read about political friends, business connections, and just plain friends. It is a rounded picture of the man, and yet the section about her father consists of less than fourteen pages.

Family Pets

To many, the mention of a family pet immediately brings a smile. Mother has a genuine fondness for her cats. At present she has Dolly, a Siamese who thinks the house belongs to it. Before that, it was Baby, an alley cat that I rescued from an old tom and stitched back together with an embroidery needle and dental floss. Smokey was the cat of the family when I was a girl. It sucked its claw the same way a child sucks its thumb.

In your family you may have your stories of favorite horses, dogs, lambs, pigs, or whatever. In some families the pet becomes a part of the household and stories about them become almost legendary. Mother tells the story of her old cat, who, after catching a mouse, would transport it to a special tree. There it forced the mouse to run in circles around the tree until the mouse dropped

[7] Dixon, op. cit., p. 10.

in exhaustion, at which time the cat finally ate it. I'm sure the story has become enlarged, but it has become a part of her repertoire.

Death Information

Catherine Drinker Bowen talks about death and how to discuss it:

> . . . Somerset Maugham, has said, "It imports us as much to know how great men die as to know how they live . . . That last step has a fascination . . . which no previous event can equal." A biography is disappointing if it does not include the death scene. Yet biographers are often guilty of this omission. Failing evidence on which to build a scene, let us at least be told how the hero died, of what disease, did he have a splendid funeral, was he greatly mourned?[8]

Death is a major fact of life that influences all of us. No one can avoid death, and we should not ignore discussing it. Although it may not be pleasant to write about the death of one of your family, especially someone who may have been close to you, it is most important to know certain facts about it. You should include these facts for the sake of posterity as well as giving a final statement to your sketch. You should include the date and place of death, age, and reason for the death—which might include part of a medical history. It is also vital to know if your ancestor had cancer or heart problems. This information is often needed for medical reasons. Perhaps in another generation the same problems might arise. Other health information that might prove useful to include would be data on respiratory illnesses, circulatory problems, blindness, deafness, deformities, epilepsy, or mental illness.

Beyond that, you might include the emotional or philosophical feelings by telling how the person felt about dying. Did he accept death, fear it, or fight it? Such information may be found in letters or personal papers.

Abigail Homans fails to say anything specific about her father's death in her book, even though she spends an entire chapter talk-

[8] Bowen, *Biography*, pp. 30–31.

ing about her father. Scattered in three places she says, "I was young when he died . . ." "With the advent of '94 it became increasingly evident that my father was still in poor shape . . ." and, "With my father's death in 1894 . . ." Somehow it feels unfinished to leave it this way.

Catherine Bowen talks about her own mother's death in her family history:

> In her eighty-eighth year, Mamma had a heart attack, serious but seemingly not painful . . . Mamma died that same year. And she did not go peacefully at all but raged indeed, clutching my hand with a grasp that hurt, drawing her breath in long, painful gasps, with lapses of consciousness and then the fearful return . . . Ma's eyes were terrified, they looked black instead of chestnut and deep in her head, and she fought every inch of the way down.[9]

What you are trying to do is to walk in another person's shoes for a short time. You are stepping into his past, telling his stories, meeting his friends, feeding his pets, accomplishing his deeds, and finally, reporting his death. And perhaps, when you have finished, you will understand and appreciate the person your ancestor really was.

[9] Bowen, *Family Portrait*, p. 282.

Chapter 13

PICTURE PERFECT

The difficult part of your family history is finished. You have researched the time and place of your ancestors, found a common tie among family members, told stories of each of your progenitors, and discovered their personalities. Once all this is accomplished, the writing is easy, especially if you write accurately and clearly. No matter how much you have researched, if it isn't presented well, no one will read it.

Writing skills include what you say, how you say it, and how you present it.

All the research material you have collected, the stories you have chosen and the details you include will make up what you say in your family history.

What You Say

SAY IT ACCURATELY

In history writing the material must be accurate. Your family history must contain the truth in as complete, unbiased, and objective a form as is possible for you to write. Many years ago the most important part of a biography was proving that you and your progenitors were faultless. Luckily we have progressed beyond that concept. The worth of early religious leaders was measured in the miracles performed and in a perfect image. Ninth-century Agnellus, Bishop of Revenna, did a series of sketches about his predecessors. He must have found it difficult to find all the necessary material and admitted, "In order that there might not be a break in the series, I have composed the life myself, with the help of God and the prayers of the brethren."[1]

Sometimes you think you are writing accurately and do not realize you are being tested. The material you choose to omit is that subtle test of your accuracy. Obviously you can't include everything in your history, but the material you leave out as well as the material you put in can distort the true picture. No one can be completely objective, of course, but be careful not to let personal biases color your writing. For example, if you are writing about a favorite grandmother or a hated uncle don't choose all the warm, fun stories of the favorite grandmother and all the underhanded stories of the less-liked uncle, unless, of course, that's all there are.

Think of one person whom you dislike (it doesn't necessarily have to be a relative). Would you be able to write about that person without your own prejudices showing through? The tendency of most people would be to vent their antagonism and tell about every fault and bad deed. Others (there aren't many) feel they should never say anything bad about anyone and so they give a one-sided picture of everyone. Another group of pacifists either ignore problem subjects or write as little as possible to avoid controversy. In all three solutions the truth is being stretched, avoided, or compromised. The best way is to be aware of your limitations and prejudices, realize how easy it is to distort the truth, and be on guard to try to write in as objective a way as possible.

Once you have decided what material you are going to include, and have been as objective and careful as you can to give an accurate picture of the situation as you understand it, the next problem you face is proving whether your material is truth or hearsay. In your writing you may find stories that are lively, fun, and have been told in family gatherings for as long as anyone can remember, but you have no way of knowing for sure how to go about proving the accuracy of that story.

There is a legend in the *Driggs' Family History*. The legend goes that in about 1700 there was a bad storm which resulted in a shipwreck in the waters of Long Island Sound. After the storm a young boy was found washed ashore lashed to the mast. That boy was Joseph Driggs, their progenitor. The family history does not

[1] G. G. Coultron, *Medieval Panorama* (New York: The Macmillan Co., 1938), p. 439.

go on to explain this story any further, and it is labeled as "legend."

This is a problem that you may also have to face. You will have to decide which are real stories and which are only good ones. The Driggs got around this problem by giving it the label. Legends are often based on truth, but there is that element of doubt.

Alex Haley, when faced with this problem, tests the legend of his family and discovers its truth. If it is possible to prove the accuracy of a story such as Mr. Haley did, it is much better. Whenever possible, check the facts. Be as accurate as you can and when you can't prove your facts, at least be honest in admitting your doubts. There will be many times in your writing when you come across anecdotes and there will be no way to verify the facts. If you decide to use the story, you should note that it is a traditional story that may have been altered in the telling. This way you are alerting your reader to the fact that it is a family folk story and not necessarily true. The other alternative would be to leave out those folk stories, but usually family histories are richer if you do include them.

USING QUOTED MATERIAL

One of the most difficult choices you have to make is in deciding how much you are going to use from your ancestor's source material. Should you quote that diary . . . and how much? Some authors quote the most pertinent parts, summarize events and quote again in a series of quotes and summaries. This is difficult to do and not always successful. You will be better off summarizing most of the material you want to give and then use the quote as the high point or final statement. Build your material so that the words of your ancestor become the most significant part of the section. Giving the quote the most prominent place is like placing a frame around a photograph to make it stand out or draw attention to it.

We are still faced with the problem of how much to include. One historian gives this help:

> Most novices at historical writing quote too often and at too great length putting too much burden on the work of others. Remember that for the reader a quotation is a kind of interruption.

Keep it brief and urgent unless you are presenting it as a document you wish to analyze for the reader . . . Yet a well chosen
quotation can add liveliness, flavor or conciseness where nothing
else will do as well.[2]

In theory this works well. It is more difficult when you are faced
with the actual material. Sometimes when you find writings of
your ancestors, especially from one who lived a long time ago, you
are so delighted that you want to include every sentence. If this is
the case, try typing the quote on a separate sheet of paper. Now
take a yellow felt pen or crayon and cross out anything that can
just as easily be summarized. Keep cutting the quote until you
have only the most forceful, interesting and pertinent material.
Summarize, give background material, and start to build a frame
in which to display that quote.

Are you still having difficulty in cutting the quote? Let's face it,
there will be some material that is written so well that you would
destroy it if you changed anything. This is the case in grandfather's autobiography. He gives advice to his son, and it is so concisely written that it can't be changed without destroying the
value of the quote. You may find similar quotes. In this case,
prepare the quote for the best presentation you can. The following excerpt from my family history contains background material
showing the religious climate in Sackville, Grandfather's reaction,
and finally the letter to his son:

When Charles arrived in Sackville with his family he sought
out other members of the Methodist faith. There was already a
group of Methodists who met each Sunday. Most of the churches
of the time met in the forenoon and again in the afternoon and
this was probably no exception. The ministers in those days traveled from area to area and in some cases there would be a
different minister for each meeting. At that time no church was
built and Charles Dixon took it upon himself to help build the
first Methodist Church in Sackville.

He was disturbed, however, because the members were divided
into factions all ready to say to each other, "I am holier than
thou." Because of this, he was prompted to write a letter to his

[2] Thomas E. Felt, *Researching, Writing and Publishing Local History* (Nashville: American Association for State and Local History, 1976), p. 71.

son warning him about pride and vanity. The advice still is valid
two hundred years later:

"This, my son, Charles, is written for thy and thy little sisters'
instruction, that thou be not high-minded, but remember the rock
from whence thou wast hewn, and in the future time when I and
thy mother shall be called home, and rest in the silent grave, you
may remember, that for your sakes we crossed the ocean. See that
you outstrip us in purity of heart and holiness of life, and always
let your words be the picture of your hearts. Study to adorn the
doctrine and Gospel of God your Savior, and acquaint yourselves
with God and be at peace. At peace with yourselves and with all
men, and may the God of peace be with you evermore. Amen."[3]

When you have finished with your quote be sure to give the
proper source and where that source may be found. If the material is printed and available in a public place such as a library or
bookstore, then follow any of the stylebooks in presenting your
source. Include title, author, publisher, publisher's address (city),
copyright date, and page number. Unpublished sources should
trace that material to the owner. Include identifying information.
In my grandfather's autobiography, the book is published, but is a
limited edition, and this is the only available copy that I have
found. In this case, I would include both the material for the
published book and then tell where it is available including name
of owner, address, and date—see book's first mention on page 126.

It is a simple thing to check back on the accuracy of a quote,
and yet easy to become careless. If you can photocopy those letters, personal papers, or whatever information you might have,
you have an advantage. If this is not possible, copy the quote
carefully, read it aloud to someone else for errors, and send a copy
back for verification. Both the quote and source must be accurately recorded. If a simple mistake is discovered, your entire work
is challenged.

ADDING DIALOGUE

If you look at biographies, you will notice that most of them
contain direct quotes used as dialogue. What does dialogue do for
your family history? For one thing, it gives the illusion of reality

[3] Dixon, *History*, p. 5.

to your writing. When you read dialogue you often feel that you are right there listening to events as they occur. If the dialogue is characteristic of a person, you may even receive the compliment, "I've heard Grandpa say those exact words!" The personality of a person is revealed better through dialogue than any other means. If, however, you are not accurate in the dialogue, your family will immediately criticize.

Dialogue takes the past and brings it to the present by making your scenes vivid and direct. Those words within the quotation marks are present tense whereas the section leading to it and after the quote are past tense. " 'Don't give up the ship,' the captain said." "Give" is present tense and "said" is past tense.

Another value of dialogue is that it gives variety to a page. As you look at a printed page, if it is nothing but long paragraphs your eyes become tired before you even start. Each time you use dialogue start a new paragraph.

"Make your dialogue short," he said.

You can see how this one sentence, set apart from the others, gives variety to this page.

There are some helps and warnings in using dialogue which you should remember. In telling a personal story it is often easy to remember what was said. At least you can remember generally the words. As long as you can capture the feeling and truth of the occasion you will probably be free to put quotation marks around it. Don't try to remember a long speech, however. A sentence or phrase will often be sufficient if you have prepared the reader for the quote. In order to do this you build with a summary of what has gone before and then use the quote as the high point of the story. In Catherine Bowen's story, already given in Chapter 11, she quotes the story of her brother Harry:

> There was a family story of Harry practicing in summer beside the open window with his friends outside batting balls and shouting until he put his hands over his face in misery. "Oh, Ma!" he moaned, "I wish I didn't love music so much!"[4]

She gives background and builds to the quote. The quote itself is short and to the point.

In order to be as accurate as you can in using dialogue, listen to

4 Bowen, *Family Portrait*, p. 52.

people. Concentrate on their words and how they use them. Try jotting down a line or two from something they have said and then listen to them again. Compare what you have written with what they are now saying. Are the speech patterns the same? Listen to yourself. How do you talk? Do you speak in long sentences or short ones? How often do you reply in sounds rather than words, "uh huh," "huh," "yeh"? Listening to speech patterns takes concentration and practice, but it will also make you more aware of yourself and others.

Very often a person has a pet phrase. These pet phrases should become a part of his story, if you don't overdo it. Once or twice should be sufficient to let the reader know the flavor of the speech without wearing out the taste. "Don't you kick till I do," could be a pet phrase of Mr. Adams, but it was used only once in the book. Overdoing any phrases, defects, or dialect tends to turn a real person into a caricature or comic character.

Try to use natural conversation when you quote someone else. Contractions such as "don't," "isn't," "I'm," "aren't" sound more natural than spelling such words out, unless, of course, your subject is very correct in his spoken language and would not use contractions.

Sometimes a person uses language that may not be grammatically correct and it is tempting to correct his English. Correct some grammatical errors in order to make it more readable, but be careful not to change the personality of that person. If Grandpa says "ain't" all the time and you change it to "isn't," then Grandpa ain't going to sound like Grandpa. Rather than do a lot of correcting, select carefully the quotes you are going to use.

If your family has come from another country, especially one which speaks another language, there will be language differences. Use this dialect sparingly. It is like spice. A little adds taste, but a lot is difficult to digest. A picture records the physical likeness and dialogue records the speech. Try to capture that speech that will depict your family member best.

When you have no memory of a person, it is difficult to put words in his mouth. Some biographers do give dialogue to their subjects, but others feel that in doing so they are writing fiction. If you are going to be accurate, record only that dialogue you have heard.

Quotation marks may cause a problem because they are used for dialogue as well as longer quotes from diaries, biographies, letters, and other sources. To make clear which is which, many writers solve the problem this way. If you quote from a diary or book, cite your source first: Abigail Homans says, "Between my father and his brother Charles, a short two years his junior, there was always a close relationship." For dialogue quotes, you can attribute it after or between the quotes: "Oh ma!" he moaned. "I wish I didn't love music so much!" Usually the context will clarify which is which.

AVOID A SUPERVIEW

As you write remember that you are looking at that individual with all the hindsight that time allows you. You can see his complete life even while you are writing about his early years. As you look at your own life you cannot see into the future, and there is that uncertainty or suspense as a result. As you write about your ancestors try to give that feeling of suspense.

To do this, try to re-create in your mind the circumstances surrounding the event. This is where a good background of the time is valuable to you. During the time of the Revolutionary War, the patriots had no idea that their words would be reverently handed down through the ages. They could just as easily have been hung as traitors. You need to show their fears and other possible consequences of their actions. When Grandfather Dixon arrived in Nova Scotia he had no idea what his future was. Others were selling their lands and moving because they couldn't make a living. This feeling of uncertainty needs to continue through the family history.

Beware of such phrases as, "if he had known what the future would be, he might not have . . ." or, "later on, John would laugh about this misfortune, but now . . ."

Try to pretend that you are a reporter on the scene trying to record an event. Give all the pertinent facts. Then show the results of those actions as they naturally occur. Often you want to give the ending of a story, but you add suspense and interest if you unfold it chronologically as it occurred in the life of your ancestor.

HOW MUCH TO TELL

There will come a time when you will have to make a decision on how much you are going to tell about a person's life. If you have an abundance of material it is obvious you can't use it all. On one side of my family everyone kept journals and wrote sketches of family members. I have to choose my material from a wealth of sources. You may have the same problem in writing about a parent or close grandparent. The other problem of how much to tell is an ethical one. How much are you going to probe into private lives? Let's consider each problem separately.

Perhaps you aren't worried now about having too much material, but it can become difficult to handle. The amount of material written by or about Franklin Roosevelt weighs forty tons. President Johnson had an entire library built to house his papers. I can't comprehend the amount of material now written about President Nixon.

Of course, you won't have that problem, but some members of your family are going to accomplish more than others, or they are going to keep better records. Somehow you are going to have to decide which incidents to use and which to cut. Opposite to this, you may have to fill out and search for more material. Some kind of balance must be established. If you have too much material, you will have to choose incidents in their lives that are representative of others. You will have to decide on the basis of relevance. Does it really matter that he prefers roast beef to leg of lamb? Owen Ruffhead wrote in 1758 about this:

> These industrious drudges, equal to any fatigue themselves, seem to imagine that their readers can never be tired. Their writings are like old women's stories, in which we do not lose a single How d'ye do? They, no doubt, think it the office of a faithful historian, not to omit the most trivial anecdote; and they often insult our patience with tedious relations, as uninteresting as if they were to acquaint us—That on such an hour, of such a day, in such a year, the Hero of their endless tale sat down to pare his nails.[5]

5 B. Nangle, *The Monthly Review*, First Series (Oxford, 1934), p. 147.

The other problem in deciding how much to tell concerns the private aspects of a person's life. It may not be pleasant to mention that your grandfather had a mistress with an illegitimate child or that your great Uncle Thomas was an alcoholic, or Aunt Lily was twice-divorced, but these are facts in your background whether you like it or not. Whether or not you use embarrassing bits in your history is up to you, but do not tamper with your source in case in the future this information is needed. That illegitimate child also has a right to a heritage.

James Clifford, a professional biographer, says:

> It is all very well to describe a man's bad temper, or his silly foibles, or to point out that occasionally he drank too much, but what about secret love affairs, illegitimate children, or the subject's syphilis? Or that he had been a very clever thief, who fooled all his reputable friends, while at the same time he was in the forefront of liberal causes? One may answer, "It all depends . . ." But on what?[6]

He doesn't give an easy answer. Instead he asks himself the following questions, which we might also ask:

1. Why did the subject try to keep this a secret?
2. Will this information embarrass anyone living today?
3. If I put the information in, or if I leave it out, will it distort historical truth?

It all boils down to a simple question, "Does it really matter?" And only you can decide. After all, it's your family.

Divorce, annulment, separation, and desertion can happen in any family. In 1890 one out of every eighteen marriages ended in divorce. By 1965 that figure had risen to one in every four. Today it is even higher. These statistics do not include those marriages that have ended in annulment, separation, and desertion. Statistics, however, only show that others have the same problems. We don't always want to include unhappy or difficult times in our family history, but when they happen we can't close our eyes and hope they will go away.

The causes of the break-up of a marriage are many. You may or

[6] *From Puzzles to Portraits* (University of North Carolina Press, Chapel Hill, 1970), p. 120.

may not have all the facts, or gory details, as some might say. Even if you did know all the problems involved from both points of view, you may wonder how much you should include. Before you write anything, ask:

1. How much is necessary to tell in order to preserve the truth?
2. Would my family history sound like gossip if I included it?
3. Do I really know the facts?
4. Do I know both sides of the story?
5. Would I hurt anyone by telling everything?

Often the facts become colored by emotions, and there is always the tendency to place blame. Often bitterness can exist for generations. In time the causes of a marriage break-up become history and the effects become the real issue. Emphasize the results of a marriage break-up rather than the causes.

1. What was the legal settlement in the case of divorce?
2. How did it affect the children?
3. How did it affect the self-image?
4. What damage and what good came of it?
5. Were any religious problems caused by it?
6. How did it change the financial position of both partners?
7. What housing arrangements were made?
8. Did the wife have to work outside the home as a result of the break-up?
9. How were children cared for if the mother had to leave the home?
10. How often did the children visit the other partner?
11. What relationship did the children have with both parents?
12. Did it cause remarriage problems?[7]

In divorce, annulment, separation, and desertion the effects are handled differently. Desertion takes on additional problems that

[7] William G. Hartley, *Preparing a Personal History* (Salt Lake City: Primer Publications, Box 11894, 1976), p. 28.

must be faced by the remaining partner, such as: Is the other partner dead or alive? Will the partner return? How long before I can remarry? What legal problems must I face? If there has been a divorce, you should include the names of subsequent marriages and additional children born of those marriages. This may be all you would want to include. Use tact, consideration, honesty, and relevance in your writing.

What you say about your family includes many things: their anecdotes or stories, their achievements, problems, personalities, human qualities, background, vital statistics, dialogue, and quotes. Your attitude and honesty will also become a part of your family history. Treat your family well. Be objective, careful, and accurate. Remember that someone in the future may update the work you have done and you may find yourself in a family history as written by one of your descendents. How would you like to be presented to your posterity?

How You Say It

All this material accurately gathered and presented is the clay or basic building block with which to work. The next step is to write it so clearly that you communicate to your readers what you have to say. How you say it then becomes as important as what you say. The two must work together.

When I first started writing this section on writing clearly, I was tired. It was nearly midnight, but I was pushing to finish. Everything I wrote was correct, but somehow it didn't hold together. All the right words were there, but it didn't say what I wanted it to say. Finally, one of the statements I had written took on a personal meaning, "In order to write clearly, you have to think clearly." I was not communicating because I wasn't taking my own advice. When you become tired you should stop your work for a while. In both research and writing your mind cannot be forced beyond its limit. Careful writers know that when they become tired they are not functioning; their eyes scan over material they should be studying; their words and sentences become vague and unfocused. After resting, ask yourself the question, "Just what is it I am trying to say?" and then, start over.

Sometimes this is not easy to do. When you are having trouble with a section of your family history, examine your material. Perhaps you haven't thought out the material carefully enough. Analyze it and ask yourself:

1. Am I trying to say too much? Instead of lumping this together, maybe I should separate the ideas and spend more time and space on each thought or story.

2. Is this section necessary? Maybe it doesn't belong and I am trying to force it in.

3. Is this material in the wrong place in the book? Maybe it should come earlier—or later.

4. Do I have enough material? Should I fill it out more, find more details, give more background?

5. Have I approached the material with the right attitude? Am I antagonistic when I should be sympathetic? Am I flippant when I should be serious? Or am I too serious?

When you write clearly you are creating a bridge from your mind to that of your reader, allowing him to share your understanding, knowledge, and enthusiasm.

CLARITY THROUGH CONTINUITY

Because your family history involves many people it is important for you to present each member clearly. The lives of children, parents, grandparents, and great-grandparents intermingle, and yet in a family history there must come a time when you focus on each individually.

Many historical biographers solve this problem by devoting a chapter or section to each generation. This would include husband, wife, and children in one section. The beginning paragraph and heading would clearly designate which time segment and family members you are going to include. When children reach maturity start a new section or chapter for them. Another way would be to divide your book into sections with several chapters in each section:

Section One—Great, Great-Grandparents
    Chapter 1—Their Lives
Section Two—Great-Grandparents

Within each chapter you are dealing with at least two people, the husband and wife. For the sake of continuity give a brief summary of each partner. Sometimes this continuity can be made more clear by the inclusion of the ancestral chart focused on these two individuals. At this point you might also want to include pictures which relate directly to these ancestors. These might include individual or group pictures, photographs of the family home or business, a copy of the ancestor's handwriting, or any other material you might have that would be of interest. Even though you focus on the husband and wife, these individuals will also be included in other chapters as children or grandparents.

In writing your family history you will notice that time is the major unifying factor. After you have traced your ancestors and gathered their stories you have a choice as to which direction you wish to go. You can write your family history from the present into the past or else you can choose one ancestor in time and follow his descendents to yourself. Either way, you are writing chronologically and this unifies and makes it easy to follow. Alex Haley searched out his ancestors from himself through his Grandmother Cynthia and back to the "African." But when he wrote the story he began with the story of Kunta Kinte and followed those descendents to himself.

When you are writing you may find that there are gaps in a person's life. These gaps may be time or geographic lapses. Let your reader know about these breaks in time or place so he won't become disoriented. For example, you may be writing about a person who is twenty years old and living in New York. The next entry might be when he is thirty and living in Mississippi. Sometimes the technique of leaving extra space between paragraphs gives variety to a page and lets the reader know that it is another time or place. White space coupled with a word of explanation is the safest, however.

Another technique of keeping the continuity between generations is to use the family links as suggested in Chapter 11:

Universal Link: John had the same taste for adventure as his Great-Grandfather Benjamin. Only this time instead of homesteading a plot of land in Wyoming, he became an astronaut with the hope of exploring other planets.

Geographic Link: After living in nearly every state in the United States, Richard and Ellie moved back to the state of their grandparents and into the old family home.

Career or Talent Link: Marty wanted to dance. Her grandmother had been in the Royal Academie Ballet until she had married Grandpa. Grandmother hadn't been a star, but she had told Marty stories about dancing for the Queen, and Marty wanted to dance more than anything.

Historical Link: Great-Great-Great-Grandfather Stephen Jones had fought in the Revolutionary War. He had been proud of helping to form a new nation. Great-Grandfather, Stephen Everett Jones had fought in the Civil War. He wrote letters that sounded as if he had single-handedly freed all the slaves. His father, Stephen Everett Hadley Jones, had fought in World War I. He helped keep the Kaiser from taking over the world. Steve was drafted into the Vietnam War. He wasn't quite sure what it was all about, but he would serve bravely, like all those in the family before him.

These links refer us back to another time and give us a feeling of continuity.

How You Present Your Material

How you present your material is a technical process. It means making your material easy to read by following the rules of correct grammar, by typing it free of errors for duplication, and by binding it securely so that it won't be separated and scattered. The following writing rules can make a fun check-list for you. The error is contained in each sentence:

1. Subjects and verbs has to agree.
2. Don't use no double negatives.
3. In autobiographies diaries and family histories use commas to keep lists of words apart.
4. Don't mispell words.
5. Don't abbrev.
6. Be sure you don't any words out.
7. Its necessary to know how to use apostrophe's correctly.
8. When you write sentence fragments.
9. Each pronoun should agree with their antecedent.
10. When dangling, don't use participles.

When you are writing, make sure your pronouns are clear. Too many indefinite pronouns create confusion. In my last chapter I was writing about a grandfather who seemed perfect. I wrote:

> But it wasn't until I heard the story of Grandfather getting so angry at one of his teen-age sons that he kicked him in the rear-end and broke his toe that I truly believed Grandpa was a real person.

You could probably have figured it out, but it could be confusing just whose toe was broken. I changed it to "he kicked the son . . . and broke his own toe . . ." to clarify it.

Ask someone else to check over your writing for misspelled words, awkward sentences, punctuation problems, and, generally, for technical errors you might have made. Most professional writers regularly employ this check on their work even before they send it to the editor. Often we are so involved in *what* we are saying that *how* we say it suffers. An outside reader will help you catch those minor errors.

When I was writing the Charles Dixon family history, I wrote:

> Fort Cumberland was originally a French Fort called Fort Beausejour built in 1750–51 and captured by the British in 1755. It was built on high land overlooking the Tantramour marshes. At first glance, according to Charles Dixon's account, "things wore a gloomy aspect. There were few of the inhabitants but wanted to sell their lands and go hence."

As I look back on my writing I realize that I had been discussing the land and marshes and then the next sentence I say is that "things wore a gloomy aspect." It sounds like the marshes were gloomy when in reality it was the circumstances of the inhabitants leaving that was gloomy. I should have said, "Conditions within the Fort and reports from Sackville were not encouraging . . ." I also need to fix my paragraphs so that one paragraph discusses the fort and its location and the next paragraph discusses the conditions outside the fort. Make sure you say what you really intended.

Chapter 18 goes into detail on preparing your manuscript for duplication and the various methods of reproduction. Whichever way you decide to reproduce your material—by mimeograph, photocopy, or by offset press—you will still need to make your copy readable. Type it double-spaced on one side of the paper with good margins. Leave 1½″ on the left side to allow for binding. You may decide to bind your manuscript permanently as discussed in Chapter 18 or to bind it in such a way as to allow for new material to be added later on.

You have finished writing your family history. You have spent a long time in researching, writing, and preparing your manuscript. You have spent time and energy, but what have you gained?

You have gained a greater interest in history. Now it has a special meaning to you. You have become acquainted with some very interesting people, your ancestors. You have a better understanding of your own heritage and why it is significant to you. Perhaps you have even clarified your own goals. You can leave a memorable record for your descendents. Your record tells about the lives of your people, who they were, and what they accomplished. You have become a link between the past and the present. Your history will help weld families closer together.

A family is a very special organization. It is the basic unit of all human life. It is more than biological. It embraces the physical, mental, moral, and spiritual training of every person on earth. Some parents ignore these obligations and the family pieces scatter and become lost. A family history gathers up those pieces and places them where they belong. Guard it well for a family history is not only your past, but your future.

Section Three

WRITING YOUR DIARY

I have started diaries before, during childhood and girlhood, but they have not survived. My nephew Joe Gargan, who spent many summers with us, recalls: "One of my memories of Aunt Rose is her saying we ought to keep diaries, because they would be so interesting for us later. But we didn't quite get around to it. And now, all these years later, of course I'm sorry. I wish we had taken her advice." I wish that I had taken my own advice; for the fact is that I did not keep a full diary until the time of Joe's ambassadorship.

Yes, let us now be thankful for small blessings, among them the 1923 diary . . . my diary summons all sorts of memories. Disordered memories. Bits of time I remember.

Rose Fitzgerald Kennedy
Times to Remember

Chapter 14

PORTRAITS IN MINIATURE

Writing Your Diary

Why, you might ask, do you include a section on diary writing, and why does it follow autobiography and family history?

Both autobiographies and family histories are a gathering, sorting, and remembering of the past whereas diaries record the present and are a continuing process in your life. An autobiography is a selection of the important events in your life and is written for others to read. It has the value of the distancing of time to allow you to evaluate your life. A family history tells all the stories and traditions of your progenitors and shows how you fit into your heritage. Family histories help you bridge many generations and time is shortened and brought into perspective. A diary or journal, on the other hand, is written soon after the event takes place. It is not written to be read by others, except at your invitation. It is impulsive, and though honest, is incomplete. In a diary you catch the excitement of each event because the emotion is fresh. The diary is spontaneous, uncalculated, and persuasive because the event has just occurred. This sense of immediacy is the value of a diary and gives the feeling of newly discovered truth. Facts are more likely to be accurate because events are happening with people you know, and the time is now and the place is here.

But diaries have an additional value far beyond the recording of facts. You can write to someone who listens patiently, never condemns, allows you to rationalize, and never gives advice (your diary). This process of "getting it off your chest" has proved to be a safety valve for many people.

Nearly every person has at least started a diary. Perhaps you started one when you were thirteen or fourteen in one of those five-year diaries that gives you the amazing space of one inch a day to record all your thoughts, actions, and dreams. But perhaps you gave it up and didn't even fill up that limited space. Some have written faithfully for many years. Others have begun and stopped, perhaps losing the book or even throwing it away when they were in one of their "cleaning up" moods.

You might say, "Diaries are important if you are an important person doing important things. But I go about every day and one day seems like the rest. What could I possibly write about myself?"

But each person is important to himself. And that is the purpose of a diary. It captures your thoughts, records your worries, questions your actions, and allows you to brag and whine and laugh about yourself. It is not written for anyone else to read. That is where it is different from any other kind of writing. Its very private nature is its strength.

Each diary has its own power and personality as each person has his own power and personality. The outward appearance of a person is not necessarily the person himself. My giggly, out-going, teen-age daughter shared her diary with me, and it revealed a serious, thoughtful young adult. To hear her talk you would not have had any idea that she had a serious thought in her head. Anne Frank mentions in her diary that "the more quiet and serious I feel inside, the more noisy I become on the outside."[1]

I was going to share a portion of my own diary with you, so I went back and reread some of the entries. But I found that they were far too personal and I was unwilling to make them public. I decided to write a "pretend" diary:

> Today I start my diary. There's so much for me to remember to include. Right now the vital thing is finishing this book. Why are there so many interruptions? I resent the pollsters calling to ask how I'm going to vote, and some furnace cleaner inquiring on the cleanliness of my air ducts, or my next door neighbor's three-year-old ringing the doorbell to find out when Billy is getting home from kindergarten. So little time for my writing. Oops, a fragmented sentence! Who cares! This is a diary and I can fragment

[1] Otto H. Frank, *Anne Frank: The Diary of a Young Girl* (Garden City: Doubleday & Company, Inc., 1952), p. 180.

all I want. And misspell. How do I spell mispell? I can't go on, not without rewriting! I mean, what about all those people peeking over my shoulder!

But as you can see, a pretend diary isn't the same. I am too much aware of an audience. A pity that my career in professional diary writing should be so brief! But it does prove a point, and that is that a diary is personal, and when it is written knowing that it will be published, it changes in content, form, and self-consciousness. My real diary will remain hidden away.

Why Do You Write?

We write with as many motives and needs for a diary as there are diaries. Perhaps you write because you need a friend; you write because you need to explain your actions or ideas; you might need to ask yourself those questions that no one else could hear; you need to feel your way into your fears or doubts or questions; you record your feelings because you're afraid you will lose your identity; you might feel that the events or trials you are now going through will be lost if you don't record it; or you have a need for self-expression. But perhaps you are like Francis Kilvert who wrote in the mid-1800s that he kept his journal because life was such a "curious and wonderful thing."

In your diary you can be very practical and present the facts in a no-nonsense way, or you can tell how you feel about a situation. It is easy to categorize them into these two classifications but not so easy to draw the line between the two. Usually diaries are written with no thought to their purpose. They are divided now only to show the wide range of possibilities and open a new vision to those who want to start.

A good example of a very practical diary comes from a friend of mine, Doug Snarr. Doug keeps a most complete and interesting diary. In the upper left-hand corner of a standard-size diary he writes his goals for the day, which are crossed off as he accomplishes them. Phone calls and interviews are summarized; brief accounts of current events are pasted in his book; small photos of friends, family, business associates, places, or events are placed on each page; important graphs and tables are folded to fit inside; social, business, religious, and civic events are all included. In other words, everything that is significant to him for that day is written in very minute handwriting into his diary. It includes international, national, family, religious, and local information. It is the world for him in capsulized form on each particular day. He considers his diaries so valuable that he keeps past diaries locked in a safe when not in use. Because of his thoroughness he has been able to use material recorded in his diary in court cases. It is indeed a very valuable record, which he uses for practical purposes.

Most of you will not be as organized as Doug. Instead, you might be like another friend who has kept a diary since she was a child. I asked her what she did with her diary.

"I write in it every night."

"Do you ever reread what you have written?"

"Oh no. I never look at it again."

For her, the diary is release of tensions, an unwinding of a day's happenings. There is nothing wrong with this. Perhaps someday she will want to go back and read it. Maybe she will even use it for reference. When she does, all the basic material is there waiting for her.

A thirteen-year-old girl shares her reasons why she is writing her diary:

> I haven't written for a few days, because I wanted to think about my diary. It's an odd idea for someone like me to keep a diary, not only because I have never done so before, but also because it seems to me that neither I . . . nor anyone else for that matter . . . will be interested in what a thirteen-year-old girl has to get off her chest. So what? I want to write. But more than that, I want to bring out all kinds of things that lie buried deep in my heart.
>
> Now I come to the root of the matter, the reason for my starting a diary: I have no real friend.
>
> Let me put it more clearly because no one will believe that a girl of thirteen feels so alone in the world. I have darling parents and a sister of sixteen. I know about thirty people whom one might call friends. I have strings of boy friends, too. I have relations . . . aunts and uncles . . . who are also darlings, and a good home. No, I don't seem to lack anything. But with all my friends

it's the same . . . just fun and joking, nothing more. We don't seem to be able to get any closer than that. Perhaps I lack confidence, but anyway, there it is. It's a stubborn fact, and I don't seem to be able to do anything about it.

Therefore, this diary. I don't want to just write down a series of dull facts like most people do. I want this diary to be my friend, and I shall call my friend Kitty. No one will understand what I'm talking about if I just begin my letters to Kitty, so I will start by briefly sketching the story of my life . . .[2]

That young girl, if you haven't already guessed, is Anne Frank. She writes this entry in her diary a few days before she goes into hiding from the Nazi army and with no knowledge of her future.

Adding the Human Element

How many times have you read entries such as "Got up, went to school, came home, went to bed," or, "went shopping, met a friend?" What is the difference between these entries and those that are interesting? Often it is as simple a thing as adding a few details. Anne Frank shows us how she observes those around her and then includes these details in her diary:

The VanDaans have been sleeping on the same sheets the whole winter. You can't wash it because there just isn't enough soap powder. Daddy goes around in ripped trousers, and his tie is beginning to show signs of wear too. Mummy's corsets have split and are too old to be fixed, and Margot wears a brassiere two sizes too small for her. Mummy and Margot have managed the whole winter with three undershirts between them. Mine are so small they don't even reach my tummy.[3]

Without these details, the diary could read, "We need new clothes," or, "My undershirt is getting too small." Anne Frank uses concrete details such as, daddy's ripped trousers, mummy's split corset, Margot's brassiere two sizes too small, and her own undershirts so small that they don't reach her tummy.

You need to train yourself to see in specifics instead of general

[2] Ibid., pp. 12, 13.
[3] Ibid., p. 91.

terms. If you meet a friend, give the name; if you attend a party, tell about it; if you are bitten by a dog you ought to tell us if it was a German shepherd or a miniature poodle. In other words, use specifics instead of classifications—Aunt Gladys Smith instead of aunt; Macy's instead of store; Girls Preference Ball at Skyline High Gym instead of dance. Observations include using all your senses. Tell what you see (four-point buck standing not more than thirty feet away); smell (crispness in the air, autumn leaves decaying underfoot); hear (rifle shot so close you can't tell the direction); taste (mouth felt sour, as though you were trying to hold onto your stomach and hadn't quite made it); feel (confused, life is so precarious!). Using your senses can help you describe the events that are going on around you.

Samuel Pepys was a common man who lived in England in the 1600s. If he were living today he would be upper middle-class. And yet, because he wrote what he honestly saw and recorded it in his diary, he has given us today a whole new appreciation and understanding of what it was like to live in England during the mid-1600s. He sees life and examines it in his diary. He writes:

> October 13, 1659–60 . . . I went out to Charing Cross, to see Major-general Harrison hanged, drawn, and quartered; which was done there, he looking as cheerful as any man could do in that condition. He was presently cut down, and his head and heart shown to the people, at which there was great shouts of joy.[4]

These details tell us a lot about the mid-1600s. Samuel Pepys, Anne Frank, and others, have demonstrated the use of specific detail. In your writing, don't say, "I'm so unhappy," or "something strange happened today" unless you are willing to give examples. You will find that your diary will be more interesting and valuable if you include names of people and places and stories of what you do. Doug Snarr's diary, mentioned earlier in this chapter, is packed with specific details complete with pictures to illustrate visually as well as verbally.

In addition to giving us details, Samuel Pepys also adds another necessary ingredient—his feelings.

[4] *The Diary of Samuel Pepys*, edited with additions by Henry Whealley (New York: Random House, 1946), p. 547.

From the moment we wake up until we fall into bed at night we cry, laugh, yell, hug, love, advise, scold, spank, gossip, listen, and occasionally think. Emotion fills our days; even when we are sitting watching television we are reacting in some way. Even lack of reaction is a reaction itself.

In every diary the reactions of the person to his situation are most evident. The diarist was worried, upset, angry, happy, bored, afraid, confused, or a combination of several emotions. When Anne Frank writes we see the gamut of emotions. We are drawn into her life, seeing her life through her eyes and feelings and made a participant for a short time.

Samuel Pepys is candid about his own feelings, but is also a little uncomfortable when his wife expresses herself. Without details and feelings Samuel Pepys might have written, "I had a fight with my wife today." Instead, we have a rich insight into a very candid man:

January 9, 1662–63
Waking in the morning, my wife I found also awake, and begun to speak to me with great trouble and tears . . . and called for Jane to reach her out of her trunk, giving her the keys to that purpose, a bundle of papers, and pulls out a paper, a copy of what, a pretty while since, she had wrote in a discontent to me, which I would not read, but burnt. She now read it, and it was so piquant, and wrote in English, and most of it true, of the retiredness of her life, and how unpleasant it was; that being wrote in English, and so in danger of being met with and read by others, I was vexed at it, and desired her and then commanded her to tear it. When she desired to be excused of it, I forced it from her, and leapt out of the bed and in my shirt clapped them into the pocket of my breeches, that she might not get them from me, and having got on my stockings and breeches and gown, I pulled them out one by one and tore them all before her face, though it went against my heart to do it, she crying and desiring me not to do it, but such was my passion and trouble to see the letters of my love to her, and my Will wherein I had given her all I have in the world when I went to see with my Lord Sandwich, to be joyned by any body. Having torn them all, saving a bond of my uncle Robert's, first letter that ever I sent her when I was her servant, I took up the pieces and carried them into my chamber,

and there, after many disputes with myself whether I should burn them or no, and having picked up the pieces of the paper she read today, of my Will which I tore, I burnt all the rest, and so went out to my office troubled in mind . . .[5]

Through Pepys' expressed emotions we see a man wrestling with his conscience. He tells us he is "troubled in mind" and has "many disputes with himself." His writing is uniquely his because of his feelings, just as your writing will be uniquely yours for the same reason.

The statements, "President John F. Kennedy was shot today," or "Today the first astronaut walked on the moon," show us nothing of your feelings about these events. They could be interpreted, perhaps, as numbness, grief, extreme emotion of some kind that prevents you from telling how you felt. However, how much more valuable if you had said how you felt at the time, and wouldn't it be interesting to go back and reread your observations at that time and compare them with how you feel today. How would Samuel Pepys have described the event?

Emotions are the common bond between the past, present, and future. How you feel about a situation, what you observe, and how much of your observations you include are important in making your diary the kind you want to reread and remember.

Beginning Your Diary

The best part of writing a diary is that you can start today. You don't need to check any of your records for dates or hunt for certificates. You are going to be writing about things you remember very well. Yesterday is over now and you probably have forgotten what it was that excited you.

We tend to forget even important happenings. At the time of the event dates, details, people, and feelings are vivid in our minds. This is the time to record. As time goes by we forget many of the details and dates. The event itself is put into perspective with that which went before and the events following. The emotions are re-evaluated into what you wanted to feel or what you think you should have felt. Or maybe you laugh indulgently at

[5] Ibid., p. 176.

yourself for even having these feelings at all. For example, I had a boy friend, a very possessive young man, who threatened anyone who might look my way. Finally, I told him I didn't want to see him again, but I was so upset, I cried all night. Looking back, I can say quite sensibly that I didn't really like the boy that much; that he needed to realize he shouldn't bully others; that I was reacting sentimentally; or that I was simply experiencing an emotional release. Although I remember the incident generally, I cannot re-create the experience. The ironic part of it all is that I can't even remember the boy's name! This particular event was not that important to me as I grew older, but other events were, and I didn't write them down. If I had written a diary as a young person, I would have been able to go back and remember dates, facts, and people. But I didn't, and I am the loser.

"If I had written it down," a fatal statement. The past is behind us. There is no need to catch up on those twenty or thirty years you haven't kept a diary. Start today.

Many people think that to write a diary you need a special book printed for that purpose, but it isn't necessary. I prefer a notebook with lined pages and no limiting factors to tell me how much I have to write. Some days I feel like writing three or more pages and the next day maybe I'll feel like writing a paragraph. I find it most annoying to be limited in how much I am going to say. If you do use a notebook, though, be sure to date your own entries. Write with a pen rather than a pencil. My grandmother's diary was partially written in pencil and has become smudged and difficult to read. You don't need to rewrite, so you won't be going back to correct or erase anyway. For those who type, you might want to use a loose-leaf notebook so you can add typed pages daily.

Write About One Event a Day

How can you write then, and make your words interesting? First of all, don't let the idea of writing overwhelm you. At the end of each day, reassess what has happened to you and what you feel most strongly about. It may be an event, a relationship with another person, or it may be your reaction to a current event. Write clearly and in detail about one thing. Include your feelings or reactions to that event. Try to re-create exactly what happened and how you felt about it. Don't try to list your entire day's happenings, only the one that impressed you the most. Once you get into the habit of putting your thoughts down, the easier you will find it, and the more you will want to write. The stumbling block for most people is that they think they have to write about everything that happens to them, and the enormity of it stops them from writing anything at all.

Remember all those sections in the autobiography and family history about rewriting and readability? Those rules don't apply here. You can split your infinitives, fragment your sentences, and even abbrev. words. Your writing can have complete freedom. There are only two rules that should be remembered in writing your diary:

1. Write regularly, daily if possible.

2. Write accurately. Keep your facts straight. You may want to check back.

Because you are writing about what is happening to you each day you may discover that you are observing what is going on around you and becoming more aware of the events in your life and your reactions to them.

Section Four

SEARCHING, ORGANIZING, AND PRESERVING THE MATERIAL

Chapter 15

BEGIN AT HOME TO FIND RECORDS

An individual who was discussing personal history was overheard to remark, "Why spoil a good story with the truth?" Unfortunately, that's the prevailing philosophy among too many story-tellers. But when you write your autobiography or family history, and when you record highlights of your life in your diary, you want accuracy—not just a good story.

One woman, in her life story, left a vivid account of the memorable storm of 1888 in her locality. Her children were deeply impressed until the facts were put down in black and white, and it was discovered that the storm of '88 actually preceded her birth. Your story must be built on facts.

As this section progresses, we will deal more extensively with these facts and their evaluation. Included herein is only a brief overview. For additional help, consult the Appendix and Bibliography, where we have listed a few of the many books that will aid your in-depth search on your ancestral lines.

The logical place to begin searching for those facts is at home. Of course, no individual or generation stands alone. We are all pivot points of what has *preceded* us and what *proceeds* from us. Our parents' lives and their stories are part of our heritage, and we are part of them—connecting links.

If you followed the suggestions in Chapter 2, you should already have your "bone collection" pretty well compiled from within your own four walls. The next step is to contact your immediate family members: parents, siblings, your children living away from home. Explain what you are attempting to accomplish so that nothing will be overlooked. Ask them to explore the attic. What's tucked away in those dresser drawers or cupboards? Is there a safekeeping metal box? Old black trunks are a favorite. Some people even keep their valuables in an old shoe box.

What will you look for in your home or the home of your relatives?

A. *Vital statistics:* Birth certificates, christening records, citizenship and naturalization papers, death certificates, divorce papers, family Bibles (some include many generations), marriage certificates and licenses, memorial cards, mortuary records, military records, obituaries.

B. *Historical records:* Awards of all kinds, baby books, biographies, diaries, diplomas, family histories, favorite old books that may contain valuable inscriptions and comments, journals, notebooks, newspaper clippings, old letters, photos, school records (report cards, etc.), Sunday school prizes, telegrams, service medals, yearbooks.

C. *Legal, financial and professional records:* Apprenticeship, business and professional licenses, club membership cards, deeds, hospital receipts, insurance papers, land grants, leases, letters of administration, obsolete savings passbooks, passports, pension records, tax records, wills.

These all furnish clues to official records.

D. *Pictures:* Pictures tell important stories and support facts. Discovering and discussing pictures can also open doors for obtaining some of the above-mentioned records as well as vital reminiscences. The only time we could ever coax Mother to talk about the past was to get out the old brown varnished picture box, which my father had made early in their married life. She relived nostalgically, for the present generation, some delightful—and some not so delightful—memories.

A family picture party can be historically rewarding. Invite aunts and uncles and/or cousins to a picture party. Suggest they bring their old photos along. Listen while the stories multiply! Be sure to take notes, or have a tape recorder running because you'll never remember all that comes out of that gathering. Undoubtedly there will be some differences of opinion, and then you will appreciate the value of documents to establish the authenticity of your own story.

Those old family pictures will do a lot to enliven your autobiography and family history, but the owner will never part with them—small wonder. Negatives are seldom available. But did you know that it's possible to have copies made of the original picture? Keep the negative and you can have as many copies made as desired for other family members. This is a wise precaution, especially for rare pictures, because all too often they mysteriously disappear, and then the whole family is out of luck. That idea may be a wedge to convince the owner to part with the picture temporarily.

A picture party will also convince you that you must do some interviewing of your relatives to obtain stories and background for your family history, or for the early facts of your autobiography. DON'T DELAY. How many times I've resolved to visit or write a relative and have procrastinated too long.

Pursuing Home Sources

I wanted to gather the facts concerning my paternal grandfather, whom I hadn't seen in many years. We had corresponded intermittently, and he had occasionally sent me bits and pieces of genealogy and family history. Then I learned that he was at the home of my aunt, not far distant. Armed with my shorthand notebook (this was before tape recorders), I called at Aunt May's home. I was totally unprepared. Grandpa had suffered a stroke and was bedfast, but he could still talk. When I asked him to tell me about his life, tears came to his eyes. "I can't remember anything. It's gone. How I wish you had come sooner."

Several years ago, in one of my classes, an older student submitted her life-story assignment, which filled only part of one side of a loose-leaf sheet. "That's all there is," she insisted.

I knew that woman had raised ten fine children and had lived from horse-and-buggy days to putting a man on the moon. I took her aside and began asking questions about her life on the ranch as a bride, and adjustments as each child was born. I knew she had been very active in her church, a thorough Christian woman, who had traveled on horseback to administer to the needs of her scattered neighbors, whether it was birthing or dying, or points in between. She told me gripping stories in her self-effacive way, of

following her hunches and arriving at critical moments to relieve
or to share a burden.

Yet here was a woman who insisted that her life was uninterest-
ing, and had written it all on one side of a page. She is gone now
and so are many of the truths and motivations she might have left
with her posterity.

In gathering any records or memoirs from public or private
sources, especially from the old-timers, time is the single most important factor. Records can be burned or otherwise destroyed,
memories can fade, individuals die, and our links with the past
are broken.

This point is illustrated by Alex Haley in *Roots*. He relates
how, as a boy, he used to listen to the graying, wrinkled old ladies
as they talked and rocked on the front porch: Grandma, aunts,
and Cousin Georgia, the youngest.

From the clues remembered in those long evening conversations, he pursued the trail to his beginnings, through plantation
records, wills, census records.

By the time his occupational situation permitted him to dig
into the past in depth, Grandma and all the other old ladies who
could help him were gone—all but Cousin Georgia who was in
her eighties, living in Kansas City, Kansas.

When he visited Cousin Georgia she said in a very moving way,
"Boy, your sweet grandma and all the rest are sitting up there
watching you . . ."

Cousin Georgia became his psychic support—wrinkled, gray,
wizened, full of all kinds of enthusiasm—that charged him up as
he pursued their common ancestry into Africa to the Mandinka
tribe.

Mr. Haley relates:

> . . . The last time I saw Cousin Georgia she had had a stroke
> about two weeks before. I was getting ready to leave for Africa,
> the time I was going into that little village where I would meet
> the old storyteller who made the connection with my seven gener-
> ations in the United States. Before I left, Cousin Georgia said,
> "Boy, I'm a soldier on God's battlefield and I've been hit. Now
> you get on out of here and do what you got to do."
> When I went to Africa I had this tremendous experience. Then

when I got back to New York, I called my brother and he told me Cousin Georgia had died while I was away. Later I was sitting with the papers my brother gave me . . . I was looking at the hospital report and it had the time of death. I began transposing time from Kansas City, Kansas, to West Africa and it hit me like a shot that Cousin Georgia had died literally within the hour from the time I set foot in that little village. And it has always seemed to me that her mission and her role as the last survivor of those old ladies who told that story when I was a little boy was to see me in the village and then she went and joined the rest, sitting up there watching me.[1]

Mr. Haley's book became far more than a family history or a genealogical compilation. He says:

This isn't the story of a family, it's the saga of a people . . . I have charted the history of every black American, since every one of us is descended from an African who was taken from his homeland, brought to America in the hold of a ship and sold as a slave.[2]

To further illustrate the urgency of exploring home sources, consider one of our experiences. We possessed practically no information on our Flack line. (Note the Flack Pedigree Chart in Chapter 18, "Genealogy Forms Organize Research.")

When my husband was only five, his father died. His mother knew very little family history—only sparse unrecorded family tradition. When his Aunt Minnie was still alive, we visited her many times in an effort to obtain data. But she was reluctant to talk about it, and always changed the subject. We knew she had a small trunk, which we hoped would prove to be a genealogical treasure chest—if we could just get into it.

In her aging years, afflicted with Parkinson's disease, Aunt Minnie was too ill to help us. But she said, "When I'm gone, I'll give the trunk to Allie, and you can get the things you need from her."

Shortly after Aunt Minnie's death, we made an appointment to see Cousin Allie. She brought out the trunk, eager to help us. We

[1] A tape recording made by and in possession of the author, of his address before the League of Utah Writers at the University of Utah, Salt Lake City, Utah, November 17, 1976.
[2] "Roots: A Major Break-Through for Black Genealogy," *Genealogy Digest*, August 1976, p. 108.

pored over its contents: hundreds of old pictures, many of them having been taken in England, as far back as the mid-1800s; scraps of paper with names and dates scribbled on them; pages ripped out of family Bibles (whose, we didn't know); grandparents' pictures that we recognized; Grandma Flack's black hair woven into a chain, daguerreotypes; a marriage certificate from St. Martin's Parish in Birmingham, England, clear back in 1839; citizenship papers; a handwritten divorce decree, which told a fascinating story; a hand-painted miniature of a second great-grandmother whose name we didn't even know at that time and there was none written on it. That was the trouble, not a name was written on one of those hundreds of pictures.

"Who are they?" we asked Allie.

"I don't know. I can remember only a few," she confessed. "Aunt Minnie went over every one with me and I thought I could remember."

What a pity we couldn't have received the knowledge Aunt Minnie took to her grave. Those pictures would have furnished valuable clues if a name and date had been written on every one. Some day even your pictures will be old. Label and date them now for those who come after you. There is not one single living person who would know those pictures of Aunt Minnie's. They are all gone. Too late! Too late!

However, with what clues we did find, we searched microfilmed records at the Genealogical Society and also obtained birth and death certificates from the General Register Office in England to fill out the family group sheet of Joseph Burchell and Mary Llewellyn as shown in Chapter 18. We still have more searching to do. But this gives you an idea of how you begin to follow clues in "home sources" in order to complete your sheets as a guide in writing your accurate family history.

Rules for Letter Writing

But what do you do about the relatives who live so far away that you can't visit or interview them personally? They are still a part of your "home sources" because of their relationship. Of course you'll have to write letters. But if rules of good letterwriting are not practiced, you may never get an answer.

1. *Put yourself in the place of the person to whom you are writing.* Ask yourself the question, "What kind of a letter would I like to receive?" Create a good first impression. WARMTH should be part of your letters. A form letter is often relegated to the if-I-get-around-to-it pile.

2. *Be genuinely interested in your correspondent.* Respect him and let him know you do. Your relative is not obligated to help you, so build good rapport. When you seek genealogical information, you are asking for confidential data which he may not want to share. You will find skeletons in many closets and in most families' records. So don't make a big thing of it or cause unnecessary embarrassment by your reactions.

3. *Letters should be clean and attractive in appearance.* Type whenever possible for easier reading. Use a black or blue-black ribbon. Never write a letter with the red side of a ribbon. Clean the type keys frequently. Letters written in pencil create a bad impression. Use clean paper of good quality. Letters hastily scribbled on a crumpled or dog-eared piece of scratch paper are an insult to the recipient. On the other hand, letters written on a letterhead may tend to intimidate the recipient, especially if he is older, so use plain paper.

4. *Plan your letter carefully.* Include return address at the top of your letter, in case the letter becomes separated from the envelope.

Use informal personal language. Avoid formal introductory statements, such as: "According to my records . . ." or, "At an early date . . ." or, "For your information wish to advise . . ."

If possible, refer to some past association to start the nostalgia thought patterns working and to create a warm responsive feeling.

Know exactly what information you need. Write a first draft. Make necessary improvements, then type the final copy neatly and accurately. Reread your letter to make sure it says what you want it to say.

Be courteous. Never demand. Be clear and concise. If he does not understand what you want, he can't help you. Be specific, but also reasonable. Don't expect too much of him. Remember that it takes time, and sometimes great effort, even to copy information your correspondent already has at hand, let alone any he may try to collect for you. Don't ask for too much at one time or you'll get nothing. Never ask for "all the information you have on this family." That's like waving a red flag in front of a dedicated genealogist. Listed questions of needed information, followed by blank spaces, are easier for most correspondents to fill in, such as:

1. Where did Grandfather go to school? _____
2. Did Grandfather have farm holdings in addition to the original homestead? If so, where? _____

A little expressed appreciation goes a long way. Offer to exchange information you have in return for what you hope to receive from him.

Give a reason for a deadline in order to get a quick response, such as: "I'm trying to finish my life story/family history to give to my children for Christmas." The longer people delay their answer, the less chance you have of receiving one.

Always include a self-addressed, stamped envelope for reply.

Always keep a carbon copy of your letter in a "suspense file"— letters waiting for replies. Check this file every couple of months, so you don't forget what is still outstanding. If you haven't received an answer, send a gracious follow-up reminder.

Some people freeze when they see a form to be completed, so a printed family group sheet (see Chapter 18) may frighten them. This is especially true of elderly people or those with limited education. But in order to keep records straight, you may have to risk it. If you think the person will respond to a family group sheet, enclose one. It looks quite crowded at first glance. Your correspondent may feel easier about filling in a questionnaire which you can formulate similar to the one shown. Leave adequate space between names so the recipient does not feel confined.

In writing your autobiography/family history, you will undoubtedly refer to your correspondent's brothers and sisters, grandparents, aunts and uncles, etc. Do you know which family tree they belong to? Family Group Sheets and Pedigree Charts (Illustrations 4, 5, 6) are the surest system of organization (see Chapter 18, "Genealogy Forms Organize Research"). For accuracy, you'll

Dear Friend and Relative,

I am trying to gather information on my family, both to preserve it and to make it available to others. I would be most grateful if you would fill in the chart on the back of this letter as completely as you can and return it to me; I have provided a self-addressed, stamped envelope for your convenience.

Genealogy is the fastest-growing hobby in the world, so you may also be interested in our ancestors. I will be glad to share what I have with you; three generations of my family are presented below.

While I appreciate any help you may give me, I don't wish to impose on you; but if you could refer me to others who might help, or if you have precious documents (Bible records, certificates, journals, etc.) that I might copy, I would be indebted to you. I want to preserve our family's history as accurately and completely as possible.

Thank you; your interest, time and help are appreciated.

Respectfully,

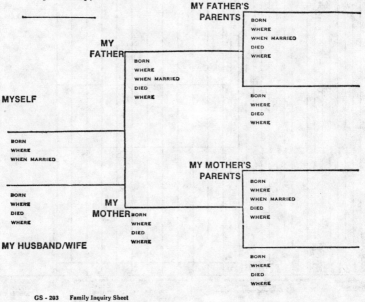

MY FATHER'S PARENTS
BORN
WHERE
WHEN MARRIED
DIED
WHERE

MY FATHER
BORN
WHERE
WHEN MARRIED
DIED
WHERE

BORN
WHERE
DIED
WHERE

MYSELF

BORN
WHERE
WHEN MARRIED

MY MOTHER'S PARENTS
BORN
WHERE
WHEN MARRIED
DIED
WHERE

BORN
WHERE
DIED
WHERE

MY MOTHER
BORN
WHERE
DIED
WHERE

MY HUSBAND/WIFE

BORN
WHERE
DIED
WHERE

GS - 203   Family Inquiry Sheet

4

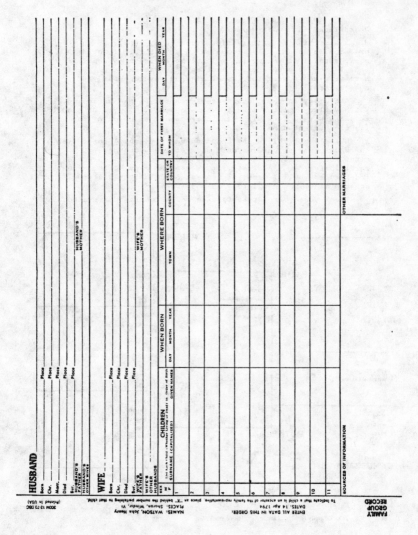

HUSBAND

Born _____ Place _____
Chr. _____ Place _____
Marr. _____ Place _____
Died _____ Place _____
Bur. _____ Place _____
HUSBAND'S FATHER
HUSBAND'S OTHER WIVES

HUSBAND'S MOTHER

WIFE _____

Born _____ Place _____
Chr. _____ Place _____
Died _____ Place _____
Bur. _____ Place _____
WIFE'S FATHER
WIFE'S OTHER HUSBANDS

WIFE'S MOTHER _____

CHILDREN	WHEN BORN			WHERE BORN			DATE OF FIRST MARRIAGE		WHEN DIED		
(List each child (whether living or dead) in Order of Birth) SURNAME (CAPITALIZED) GIVEN NAMES	DAY	MONTH	YEAR	TOWN	COUNTY	STATE OR COUNTRY	TO WHOM		DAY	MONTH	YEAR
M F											
1											
2											
3											
4											
5											
6											
7											
8											
9											
10											
11											

OTHER MARRIAGES

SOURCES OF INFORMATION

FAMILY GROUP RECORD

300M 12-73 DBC
(Printed in USA)

To indicate that a child is an ancestor of the family representative, place an "X" behind the number pertaining to that child.

ENTER ALL DATA IN THIS ORDER:
NAMES: WATSON, John Henry
PLACES: Sharon, Windsr, Vt
DATES: 14 Apr 1794

5

Pedigree Chart for your convenience,
Please Complete and Return.

☐ Great Grandfather
BORN
WHERE
WHEN MARRIED
DIED
WHERE

☐ Great Grandmother
BORN
WHERE
DIED
WHERE

☐ Great Grandfather
BORN
WHERE
WHEN MARRIED
DIED
WHERE

☐ Great Grandmother
BORN
WHERE
DIED
WHERE

☐ Great Grandfather
BORN
WHERE
WHEN MARRIED
DIED
WHERE

☐ Great Grandmother
BORN
WHERE
DIED
WHERE

☐ Great Grandfather
BORN
WHERE
WHEN MARRIED
DIED
WHERE

☐ Great Grandmother
BORN
WHERE
DIED
WHERE

Your Father's Father
BORN
WHERE
WHEN MARRIED
DIED
WHERE

Your Father's Mother
BORN
WHERE
DIED
WHERE

Your Mother's Father
BORN
WHERE
WHEN MARRIED
DIED
WHERE

Your Mother's Mother
BORN
WHERE
DIED
WHERE

Your Father
BORN
WHERE
WHEN MARRIED
DIED
WHERE

Your Mother
BORN
WHERE
DIED
WHERE

Your Name
BORN
WHERE

Your Spouse

Please estimate dates if not known.
Indicate estimated dates with a '?'.

6

QUESTIONNAIRE FOR FAMILY INFORMATION

Will you please fill in as much information in the spaces as you can, even if it is not complete?

Your father's name (my grandfather) _____

His birth date _____ His birth place _____

His death date _____ Where did he die? _____

Your mother's maiden name (my grandmother) _____

Her birth date _____ Her birth place _____

Her death date _____ Where did she die? _____

Their marriage date _____ Where were they married? _____

Do you have information about their children:

Name in full	Birth date	Birth place	To whom married?	Mge date	Death date
1.					
2.					
3.					
4.					
5.					
6.					

What else do you recall about places this family lived? What was their work? What church did they belong to? Were they active in the community? Do you know of any outstanding accomplishments or positions held? Please use the reverse side if you can supply any of the suggested or additional information.

need these for as many generations as your family history includes.[3]

Or you can create your own form as desired, using Illustration 7 as your guide.

Now that you have accumulated all this information from your home sources, how can you determine what tidbits are correct, or are more likely to be correct, than others? Undoubtedly you have found conflicting data. You can't possibly evaluate it without understanding the differences between Primary and Secondary Sources.

A *Primary source* is an eyewitness record or account of an event or circumstance, written or stated, at or near the time of happening. Or it can be recorded at the time of the event from your own knowledge. For example, I was not an eyewitness to the birth of my niece, but my sister telephoned and told me, and I recorded it in my journal immediately following the conversation.

A *Secondary source* is a record or account of an event or circumstance made or stated by a non-eyewitness or by one not closely connected with the event, recorded or stated sometime following the event, making fallibility of memory an important consideration.

Primary sources include:

1. Eyewitness accounts. (However, different eyewitnesses to the same event may report conflicting impressions.)
2. Diaries and journals.
3. Vital statistics.
4. Deeds.
5. Military records. (Early militia rolls are filed in county offices; some are filed in the State Archives; most are in the National Archives in Washington, D.C.)
6. Cemetery records, tombstones, and sexton's records. (Although these are Primary Sources, most of the information included is secondary, such as birth and parentage, which may have been supplied by a fallible informant. An informant is one who supplies information for a rec-

[3] A handy printed inquiry form is available through the Genealogy Club of America and The Everton Publishers, Inc. listed in the Appendix.

ord, and is usually so designated on the form. No written
record is better than its informant. If he is a member of
the family, the information would be more reliable than
a neighbor's word, who might be listed as the informant
on a death certificate, for example.)

7. School records.
8. Printed funeral programs.
9. Birth announcements.
10. Certificates.
11. Church records. What do you do if the church burns
    down with the records in it? It's a vicious circle. You're
    back to Vital Statistics (see Chapters 16 and 17, "Civil
    and Public Records" and "Church Records").
12. Newspapers. (They are subject to considerable error even
    though the record was reported at the time of the event.
    The typesetter may commit an error, and the information
    given to him may have been secondary, or erroneous in
    the first place. Read accounts of the same event in two
    newspapers and note the differences.)
13. Letters. (They are most helpful, if date and place are
    stated.)
14. Photographs. (They furnish many clues if labeled and
    dated, which is rare.)
15. Telephone and city directories.
16. Personal records.
17. Marriage proclamations and wedding invitations. (Re-
    member that not all marriages actually follow issuance of
    an invitation or announcement.)
18. Pamphlets of historical or family significance.
19. Oral history.
20. State and Federal Census Records. (The census itself is
    Primary, but some of the information included is Second-
    ary—given long after births, for example. We seldom
    know who the census informant was—it could have been
    a neighbor or an older child who didn't know the right
    answers. Also remember that the census recorder wrote
    the information as he heard it.)
21. Land records.

22. Court records.
23. Naturalization papers.

When searching any of these documents or papers, always ask yourself some questions about how the record came to be made. Is it authentic? You must make value judgments of the author or the maker of such records. How accurate are they? Some record-keepers, especially amateur, wish to hide the truth of conditions and events. Evaluate honestly, if you can.

Secondary sources include:

1. Testimony recorded at a time *removed* from the event.
2. Obituaries are only as accurate as the person giving the data, as well as allowing for possible typesetting errors.
3. Printed family histories.
4. Printed county records are only as accurate as the compiler.
5. Transcribed records.
6. Compiled records.
7. Copied records.

Of course, the last three named designate records that have been copied from either an original record or from other transcribed, compiled, or copied records. Human error creeps in each time a record is copied. This is why photostats of original records are desirable. You have an actual picture of the original, removing chances for human error.

As you study the next two chapters on civil and church records, keep these facts in mind, and you will be able to more intelligently evaluate what is recorded there.

If you need personal help, check with nearby colleges and universities. Many of them now teach genealogy and related classes. Local state and county historical societies can also help, because some of them conduct training classes. Many of them have excellent libraries on the subject. Your principle sources of information will be located in three kinds of depositories. In this and the following two chapters, we will discuss three kinds of records: (1) personal, or home sources, (2) public, or civil, (3) religious, or church.

Chapter 16

CIVIL AND PUBLIC RECORDS

Government agencies constantly accumulate data that reveal the course of citizens' lives from birth to death. The moves from one locality to another are reflected in birth, marriage, and death records which, by law, are to be kept through civil vital statistics. This has not always been the case, especially in America. Military service becomes part of local and federal records. A "military jacket" (the packet in which all papers are filed pertaining to a specific serviceman or woman) are generally filed in the National Archives. They sometimes disclose a great deal of individual history regarding service assignments and, if dead, the problems of survivorship, listing names, addresses, and relationships.

Land ownership and transfer records trace moves from one locality to another, giving clues for specific searches. Employment records and licenses of all kinds pinpoint an individual in his livelihood and provide more specific identification, especially when there are similar names. For example, I have a great-great-grandfather named James James in Wales. I have located three men in the same parish named James James: one an agricultural laborer, one a tailor, and one a shoemaker. Any one of the three could fit my pedigree agewise, but I can prove nothing.

Taxes, inheritances, bankruptcies, lawsuits, and wills all have possibilities for family links and interesting family history data.

A confusing aspect is that records are created and preserved at different government levels—town (or township) or city, county, state, federal. Yet what is recorded and preserved at specific levels of government is not always clearly defined, and to further complicate the picture, it varies from state to state. Record-keeping agencies differ in each country, but each has its counterparts of town, county, and national jurisdictions. However, knowing in which agency the specific records are kept doesn't always open the door.

Because of the right to privacy, all records—such as welfare records—are not open to public scrutiny. Census records since 1900 are not available for search, for the same reason. Adoptions are sealed. So keep this in mind as you try to obtain information from public-record repositories.

Another stumbling block is that many public offices are subject to political change, and a continuity of skilled help may be lacking where the employee turnover is affected by elections rather than capability. So be prepared for occasional inefficiency.

This turnover may account for the fact that some records cannot be located in the right place. They may be stored in another repository, unknown to the current employee. In fact, even some local information can be found in the National Archives or in the State Archives. So keep looking.

Undoubtedly you will have to search in various areas beyond your own state, and jurisdictions different from your own locality may be confusing.

> If you are working on strange territory outside your own state, it is helpful to know something about the several main patterns of local government across the country. Every state is divided into counties except Louisiana, which calls its comparable units parishes. The only subdivisions not included in counties are certain large cities in a few states. In these cases the cities have been given county functions, usually only in the twentieth century. The most extreme case is Virginia, which has 96 counties and 38 independent cities. New York has 57 counties and the five boroughs of New York City, each borough doubling as a county. San Francisco, Denver, Honolulu, and St. Louis also double as counties.
>
> The next complication is that the common terms in local government have no standard definitions. In the New England states, the unit with most local authority is the town. (The extreme cases are Connecticut and Rhode Island, where counties are merely court jurisdictions.) But the term *town* in New England, and in New York as well, does not mean an urban center comparable to a village or city. It means a subdivision of a county similar

to the township in the midwest—but with more important functions. Thus in these northeastern states, all farmers live in towns
even though they live in the country.

In the southeast, where early settlement was more often rural,
the county has always been the major subdivision. Townships
exist as unimportant units within counties. The Middle Atlantic
states vary between these extremes, and as the newer states to the
west were organized, they created townships in the rural areas, but
incorporated separately from them as towns those urban settle-
ments larger than villages but smaller than cities. To confuse matters further, *township* was also the term used for the land sur-
veyor's unit of six miles square. It may or may not represent the
bounds of a political subdivision by the same name.[1]

Generally you will be able to find records in civil jurisdictions,
as follows:

Birth and death, marriage and divorce records: Most states since
the early 1900s keep vital statistics on a state basis under the State
Health Department. Write to the Bureau of Vital Statistics in the
state of birth. County clerks must be contacted for births and
deaths that occurred before state offices were established, different
years for different states. (See Appendix for charts of where to
write for births, deaths, marriages, and divorces, and beginnings
by state.)

School records: Superintendent of Schools in the county or district. University records at the specific institution.

State Census records: County Clerk. The National Archives has
federal censuses. Most state libraries and state historical societies
also have state censuses.

Land records: County Recorder, or Town Clerk in New England.

Tax records: City (town) or County Treasurer, City or County
Auditor; County Trustee in Tennessee; Tax Collector in New
Jersey.

Military records: County Clerk for early militia rolls; the National
Archives for other.

Judicial records: County Clerk.

County histories in the public or genealogical library or histori-

[1] Thomas E. Felt, *Researching, Writing, and Publishing Local History*
(Nashville: American Association for State and Local History, 1976), pp.
44–45.

cal societies will outline the evolution of counties from their inception, showing county divisions with population growth. Studying gazetteers and maps is essential to follow your people and to know where to inquire for specific records. Maps and county histories work together.

The National Archives and Records Center, Washington, D.C. 20409 is the depository for vast federal records. However, the trend is currently to get federal records of a local nature out of Washington. Eleven branches have been set up throughout the United States to serve specific regions. (See Appendix for list of locations and addresses.)

Every country has its specific record requirements. For example, the Civil Registration of births, marriages, and deaths for England and Wales began 1 July 1837. You can get a copy of the certificate and have indexes searched by writing to: General Register Office, St. Catherine's House, 10 Kingsway, London WC2B 6JP, England. You must send £4.50 ($9.00 U.S., depending on exchange rate) for each certificate, which would include a five-year search in their records for a particular name. Send 10p (25¢ U.S.) for an airmail reply which will cover postage for up to three certificates. Use some form of international money order, such as American Express, instead of sending cash, personal checks, etc. The above fees are subject to change.

Before 1837 in England, birth, marriage, and death records were kept in local parish registers. Periodically, copies of the parish records were made and sent to the diocesan office. Such copies have become known as Bishop's Transcripts.

Certificates of birth, marriage, and death furnish not only specific data, but many clues for further search. If you haven't obtained a certified copy of your own birth certificate, by all means do it. You'll need it for a passport, and also eventually when you file for Social Security benefits.

When requesting the certificate from an agency before states assumed the responsibility, give "about" dates and places, especially if there is a question. For example, ask the County Clerk for the birth certificate for Jane Doe, born about 1890 near Omaha, Nebraska. If you are too specific, he might overlook the

real Jane Doe who was born January 15, 1891 in Douglas, Nebraska (near Omaha). You might know the individual lived in
Omaha, but learn that she was born at her grandmother's home
in Douglas. The given name is not listed. It may be just male or
female child Doe in many instances.

It's entirely possible that a doctor, due to pressures of work,
neglected to file a record of birth. In that case, church records are
the only hope for an official record. A church baptism or blessing
certificate is a proper substitute. If there is no existing church record of the event, you may obtain a "Birth Testimony." Of course,
you can make up your own form, but one is shown here.[2] This
procedure should also be followed for marriages and deaths. (See
Illustrations 8, 9, 10.)

In the case of adoptions, such records are sealed by the court in
order to protect the child and both sets of parents. No one is supposed to be allowed to examine such records. Birth certificates are
reissued with the names of the adoptive parents instead of the
natural parents.

Thoughtful examination of certificates divulges a great deal of
personal or family history.

Birth Certificate

Note the details recorded on a certified copy of a birth
certificate. We'll list them, because it's hard to spot them all,
when bunched together on the form. Of course, these are not
completely uniform from state to state.

Place of birth—city, county, and state. Hospital or at home.

Name of child. (This is often left blank.)

Sex: F or M. (Mine was marked G—for girl.)

Twin, triplet, or other.

Legitimate?

Date of birth.

Full names of father and mother.

Places of residence.

Occupations and type of business of both parents.

[2] Copies of Birth, Marriage, and Death Testimony certificates can be obtained
from Jerry D. Wells, 1122 North 800 East, Orem, Utah, for about 5¢ each.

Birth Testimony

I, the undersigned, testify that

_____
(Full Name as Given at Birth)

was born at_____
(Town, County, State or Country)

on_____, the_____
(Day, Month, Year)   (Son or Daughter)

of_____
(Father's Full Name)

and _____
(Mother's Full Maiden Name)

The person described above is my_____
(Self, Son, Father, Sister, etc.)

I obtained this information from:

_____
(Name and Address of Person or Description and Location of Document)

_____

_____

Signed_____
(Date)

Witness_____
(Date)

Number of children of this mother and number of living children.

How many fetal deaths?

Signature of informant and doctor. (Analyze the "informant" situation. Was the individual reliable? Was she/he present at the birth? Or is there a margin for error?)

Marriage Records

Application for marriage license is filled out in the office of the County Clerk (or counterpart) from information submitted by the bride and groom, usually found in the bride's locality. The application calls for the following:

Full names of bride and groom.

Dates of birth of both.

Usual residence of both (city, town, county, and state).

Race (not included on the forms in all states).

Number of marriages.

How their last marriage ended.

Education (elementary, high school, college).

Both fathers' names and where born.

Both mothers' maiden names and where born.

Race and nationality of fathers and mothers (again, race only in some states).

Date of intended marriage and who will perform the ceremony.

Signed by the deputy clerk and bride and groom.

In some states they are also asked, "Are you under any court-imposed obligation to support of minor children?" (Must answer yes or no. If the answer is yes, many more questions and answers become part of the file.)

The marriage license, in two parts, is then issued and taken to the church at the time of marriage. After the ceremony, the license is signed by two witnesses. The officiant (minister, priest, rabbi, or bishop) signs the certificate and fills in the marriage date. He gives the certificate to the couple and returns the other part to the County Clerk's office.

Both application and license are filed in the County Clerk's

Marriage Testimony

I, the undersigned, testify that

_____
(Full Name of the Groom)

and _____
(Full Name of the Bride)

were married on _____
(Day, Month, Year)

at _____
(Town, County, State or Country)

This was his_____ and her_____ marriage.
(1st, 2nd, etc.)   (1st, 2nd, etc.)

Groom's father: *_____

Groom's mother: *_____

Bride's father: *_____

Bride's mother: *_____

Married by: *_____

a (n)_____ in _____
(Title of Minister or Official)   (Name of Church or Political Jurisdiction)

The_____described above is (are) my_____
(Couple, Groom or Bride)   (Self, Mother, etc.)

I obtained this information from:

_____
(Name and Address of Person or Description and Location of Document)

_____

Signed:_____
(Date)

Witness:_____
(Date)

*Record only that information about which you are sure.

office and can be examined if both names and date of marriage are known. A copy of the license can be obtained.

The marriage certificate, which is presented to the bride and groom, of course, does not include all the foregoing information, but simply:

Names and residences (city and state) of bride and groom.

Date of marriage, signature of officiant, signatures of two witnesses.

The church certificate has the same number on it as the one issued by the County Clerk.

Death Certificate

A certified copy of a death certificate is obtained from the same source as the birth certificate. What's on it? These also vary slightly, and a recent one includes a little more detail than an old form does.

Name.

Date and time of death.

Sex.

Race (not included on the forms in all states).

Birthplace.

Birth date.

Age at death.

Citizen of what country?

Social Security number (only recently).

Marital status.

Name of surviving spouse.

Usual occupation.

Kind of business or industry.

Education.

Name of father.

Maiden name of mother.

Was decedent ever in U. S. Armed Forces?

Residence: Inside or outside city limits. City, county, state.

Mailing address of informant. (This could be a non-family member, in which case, how authentic is the information?)

Death Testimony

I, the undersigned, testify that

_____
(Full Name of Deceased at Time of Death)

died at_____
(Hospital or Street Address, if Known)

_____
(Town, County, State or Country)

on _____ and was buried on _____
(Day, Month, Year)   (Day, Month, Year)

in the_____cemetery

at_____,
(Town, County, State or Country)

_____was aged_____and was the_____of
(He or She)   (Son or Daughter)

_____
(Name of Deceased's Father)

and_____
(Name of Deceased's Mother)

and the_____of_____
(Husband or Wife)   (Name of Spouse)

The deceased was my_____
(Father, Sister, Husband, Daughter, etc.)

I obtained this information from:

_____
(Name and Address of Person or Description and Location of Document)

_____

Signed:_____
(Date)

Witness:_____
(Date)

Name of hospital or other institution where death occurred, city, county.

Physician's signature (certifier of death).

Physician's state license number.

Certifier's address.

Burial, entombment, cremation, or removal.

Signature of funeral director.

Name of funeral home.

Name and location of cemetery or crematory.

Local Registrar's signature and date accepted by local Registrar.

Cause of death: illness, accident, homicide, suicide, pending.

Date of injury.

Time of injury.

Was the injury at work (yes or no)?

Place of injury (home, farm, factory, street, freeway, office building, etc.).

Location (address).

Distance of injury away from home.

Were laboratory tests done for toxic chemicals (yes or no)?

The same questions are asked for alcohol.

Describe how injury occurred.

If motor vehicle accident, explain if decedent was driver, passenger, or pedestrian.

See how many clues there are to follow up and how much information you have found for your family history?

Cemetery or Sexton's Records

But a death certificate isn't the only important part of death records. Don't overlook cemetery or sexton's records or funeral homes. Public cemeteries are maintained under town, city, or county jurisdiction. You could tramp the cemetery over, searching for specific stones, but the sexton has indexed records to save all that trouble. Again you'll find varying degrees of information, some complete and some incomplete. What does it generally give? A plot description, telling where the person was buried:

Name of deceased.

Date of death.

Age of deceased.

A relationship of the deceased to some person, living or dead, such as "widow of."

Names of parents.

Date of birth of deceased.

Sometimes place of birth of deceased.

The offices of private cemeteries keep much more complete records. In more recent years "prearrangements" have been sold, and the company keeps a file on everyone who purchases a plot or prepaid funeral arrangements. This file could include complete vital statistics of the purchaser and his whole family, where working, where living, and obituaries, of family members who have died.

In times past families had private burial grounds, sometimes on or near their farms. Some archives have collected and preserved data from all the family cemeteries in their locality, but a visit to the locale is sometimes necessary.

Vital statistics are the skeleton of your autobiography/family history, but don't stop there.

In case you don't already know it, libraries and historical societies have not only vast numbers of books on all subjects, but they also maintain collections of old and recent newspapers (either in the stacks or on microfilm), periodicals, maps, histories of county, state, and nation, gazetteers, collections of clippings and other people's research, church records (printed and on microfilm), census records (microfilmed), unpublished manuscripts. Many of the large public libraries also have a genealogical library, notably Los Angeles, Portland, Minneapolis, New York, to name only a few.

If the library or historical society is far distant, consult the telephone directories in the local library or metropolitan telephone office for addresses. Always include a self-addressed, stamped envelope for reply. See if the library has a copy of the *Directory of Historical Societies and Agencies*, published by the American Association for State and Local History, 1400 Eighth Avenue South, Nashville, Tennessee 37203.

Through interlibrary loans you may be able to obtain the records you need which are in another library across the country, or even in another country. Books, microfilms, theses, and even some manuscripts can be requested. Go to your local public librarian and give the complete bibliographical data that identifies the record you need. If you know the library where your record is, tell the librarian. Otherwise he will know the nearest library to contact and will notify you when the record arrives. You will be charged only for postage. It is possible you will have to use the record right at the library. After you have copied the information you need, check it back for accuracy while you still have the record in your possession.

Regional Archives Centers have *Union Catalogs of Books, Microfilms, Manuscripts and Newspapers* (see Appendix for addresses).

Separate genealogical libraries and historical societies are all over the world. Some require membership to use their records, and it would be advantageous to join one such as the extensive New England Historic Genealogical Society, 101 Newbury Street, Boston, Massachusetts 02116. You would save time and money which would otherwise be spent in correspondence and travel.

The Genealogical Library, 50 East North Temple, Salt Lake City, Utah 84150, operated by The Church of Jesus Christ of Latter-day Saints, is the largest of its type in the world, and is open to the public for searching, without charge. Vast microfilming projects constantly add records from all over the world.

This library has some two hundred branches throughout the United States where anyone of any faith can go and, for a postage transfer fee, order microfilms from the headquarters library. Then you can search the film on the reading machines at the branch library near you. To find a branch library, turn to the Yellow Pages of the telephone directory and call the closest unit of The Church of Jesus Christ of Latter-day Saints to find out where the nearest branch library is. Or the July 1976 issue of *The Genealogical Helper* lists all the branches. For this magazine write to The Everton Publishers, P.O. Box 368, Logan, Utah 84321.

A Utah historian was attending a conference in the Midwest and visited with a woman who said, "We live in this tiny town in South Dakota where one would think we could never have access to historical and family history records. But we have a dedicated local librarian who is very interested in family history, and he collects every possible volume. If the volume can't be obtained, he has it photocopied. We also have a Mormon Church Branch Library nearby where we can order records from the big library in Utah. I go to our public library and study the family history collections, and my husband goes to the Mormon Church to read the microfilms we order, and we are the lucky recipients of worldwide records right in our little town."

Alex Haley recently told a historians' conference at Logan, Utah, that after visiting the Genealogical Library in Salt Lake City, he discovered he could have done most of his *Roots* research right there.

In addition to university libraries, don't overlook university records which may be valuable to you. They include account books, Registrar's records, matriculating lists, examination lists, tuition lists, subscription lists, graduation lists, degree lists, alumni, sorority/fraternity, social units, honorary society, transcripts, reports, yearbooks, directories, college publications, and awards.

National and worldwide clubs and fraternal organizations are numerous. These would give little genealogical data, but may be meaningful with details for your family history if your people have been members of some of those units. Such records give the club history, and history of members, as it pertains to the organization (see Appendix for a book listing organization names and addresses).

This book also lists other organizations which have been established for the express purpose of searching and preserving records, such as the Daughters of the American Revolution, Sons of the American Revolution, Daughters of the American Colonists, and similar counterparts of pioneers in the various states.

Chapter 17

CHURCH RECORDS

In the earlier years of expansion in the United States, even though vital statistics were kept by the county clerk, there was no strict regulation. Record-keeping was far from complete. The earliest United States Census was 1790, and the data included was sparse. But census records were often the only official record that grouped families together. However, if an individual was not living at home, he was listed in the household where he was staying, usually because of employment.

So in the absence of good civil records, church records are usually our best source from the past. One or two hundred years ago the church was the central spot of the community and the one agency that brought families together.

Since there is no "mother church" or "church of state" in America, there is no central repository for church records. Churches vary in their organizational structure, and supervision and record preservation varies accordingly. If you contact a clergyman of your faith, he can tell you where specific records would be preserved and available. If you cannot find a helpful clergyman, check the *Directory of Historical Societies and Agencies* in the library. In the index, find an organization that preserves the history of that particular denomination. Records of churches no longer in existence can also be found in this way.

In the 1930 depression years, WPA projects copied many of the old church records. So look in the state archives where your people lived, and you might find their records preserved.

Prior to the early 1900s and the beginning of state vital statistics, and especially in the western migrations, itinerant clergymen traveled throughout their assigned areas, preaching as the opportunities arose, giving spiritual aid, and also performing the services of baptizing, marrying, and performing last rites. As the clergy-man traveled, he recorded births, marriages, and deaths that had occurred since his last visit, which may have been months or even years before. He recorded these in his notebook, and upon return-ing to his headquarters after making his circuit, he transferred the data to the permanent church registers. Often long periods of time elapsed before those bits became part of the permanent rec-ords. There was always the possibility of losing some of those loose notations.

The Catholic priest registered his data on cards in the Chan-cery Office. Clergymen of other denominations followed the pat-tern of their own churches.

Many foreigners were included in the growing population, and since most could neither read nor write English they couldn't as-certain correct recording. The clergyman simply recorded as he lis-tened to the broken English. Sometimes two brothers or more in the same family spelled their surnames differently. And that spelling may persist down to the present time. Speak the name aloud and detect possible spelling variations. Especially be aware of the C and K sounds. You will immediately see the possibilities of error in the records made under these difficult circumstances. But they are still better than nothing.

What do church records contain?

Baptism and Blessings

CATHOLIC

Date of birth. (When, where, and how—an emergency is noted.)

Date of baptism. (Baptism and christening is synonymous.)

Parents' names.

Godparents' names.

Priest's signature.

Parish seal is affixed.

PROTESTANT

Protestant churches record basically the same information. Baptists, of course, do not baptize children. They practice "believer baptism." However, if desired, they do sometimes have a "dedication of children" and issue a certificate to the parents that states the date on which it occurred and sometimes the age of the child, but not always.

JEWISH

A Certificate for the Naming of a Child is given to the parents at the Jewish synagogues. The orthodox congregations issue certificates in Hebrew. Certificates issued by the Reformed and Conservative synagogues are written in the language of the country of residence. It reads:

> ". . . In conformity with Jewish tradition, child of _____ [names of parents] was named and blessed in the sanctuary of the Lord _____ [name and place of synagogue] and was given the Hebrew name of _____. May it become a name honored in the household of Israel. Ye are the children of the Lord your God.
> Date of birth and name: _____
> Signatures of witnesses: _____
> _____

MORMON (L.D.S.)

A child is given a "blessing" within weeks of birth, but he is usually "baptized" at the age of eight. Blessing and baptism certificates are issued to the parents, and the ward clerk keeps a duplicate. These records, along with other information contained in Ward Records, from mid-1800s to 1950, can be searched on microfilm at the Genealogical Library, 50 East North Temple, Salt Lake City, Utah.

Church censuses are also available for searching.

The Blessing Certificate supplies the following:

Name of child.

Parentage.

Birth date.

Blessing date.

Name of ward and stake.

Who performed the ordinance.

Signed by the Bishop and clerk.

The birth and blessing information is then placed on a permanent membership record form which remains in the ward or branch of residence all his life and transfers with him when he moves. A duplicate of the form is kept in the membership files at church headquarters in Salt Lake City, Utah. Additional items of church importance are added to the membership record as they occur during the member's life.

Whether the baptism performed is for an eight-year-old child or for an adult, the Baptism Certificate is issued and carries the same data:

Name of baptized member.
Names of both parents.
Birth date and place.
Baptism date.
By whom.
Date of confirmation.
By whom.
Signatures of Bishop and clerk.

Marriage Records

CATHOLIC

The marriage certificate, which is presented to the bride and groom, of course, does not list all the information included on the civil license, but simply:

Names and residences (city and state) of bride and groom.
Date of marriage.
Signatures of two witnesses.
Signature of officiant.

In the Catholic Parish Marriage Register, the following data appears:

Names of couple.
Baptism date and place.
Religion.
Date of marriage.
Witnesses.
Priest's signature.

However, as a result of the prenuptial interview, a great deal more information is filed in the "marriage packet," and this is confidential between the priest and the individuals involved. If the couple specifically asks for a Catholic marriage form, it can be issued, otherwise the form issued by the county clerk suffices. The marriage data is then sent to the parish of baptism. For example, if someone is married in Sacramento, California, but was baptized in St. Louis, Missouri, the information is sent to St. Louis and is then entered in that parish in addition to the baptismal information retained there.

Confirmations are also sent to the parish of baptism.

PROTESTANT

A certificate with marriage date, place, names of bride and groom, signature of officiant, and signatures of witnesses is usually given to the couple, but not always.

JEWISH

The Rabbi issues a certificate of marriage:

> On the day of _____ the sacred covenant of marriage was entered into by _____ [names and Hebrew names of bride and groom] at _____ [name and place of synagogue]. They have spoken the word and performed the rites of Jewish tradition. Marriage is declared. Signed by the Rabbi, by three witnesses, and by the bride and groom.

MORMON (L.D.S.)

No special certificate is issued if the ceremony is performed by a Bishop in a civil ceremony. The license form from the County Clerk suffices. However, when a Mormon couple is married in a "temple," a special certificate is issued, which gives the following information:

Names and place of residence of bride and groom.

Date and place of marriage and which temple.

Signatures of two witnesses.

Signature of officiant.

Date and place of issuance of marriage licence, since this could be a different locality from where the temple is located.

Deaths

CATHOLIC

The death is recorded in the Parish Register. It includes name, birth place, and date, and death date and place.

PROTESTANT

They vary in the detail of their death records. Some keep only the name, death date, and place of the deceased.

JEWISH

Recording of the death date at the synagogue is very important in Jewish tradition. The eldest son is notified on that date every year so he can say a minion and light the candles for his father, to burn from sundown the anniversary day before the father's death to sundown of the anniversary day of death.

MORMON (L.D.S.)

The name, death date, and place is added to the membership record which is retained in the ward or branch where he resides as long as he lives. At death the membership record is forwarded to church headquarters, to be added to the duplicate membership record kept there, and is transferred out of live membership to deceased members' file.

Cemetery Inscriptions

Cemetery inscriptions are often a part of church records because the cemetery sometimes surrounded the church, or was nearby.

Dedicated genealogists have systematically traced tombstone inscriptions, but many abandoned cemeteries are untouched. If you ever visit an old abandoned cemetery, you will see wooden headstones that have deteriorated until no information is left. Even on many stones the data has weathered away. In many such instances no sexton's records were kept, but the burials were part of church records. Many private cemeteries were recorded only in family records which may have been destroyed long ago.

Ethel, a relative in Buffalo, New York, took me to an old cemetery where my fourth great-grandparents, Magdalena Saltsman and John Pickle, were buried. The cemetery was over the hill from the road, and no one would have expected to find a cemetery there until he actually stumbled over fallen headstones. We scrambled through the growth and wild yellow rosebushes in bloom. After lifting up fallen stones, with the help of her boys, we finally found Magdalena's stone. Ethel remembered, from visiting the spot with her father, what the old stone looked like. The rounded white slab was flat on its face, almost covered with vegetation. When we raised it up, the inscription was completely gone. Putting our fingers in the indentations, we spelled out Magdalena Pickle. We never did find John's stone.

If a tracing had been made and preserved in some archive, while the inscriptions were clear, this would have been statistical proof. But it was too late. No sexton's records were available either. This is only one of many similar examples. Projects have been completed of transcribing cemetery inscriptions, and they have been preserved sometimes in the church, sometimes in civil records or in archives and libraries. Many old cemeteries have been demolished, the stones having been bulldozed and destroyed to make way for new burials. The church records, if they still exist, become the only burial records.

Chapter 18

GENEALOGY FORMS ORGANIZE RESEARCH

Now that you know where to find records to make your autobiography/family history as complete and correct as possible, what are you going to do with all that information once it's collected? Gathering and sorting and refinding is very confusing if you don't know how to organize it for easy reference as you write.

A binder and a few basic genealogy forms are tools so you can keep the discovered data in a logical sequence, and you can see at a glance what you lack. As you move into your writing you can easily refer to these sheets.

A binder of some kind is essential in which to keep your sheets and your autobiography/family history when it is finished. Choose either a legal-size post binder, which takes 8½"×14" sheets, or a three-ring binder, which takes 8½"×11" sheets. Any good loose-leaf will do if you wish to use the short sheets. Of course, the 8½"×11" paper is never a problem, while the legal-size post binder is hard to find, as is the paper. There are many supply houses, particularly in the Rocky Mountain west, that supply these long forms and binders. The long sheets have the advantage of carrying more mounted pictures or typed information per page. The Genealogy Club of America and Everton Publishers (see Appendix) have modified the long forms to fit a three-ring binder. There are slight variations in the forms, but the basics are similar. Both houses stock long and short forms. So, in order to avoid confusion, we include them as the sources of supply even though there are other supply houses. Send for their free price list or catalogue.

The basic genealogy sheets are:

A. Five-generation Pedigree Chart.

B. Ancestral Photo Chart (for mounting the pictures of your five generations of ancestors). The Ancestral Photo Chart fits the long post binder, and a Pedigree Portrait Chart fits the three-ring binder. Don't be confused by the difference in the names. They both accomplish the same purpose.

C. Family Group Sheet. You can choose between three styles:

(1) long $8\frac{1}{2}'' \times 14''$ are horizontal only, and fit the legal-size post binder;

(2) short horizontal, $8\frac{1}{2}'' \times 11''$;

(3) short vertical, $8\frac{1}{2}'' \times 11''$. These short forms fit any three-ring binder.

D. Mounting sheets for pictures (heavier paper, about 24-pound to support photos, etc.).

E. Plastic protector sheets for picture pages, either size.

F. Divider sheets (heavier mounting sheets to organize the contents of your book). As your book expands, you will welcome dividers for quick finding. To the edge of the divider sheets, attach divider tabs, purchased at any stationery store. Label inserts as desired. Stagger the tabs so you can locate a specific division at a glance. Suggested labeled divisions would be: Pedigree Charts, Family Groups, Biographies, Documents. Add more divisions if and when the need arises.

If you have an artistic flair or an eye for beauty, you may want to decorate division sheets meaningfully with your own artwork, or with flowers and other objects cut from old cards to make your book reflect you.

You may find your book becoming too bulky with the constant flow of family birth, wedding, and death announcements, family picture Christmas cards, snaps, newspaper clippings, relevant obituaries, and other mementos (all containing valuable family data which should be added to Family Group Sheets and Pedigree Charts). So transfer such items to a separate scrapbook.

Now, let's get your collected material organized on the convenient sheets. Then at a glance you will know what you already have and what you yet must find. Even though this may seem tedious, it will save you endless hours as you proceed with your autobiography/family history, because you will have your material organized for speedy reference. (See Illustrations 11, 12, 13.)

PEDIGREE CHART

CHART NO._____

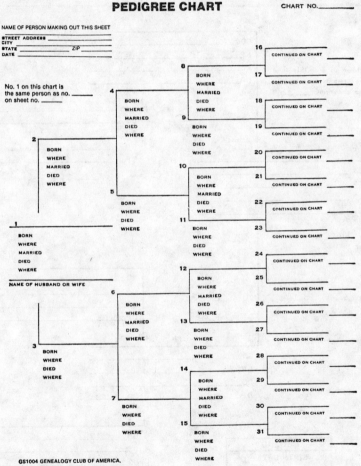

NAME OF PERSON MAKING OUT THIS SHEET

STREET ADDRESS _____
CITY _____
STATE _____ ZIP _____
DATE _____

No. 1 on this chart is the same person as no. _____ on sheet no. _____

16 CONTINUED ON CHART _____

8
BORN
WHERE
MARRIED

17 CONTINUED ON CHART _____

4
BORN
WHERE
MARRIED
DIED
WHERE

DIED
WHERE

18 CONTINUED ON CHART _____

9
BORN
WHERE
DIED
WHERE

19 CONTINUED ON CHART _____

2
BORN
WHERE
MARRIED
DIED
WHERE

20 CONTINUED ON CHART _____

10
BORN
WHERE
MARRIED
DIED
WHERE

21 CONTINUED ON CHART _____

5
BORN
WHERE
DIED
WHERE

22 CONTINUED ON CHART _____

11
BORN
WHERE
DIED
WHERE

23 CONTINUED ON CHART _____

1
BORN
WHERE
MARRIED
DIED
WHERE

24 CONTINUED ON CHART _____

NAME OF HUSBAND OR WIFE

12
BORN
WHERE
MARRIED
DIED
WHERE

25 CONTINUED ON CHART _____

6
BORN
WHERE
MARRIED
DIED
WHERE

26 CONTINUED ON CHART _____

13
BORN
WHERE
DIED
WHERE

27

3
BORN
WHERE
DIED
WHERE

28 CONTINUED ON CHART _____

14
BORN
WHERE
MARRIED
DIED
WHERE

29 CONTINUED ON CHART _____

7
BORN
WHERE
DIED
WHERE

30 CONTINUED ON CHART _____

15
BORN
WHERE
DIED
WHERE

31 CONTINUED ON CHART _____

GS1004 GENEALOGY CLUB OF AMERICA.
P.O. BOX 15784, SALT LAKE CITY, UTAH 84115

11

PEDIGREE SHEET

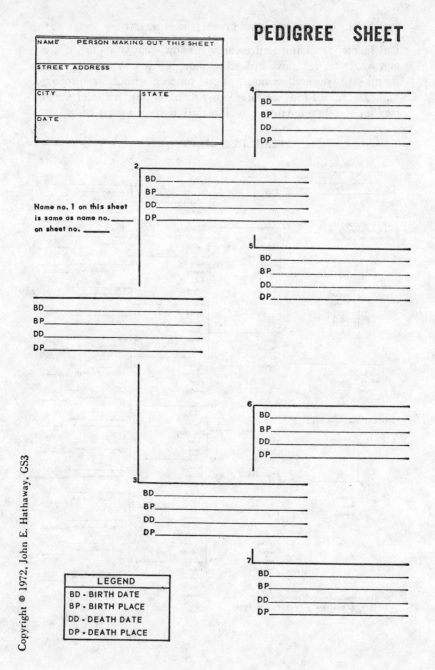

NAME	PERSON MAKING OUT THIS SHEET
STREET ADDRESS	
CITY	STATE
DATE	

Name no. 1 on this sheet
is same as name no. ____
on sheet no. ____

4
BD_____
BP_____
DD_____
DP_____

2
BD_____
BP_____
DD_____
DP_____

5
BD_____
BP_____
DD_____
DP_____

BD_____
BP_____
DD_____
DP_____

6
BD_____
BP_____
DD_____
DP_____

3
BD_____
BP_____
DD_____
DP_____

7
BD_____
BP_____
DD_____
DP_____

LEGEND
BD - BIRTH DATE
BP - BIRTH PLACE
DD - DEATH DATE
DP - DEATH PLACE

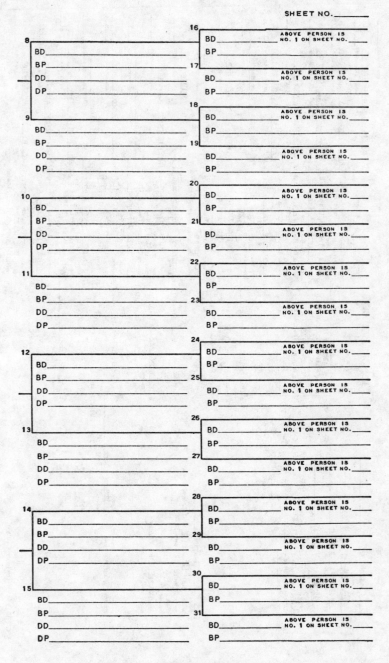

PEDIGREE CHART

Marlane Flack Smith
NAME OF PERSON SUBMITTING CHART

448 East 775 North
STREET ADDRESS

Bountiful, Utah 84010
CITY   STATE

NO. 1 ON THIS CHART IS
THE SAME PERSON AS NO. _____
ON CHART NO. _____

Gen. 1

1 FLACK, Marlane
WHERE Salt Lake City, Salt Lake, Utah
BORN 24 Mar 1954
WHEN MARRIED 12 June 1974
DIED
WHERE

SMITH, Alan Thomas
NAME OF HUSBAND OR WIFE

SOURCES OF INFORMATION

Gen. 2

2 FLACK, Alroy LeGrand
BORN 3 Oct 1920
WHERE Alpine, Utah, Utah
WHEN MARRIED 7 Jan 1946
DIED
WHERE

3 DUTSON, Dora
BORN 9 July 1919
WHERE Kimberly, Twin Falls, Idaho
DIED
WHERE

Gen. 3

4 FLACK, Alroy Mortimer
BORN .22 Mar 1882
WHERE Fairfield, Utah, Utah
WHEN MARRIED 6 Sep 1910
DIED 28 Dec 1925
WHERE Alpine, Utah, Utah

5 CARLISLE, Annie Jeune
BORN 29 May 1892
WHERE Alpine, Utah, Utah
DIED 25 Dec 1965
WHERE Provo, Utah, Utah

6 DUTSON, Alonzo Edmund
BORN 30 July 1893
WHERE Oak City, Millard, Utah
WHEN MARRIED 5 Oct 1916
DIED 19 July 1927
WHERE Salt Lake City, S-L, Utah

7 IAMES, Iona
BORN 22 Dec 1897
WHERE Park Valley, B-Eldr, Ut
DIED 17 Apr 1975
WHERE Salt Lake City, S-L, Utah

Gen. 4

8 FLACK, John Logan
BORN 2 Feb 1834
WHERE Crab Orchard, Lnc, KY,
WHEN MARRIED 7 June 1860
DIED 7 Dec 1899
WHERE Fairfield, Utah, Utah

9 BURCHELL, Emma
BORN 13 Feb 1844
WHERE Dudley, Wrcstr, Engl
DIED 19 May 1929
WHERE Fairfield, Utah, Utah

10 CARLISLE, Thomas Fields, Jr.
BORN 8 Oct 1859
WHERE Alpine, Utah, Utah
WHEN MARRIED 27 Dec 1883
DIED 7 Aug 1933
WHERE Alpine, Utah, Utah

11 SHEPPARD, Annie
BORN 30 Aug 1865
WHERE Provo, Utah, Utah
DIED 5 Mar 1943
WHERE Alpine, Utah, Utah

12 DUTSON, James Nathaniel
BORN 9 May 1869
WHERE Fillmore, Millard, Utah,
WHEN MARRIED 2 Nov 1892
DIED 14 Jan 1947
WHERE Tooele, Tooele, Utah

13 LOVELL, Suzannah
BORN 4 Jan 1874
WHERE Oak City, Millard, Utah,
DIED 17 Nov 1927
WHERE Hinckley, Millard, Utah

14 IAMES, Thomas Richard
BORN 4 Jan 1865
WHERE Lake Point, Tooele, Utah
WHEN MARRIED 5 Sep 1893
DIED 18 Aug 1939
WHERE Salt Lake City, S-L, Utah

15 CHADWICK, Mary Ann
BORN 23 Sep 1867
WHERE North Ogden, Weber, Uh,
DIED 18 Feb 1952
WHERE Salem, Madison, Idaho

Gen. 5

16	FLACK, James Madison	CONT. ON CHART
17	MONTGOMERY, Emily Jane	CONT. ON CHART
18	BURCHELL, Joseph	CONT. ON CHART
19	LLEWELLYN, Mary	CONT. ON CHART
20	CARLISLE, Thomas Fields	CONT. ON CHART
21	HOCQUARD, Fanny Sophia	CONT. ON CHART
22	SHEPPARD, George Henry	CONT. ON CHART
23	ASHMAN, Mary Ann	CONT. ON CHART
24	DUTSON, John William	CONT. ON CHART
25	(2) JENKINS, Caroline Geneva	CONT. ON CHART
26	LOVELL, George	CONT. ON CHART
27	TURNER, Martha	CONT. ON CHART
28	IAMES, James	CONT. ON CHART
29	RICHARDS, Mary	CONT. ON CHART
30	CHADWICK, Abraham	CONT. ON CHART
31	GARNER, Mary Marinda	CONT. ON CHART

CHART NO. _____
1
2
3
4
5
6
7
8
9
10
11
12
13

GS 1013 - Genealogy Club of America

First, take a Five-generation Pedigree Chart—any one of the three shown which will fit your binder. This is your road map, showing how far you've traveled and where you are headed. No matter which form you select, you'll proceed exactly the same. You'll note that the lines are longer on the horizontal forms (Illustrations 12, 13, and 14), thus providing more writing space.

In the top left-hand corner fill in your name, address, and the current date. In the space in the right-hand corner, write 1 after Chart No. __. Now back to the left-hand margin, ignore the next words and go down to the middle line which says 1.

This is YOU.

From your "bone" collection, take your birth certificate. If you always record names, dates, and places uniformly, rather than in a haphazard way, you will find them easier to read. So before writing your name, let's consider some details.

Recording names. Whether you write your name in the order it is spoken, or put the surname first, capitalizing the surname makes your record clearer, especially if you have an unusual name. For example, how would a person who picks up your work know if the name "Van Steuben" is Mr. Van (given name) Steuben (surname)? Or is it Mr. VAN STEUBEN (all surname)?

If initials instead of a full name are part of your given name, put them in quotes so anyone will know you weren't careless. Examples: EVANS, John "L," or EVANS, "JL," if that's your *real* given name.

Now, refer to your birth certificate and write your name in the space after 1, surname capitalized.

The space after *Born* is for your birth date. Wait! There are some real taboos for entering dates.

Recording dates. Always record the day first, then the month, then the year, like the military: 5 June 1945. NEVER use numbers for months, or you'll wonder which is the day and which is the month: 5/6/45. Your records must be explicit, or you'll misread data to be included in your writing. You must use the whole year (1915, 1840, 1750) or your records will really be confusing as you reach back into preceding centuries. Abbreviate the months, leaving off the periods. Your spaces are limited and you need every one.

Now, from your birth certificate, fill in the proper date on your Pedigree Chart. *Print legibly*.

Recording places. A town and state isn't enough. There are towns, named the same, in different counties of the same state in America, and in comparable geographic divisions abroad. So record the town first, then the county, then the state. In other words, proceed from the smallest area to the largest. You do not include the street address, however. In England especially, in earlier years, you might discover an identifying hill or parish listed on the record, within the town or city. It should be included. List it first, then the town or city, then shire (equivalent to American counties), then the country. In America, it would be town, county, state and you needn't add USA.

Example: a. Old Bucket Parish, in the city of Birmingham in Warwickshire in England would be recorded, "Old Bucket, Birmingham, Warws, Eng. or Engl."
          b. Ritzville (never abbreviate a town or city), Adam County, Washington, would be recorded: "Ritzville, Adam, WN."

Abbreviating the county and state is advantageous in getting the necessary information within the allotted space, but it can lead to confusion. Where possible, write out the county. You may wish to use the old-fashioned state abbreviations for clarity.

The next line is *married*. (This is not included on the horizontal forms, Illustrations 12 and 13.) There is space for date only and not a place on Illustrations 11 and 14. Find your marriage certificate. Enter the date—day, month, year.

The next two lines are *Died* and *Where*. Of course, someone else will be filling in those spaces for you.

The space with *Name of Husband or Wife* will be left blank until you're married. If you are or have been married, fill the name in, in the same order as your own. In the case of females, use only the *maiden* surname and don't add the *married* surname. On all genealogical forms a woman is identified by her maiden surname only, except in the top spaces indicating the person who makes out the sheets. Only there she is known by her full name, including married surname: Jane Evans Smith.

If you've been married more than once, put 1 in parentheses before the maiden surname: (1) JONES, Mary Ann. That marriage date on the form refers only to your first marriage. So if you've been divorced, write "div" after the name of the husband or wife. You will find sufficient space at the bottom to fill in subsequent marriage names and dates.

But, you ask, "Where do I put my children?" This is a Pedigree Chart on which you will list only your *direct ancestry*—parents, grandparents, etc., no children, cousins, aunts, or uncles. Your children are your *descendants,* and are listed on the Family Group Sheet, with you as a parent. Your aunts and uncles are the children of your direct ancestors. Your cousins are their children and all will be included on a Family Group Sheet, with their own parents.

Now that box ⚹1 is completed as far as possible, look at your birth certificate for the names of your parents. Compare the names with their birth certificates, if you have them, but be sure you have the correct names.

As your eye follows the little boxes on the Pedigree Chart, you'll note there are even numbers and uneven numbers. Except for YOU in ⚹1, which can be either male or female, *the even numbers are always for male entries, the uneven for female entries.*

So, in space ⚹2 put your father's name. Try to substantiate the name and spelling with "official" records, vital statistics, or church records.

In space ⚹3, enter the *maiden* name of your mother with her other vital data. You'll note "married" appears only under the male name. You don't have to repeat the marriage date in your mother's data.

Go on to spaces ⚹4 and ⚹5. These are your paternal grandparents. Spaces ⚹6 and ⚹7 are for your maternal grandparents. Be sure you get the right people in the right spaces.

The average person won't have nearly enough information to complete this five-generation Pedigree Chart until he's been "gathering" for quite a while. If you're the exception and can go farther, we suggest you order the large Eight- or Twelve-generation Pedigree Chart that folds up to fit into a legal-size book.

Ancestral Photo Chart

Now to the real fun of a Pedigree Chart—your family tree in pictures. The long form (Illustration 16) is called an "Ancestral Photo Chart." The short one (Illustration 15) is called "Pedigree Portrait Chart." You will see immediately that the long form is easier to follow.

First let's consider the long form. Before mounting any pictures at all, if you are typing your records, you'll definitely need a long carriage. Otherwise print your name under the box marked "self" or "child." Numbers 2 and 3 are for your parents. Record their full names under the boxes—your mother's *maiden* name only. Type these as you speak them, instead of surname first and capitalized. On the lower lines, space is limited for names. These boxes correspond to the spaces on your Five-generation Pedigree Chart. Seldom will you be able to find pictures beyond your second-great-grandparents. If you do find more, mount them on the back and put the names under them. A straight line for your third-great-grandparents will probably be sufficient. Under that another line would be for pictures of your fourth-great-grandparents. But this is a rare exception! Good luck.

If using the short form, YOU are in the position of "Child." Enter your name on the line after child. "BP" stands for birth place, and "BD" stands for birth date. Follow the heavy solid lines over to ⚹2 (your father) and ⚹3 (your mother).

At a glance you can see that pictures of all your father's ancestors are to be mounted on the *upper* part of the page and your mother's people are to be mounted on the *lower* part of the page.

A close look at a Pedigree Portrait Chart will usually point out similarities in facial characteristics. You'll know which ancestor you can credit for your big nose, or close-set eyes, or square jaw, or smile. They become more than just names on a sheet.

Finding these old pictures is a real challenge, but a rewarding one. Of course, home sources are probably the only place you'll find them. If you can't find a photographer in your area to copy pictures and reduce them to 1"×1¼" for your Pedigree Portrait

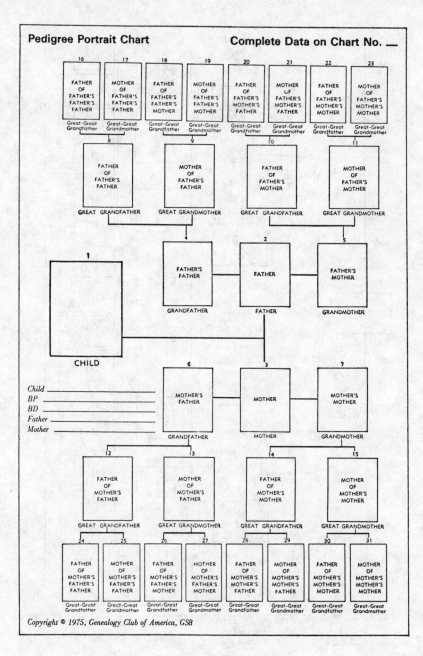

Pedigree Portrait Chart

Complete Data on Chart No. __

| 16 | 17 | 18 | 19 | 20 | 21 | 22 | 23 |

FATHER OF FATHER'S FATHER'S FATHER — Great-Great Grandfather

MOTHER OF FATHER'S FATHER'S FATHER — Great-Great Grandmother

FATHER OF FATHER'S FATHER'S MOTHER — Great-Great Grandfather

MOTHER OF FATHER'S FATHER'S MOTHER — Great-Great Grandmother

FATHER OF FATHER'S MOTHER'S FATHER — Great-Great Grandfather

MOTHER OF FATHER'S MOTHER'S FATHER — Great-Great Grandmother

FATHER OF FATHER'S MOTHER'S MOTHER — Great-Great Grandfather

MOTHER OF FATHER'S MOTHER'S MOTHER — Great-Great Grandmother

8 — FATHER OF FATHER'S FATHER — GREAT GRANDFATHER

9 — MOTHER OF FATHER'S FATHER — GREAT GRANDMOTHER

10 — FATHER OF FATHER'S MOTHER — GREAT GRANDFATHER

11 — MOTHER OF FATHER'S MOTHER — GREAT GRANDMOTHER

4 — FATHER'S FATHER — GRANDFATHER

2 — FATHER — FATHER

5 — FATHER'S MOTHER — GRANDMOTHER

1 — CHILD

Child _____
BP _____
BD _____
Father _____
Mother _____

6 — MOTHER'S FATHER — GRANDFATHER

3 — MOTHER — MOTHER

7 — MOTHER'S MOTHER — GRANDMOTHER

12 — FATHER OF MOTHER'S FATHER — GREAT GRANDFATHER

13 — MOTHER OF MOTHER'S FATHER — GREAT GRANDMOTHER

14 — FATHER OF MOTHER'S MOTHER — GREAT GRANDFATHER

15 — MOTHER OF MOTHER'S MOTHER — GREAT GRANDMOTHER

| 24 | 25 | 26 | 27 | 28 | 29 | 30 | 31 |

FATHER OF MOTHER'S FATHER'S FATHER — Great-Great Grandfather

MOTHER OF MOTHER'S FATHER'S FATHER — Great-Great Grandmother

FATHER OF MOTHER'S FATHER'S MOTHER — Great-Great Grandfather

MOTHER OF MOTHER'S FATHER'S MOTHER — Great-Great Grandmother

FATHER OF MOTHER'S MOTHER'S FATHER — Great-Great Grandfather

MOTHER OF MOTHER'S MOTHER'S FATHER — Great-Great Grandmother

FATHER OF MOTHER'S MOTHER'S MOTHER — Great-Great Grandfather

MOTHER OF MOTHER'S MOTHER'S MOTHER — Great-Great Grandmother

15

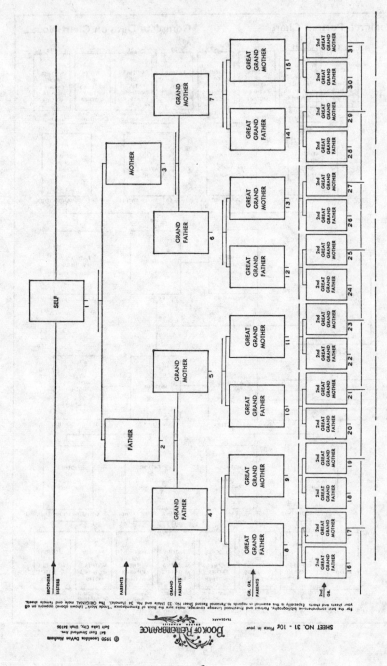

© 1950 Leondas DeVon Mecham
541 East Stratford Ave.
Salt Lake City, Utah 84106

BOOK OF REMEMBRANCE
TRADEMARK

SHEET NO. 31 - 10¢ Place in your

Chart, you can send them to Simmons Photo, a genealogy photo specialist (see Appendix).

As your research proceeds, especially as you consult printed records for your ancestry, you may encounter some different kinds of pedigree charts, the most common being a *descendant* chart. This is the reverse of the ancestral Pedigree Charts shown here. They list the ancestor farthest back and then show his descendants as they spread out with each generation. They take some real studying and you will appreciate the simplicity of the forms included here.

Now that you're following your road map in your Pedigree Charts, isn't that enough? Of course not. Where do you list your children?

Family Group Record

Pictured are two different forms of a Family Group Record (or Sheet), and instructions follow to guide you with each one. They cover the same information, with different amounts of space in which to work. The short vertical sheet (Illustration 17), for a three-ring binder, has small spaces, but you can read it without turning the binder. If you have a legal-size book, you'll use the long horizontal form (Illustration 18), which is the easiest.

Enter names, dates, and places as explained under Pedigree Charts.

If you're using the sheet in Illustration 19, first write your name and address under "Name and address of person submitting this sheet:"

In the space provided, be sure to detail where you obtained each bit and piece of data filled in on your sheet.

Example: 1. Family records compiled by and in possession of Marilla Evans, 1901 "I" St., Sacramento, CA
2. St. Vincent Parish Records, 1375 Spring Lane, Murray, Utah

List additional marriage and divorce information of the children under "Necessary explanations" on Illustration 18, or on the reverse side of Illustration 19.

GS 1025
Copyright © 1969 – Genealogy Club of America

FAMILY GROUP WORK SHEET

HUSBAND_____

Birth	Place	
Chr	Place	Jurisdiction
Death	Place	
Burial	Place	Date of Search
Mar	Place	
Father	Mother (Maiden Name)	...... Recorded Copy Miscellaneous Notes

WIFE _____

Birth	Place	........Transcribed Copy
Chr	Place	...... Extract
Death	Place	
Burial	Place	...... Original
Father	Mother (Maiden Name)	...... Legibility

DOCUMENT DATED: _____

RECORDED: _____   Enc. No._____ Search No._____ Calander Page _____

Male or Female	No.	CHILDREN	WHEN BORN Day Mo. Yr.	WHERE BORN Town	County	State or Country	DIED Day Mo. Place Yr.	MARRIED Date Place To
	1							
	2							
	3							
	4							
	5							
	6							
	7							
	8							
	9							
	10							
	11							
	12							

17

If you are unmarried, go to the column marked "Children."
Where do you fit numerically in your family? You're the second
child? Indicate your sex (F or M) appropriately in the first column. Then record your name in space 2. Capitalize your surname.

Yes, there are children of different surnames in the same family.
We'll discuss this a bit later.

Never use the diminutive form of a given name, such as Betty
for Elizabeth, if the real name is known. If the diminutive form is
the *actual* name, underline it, indicating that it is the real name.

Example: WALL, Betty.

Underline unusual names. Example: WELCH, Aldythe.

Where a name is used for either sex, indicate in the sex column

Family Group Record

SOURCES OF INFORMATION

HUSBAND (1) BURCHELL, Joseph ②

Born	abt 1811 ②	Place of Dudley, Worcs., Engl ②
Chr.	30 May 1813 ②	Place Dudley, Worcs., Engl
m.	18 July 1839②	Place St. Martin's Parish, Birmingham, Warws., Engl ②
Died	27 July 1847②	Place Oldbury, Worcs., Engl
Bur.		Place

HUSBAND'S FATHER BURCHELL, George ② ②
HUSBAND'S MOTHER FOXALL, Esther ②

OTHER WIVES

WIFE LLEWELLYN, Mary ②

Born	1 Aug 1813 ②	Place Dudley, Worcs., Engl ②
Chr.	23 Jan 1899②	Place Fairfield, Utah, Utah
Died		Place
Bur.		Place

WIFE'S FATHER LLEWELLYN, Samuel② ② Mary ②
WIFE'S MOTHER

OTHER HUSBANDS (2) ROSSITER, Solomon (miner) - div. 7 Mar 1857 ②

① Marriage certificate of husband and wife.
② Death certificates of husband and children #1 and #4.
③ Birth certificates of children #1, #2, #3, #4.
④ Christening records of Dudley Parish, by correspondence.
⑤ Divorce decree to Solomon Rossiter and Mary (Llewellyn)Rossiter.
⑥ Naturalization Declaration of Intention for child #2.
⑦ Obituary notices of children #2 and #3.
All of above in possession of A. LeGrand Flack, 448 E. 775 No.,
Bountiful, Utah 84010.

NECESSARY EXPLANATIONS

(list any other marriages of children in this space)

SEX	CHILDREN	WHEN BORN			WHERE BORN			WHEN DIED				WHERE DIED	MARRIED TO	WHEN MD.
		DAY	MONTH	YEAR	TOWN	COUNTY	STATE OR COUNTRY	DAY	MONTH	YEAR		Place		
1 M	BURCHELL, Henry Thomas ③②	4	June	1840	Dudley	Worcs. ②	Engl	30	Aug	1848 ②		Dudley, Engl	To / Where	
2 M	BURCHELL, Charles ③②	1	Apr	1842 ②	"	"	"	1	June	1900②			To FLACK, John Logan ② ②	7 June 1860②
3 F X	BURCHELL, Emma ③	13	Feb	1844 ②	"	"	"	19	May	1929②		Fairfield, Ut. Ut.	where Bates, Tooele, Utah	
4 M	BURCHELL, Abraham George	25	Aug	1846	"	"	"	21	Feb	1847②		Dudley, Engl	To / Where	
5													To / Where	
6													To / Where	
7													To / Where	
8													To / Where	
9													To / Where	
10													To / Where	
11													To / Where	
12													To / Where	
13													To / Where	

and also underline the name. Example: "M" for male, RAN
DALL, Beverly.

If the person was known by a nickname, it can be put in
parentheses following the proper name.

If a person was known by a title during his lifetime, include it
in parentheses.

Example: SMITH, (Rev) Samuel, or
              SMITH, (Dr) Abel.

Now, back to you as that second child. Your name is entered.
The next column says *Day Mo. Year*—a reminder for the order of
recording dates. Record where you were born. "B" means your
birth date. "D" means when you died. (Of course that will be
filled in by someone else in the future.)

At this point we still presume you are an unmarried child, so
leave the "Spouse" column blank.

Other children are listed in their numerical order in the family.
If a child was stillborn, list the word "Stillborn" in the space for
names, and record the date.

In the case of twins or triplets, write the word in parentheses
after the names.

Since you are presumably that #2 unmarried child, now go to
the top of the page and record the name of your father and his
birth date and place. You'll note a space for christening in addition to birth date and place. Fill it in if you have it, but it isn't
vital if you have a birth certificate. Especially as you go farther
back on your pedigree, you may find a christening date in a
church record but no actual birth date. So this must substitute for
a birth date. On the Pedigree Chart, you'll write *chr* before the
date, to indicate that this is a christening and not a birth date.

Next is a space for marriage date and place of the Husband and
Wife.

On your Pedigree Chart you filled in the space for death date
for an ancestor. But here on the Family Group Record is a space
for burial date and place also. Record both dates whenever found.
But sometimes the burial date must be substituted in the absence
of the actual death date.

Under "Note," on Illustration 17, list any other marriages of the Husband and Wife.

Example: (2) 3 Mar 1945 ANDREWS, Margaret

Illustration 18 has a line for other marriages of Husband and Wife. Pedigree Charts do not have lines for additional marriages.

In the case of multiple marriages, the children of each marriage should be listed on separate sheets with their own parents. If a mother has been married twice and has children by both husbands, fill out *two* Family Group Sheets, listing the children of the first husband and the mother, with that husband's data at the top, and the children of the second husband on a separate sheet with that husband's data at the top. The mother will be listed as the wife in both cases. Place 1 in parentheses in front of the first husband's name and 2 in front of the second husband's name.

Example: (1) ADAMS, Jonathan Douglas

Of course the appropriate marriage date of each husband would be on the different sheets in the appropriate spaces.

The long form (Illustration 18) is self-explanatory after reviewing instructions for the short form (Illustration 19).

If you are married (instead of being that unmarried ⚹2 child previously mentioned), list the data on you and your spouse in the spaces at the top of the sheet, and then list your children and their vital data on the lower part of the page. You will be able to adjust to the minor differences in Family Group Sheets and Pedigree Charts, depending on your source of supply. Two are listed in the Appendix.

As you move into the past on your Pedigree Chart, make a Family Group Record for each couple on your chart. Even if you have nothing but names and a child or two, make a sheet for them. Then in the space where their child (who is your ancestor) appears, place X in front of that name, so you can quickly spot your direct ancestry.

These Family Group Sheets, together with your Pedigree Charts, are your organization, so you can spot at a glance where you need to work to complete information for your family history.

Note-keeping Systems

Keeping track of the material you use to substantiate the entered data on your Family Group records is vitally important. When you're concerned with only the first couple of generations, this isn't difficult. But as you move into preceding generations on your Pedigree Chart, the information is not as plentiful or as easily documented. At all times you should be able to identify the source of each separate bit of data.

The simplest note-keeping system, when you have only a little information, is to number each source in the "Source of Information" box. Then in every space on the Family Group Record, put the corresponding number in a circle, where data has been entered from that particular source. Write the numbers small because you may have two or three circled numbers in a space where the information is recorded, since that name or data may be listed in several of your sources. *Never* throw away your Work Sheet on which you have entered all these footnotes, because it is a key to your proof. Also keep the note paper on which you copied from original sources and, for future reference, always detail the source completely. Keep all documents that substantiate your data.

As your records increase in volume and complexity, the simple note-keeping system is not sufficient. If you intend to do much searching on your genealogy to support a lengthy family history, you should get organized early in the game with a more detailed system. The earlier you start these organizing techniques, the easier it is to keep your records straight. The following procedures are here when you're ready for them, but don't be discouraged by taking on too much all at once. You learn by degrees.

A more efficient note-keeping system is to maintain a "calendar." Obtain a supply of manila file folders or envelopes—files are easier to work with, if you have a filing cabinet or an adequate box in which to store them. Also have a good supply of "Family Group Work Sheets" (Illustration 19) on hand. Note additional space at the top for sources which makes them different from an ordinary Family Group Record. If you have a good note-keeping

HUSBAND _____

Birth _____ Place _____

Chr. _____ Place _____

Mar. _____ Place _____

Death _____ Place _____

Burial _____ Place _____

Father _____

Mother _____

NOTE _____

WIFE _____

Birth _____ Place _____

Chr. _____ Place _____

Death _____ Place _____

Burial _____ Place _____

Father _____

Mother _____

NOTE _____

Name and address of person submitting
this sheet:

_____

_____

_____

_____

_____

Where was information shown on this
family record obtained?

_____

_____

_____

_____

_____

_____

_____

19

Family Group Sheet

SEX	CHILDREN	DAY MO. YEAR	CITY	COUNTY	STATE	SPOUSE
1.		B.				Date
		D.				To
2.		B.				Date
		D.				To
3.		B.				Date
		D.				To
4.		B.				Date
		D.				To
5.		B.				Date
		D.				To
6.		B.				Date
		D.				To
7.		B.				Date
		D.				To
8.		B.				Date
		D.				To
9.		B.				Date
		D.				To
10.		B.				Date
		D.				To
11.		B.				Date
		D.				To
12.		B.				Date
		D.				To

Date of search	Search number	Enclosure number	Source of Information	Nil or no. of W. S.
30 Mar 1972	1	1	Utah Bureau of Vital Statistics, Birth Certificate; my vital data; parents' names.	1
6 May 1972	2		Parents' records; many records of ancestors in varying stages; not much on Flacks.	20
30 June 1972	3		With parents visited Dad's cousin, Allie Larsen, Vernon Utah, to see Aunt Minnie Flack's trunk. Many unnamed pictures;	
		2	Loose family Bible sheets;	3
		3	Mge. ctf. Joseph Burchell-Mary Llewellyn	3
		4	Divorce decree. Mary Llewellyn Burchell and Solomon Rossiter; when did she marry Rossiter? When did she come to America?	1
		5	Mge. ctf. Emma Burchell —John Logan Flack	1
21 Aug 1972	4	6, 7	From Somerset House received birth and death ctfs. for Henry Charles Burchell and	
		8, 9	Abraham George Burchell; birth ctfs. for	
		10, 11	Charles and Emma Burchell; death ctf.	
		12	for Joseph Burchell	
1 Oct 1972	5		Searched Oldbury Parish Register on microfilm, Genealogy Library, Salt Lake City film # -------------.	4

system, anyone picking up your work in the future will not have to retrace your steps.[1]

Keep a Calendar sheet(s) (Illustration 20) in the front of each folder. You will note that you could rule any piece of lined notebook paper and make your own headings. At the top of the page, put the surname on which you are researching. Keep a file on each surname, or as you move back in time, a file for each country might be better.

This Calendar becomes your organization of notes to yourself and an organization of source material and documents on that particular line.

Study the picture of the Calendar and you'll be able to see how it can help you.

Date of search: Self-explanatory.

Search number: Every time you write a letter to a relative or a civil authority, or anyone else, this becomes a "search." Number it. For example, put a ⌗1 in red pencil on your letter to the Bureau of Vital Statistics for your birth certificate. This is Search ⌗1. Put that letter in your file. When the birth certificate arrives, it becomes Enclosure ⌗1. Number it and put it in a large manila envelope, to which you will add subsequent "enclosures." Or enclosures can be punched with a two-hole punch and anchored to the side of the file folder with a metal prong fastener. But don't punch current legal documents.

Source of Information: "Utah Bureau of Vital Statistics, Birth Certificate; my vital data; parents' names."

Nil or no. of W.S.: "Nil" means that a particular search yielded nothing on the surname you're working on. But do record it when applicable. At least you know nothing of value to you is in that source, and you won't spend time repeating the effort by mistake. "W.S." means work sheet. From your birth certificate you can make out a work sheet—a Family Group Work Sheet (Illustration 19) with your mother and father in the "husband" and "wife" spaces and you as a child in the appropriate space at the

---

[1] For a complete explanation of more technical ramifications, refer to Floren F. and Phyllis T. Preece, *The Sure Guide to Genealogy Research* (Mendon, Utah: Genealogy Club of America, 1969).

Or, Vincent L. Jones, Arlene H. Eakle, and Mildred H. Christensen, *Family History for Fun and Profit* (Salt Lake City, Utah: Publishers Press, 1972).

bottom, together with any other information given on the birth certificate. Check *Vital Statistics* in the top source box, and enter *nothing else* on that particular work sheet.

Each time you make a "search," record it in this manner. Other random entries are given on the sample Calendar of Genealogical Research shown (Illustration 20) so you'll know how to handle a variety of sources.

Number each subsequent effort as a search, starting with the #1 of your birth certificate.

Each document, photocopy, picture, scrap of paper on which you copied something, newspaper clipping, etc. becomes an enclosure. Number them consecutively and file in sequence. Enter the enclosure number on the Calendar by your statements concerning that specific search and, as a cross-reference, also on the work sheets made from that enclosure.

The Calendar tells *where* the information was found, and the work sheets tell *what* was found. A total stranger picking up your file could tell what you have done and what you have found.

Only one family should be recorded on a Work Sheet. If several families are included in one particular source (for example, a family record or a church record), make a separate work sheet for each family, from each separate source. You may have duplicate family entries with varying amounts of information. Even though this requires numerous work sheets, you'll see, when you move into it, that it facilitates evaluating the data. You'll be able to analyze it according to whether it is Primary or Secondary Source material.

Do not edit the information you find. Record it exactly as you find it. Make any necessary notes to yourself to guide you in evaluating it later.

Work sheets on any one family can be filed in a three-ring binder or a manila folder alphabetically according to surname, then the given name. A manila folder for each ancestral family can be kept as the number of sheets increases. Be sure to keep an accurate record of the complete source on each work sheet.

Chapter 19

USES OF TAPE RECORDERS:
Oral Interviewing and Taping
Your Autobiography

Since oral interviewing is a comparatively new field, I had to learn by much trial and error. In fact, it's a continuous learning experience. Some of my old tapes are awful. They must be listened to with intense concentration. I had not been careful enough in preparations and setting up the equipment. It's hard to hear the intent of some of those tapes because I was not assertive in eliminating and minimizing noises, which included the visiting in the room, rising and falling in cadences, loud bursts of laughter, doors banging, chairs scraping. In spite of the problems, however, those tapes are still valuable.

A tape recorder properly used is the best single aid to effective interviewing as you gather material for your autobiography/family history from home sources and other knowledgeable individuals. Without it you must be an expert notetaker with a skill in shorthand, or your own brand of speedwriting. A keen memory is invaluable.

Consider the following points in purchasing a tape recorder:

1. *What kind?* Of course you need a portable unit. *Cheap* cassettes are not very satisfactory for interviewing, and the results of the interview are disappointing. Invest in a good one, if at all possible. The field of tape recorders is rapidly changing, with constant improvements. Cassettes have largely replaced reel-to-reel recorders for personal use, but reel-to-reel do have some advantages. Schools and other institutions, especially historical societies, still buy them. If you want a reel-to-reel recorder, find a dealer who handles Sony products.

2. *Microphone.* Most cassettes have built-in microphones. Be sure it's a good mike.

3. *Fidelity of sound.* An expensive cassette or reel-to-reel recorder usually has excellent sound. Test before you buy.

4. *Progress.* At a glance the operator with a reel-to-reel recorder

can see how much tape is left, if it's tangling, if it's moving. These situations are hard to detect on a cassette.

5. *Tape.* Buy only good-quality tapes of known brands. Inferior tape can damage the heads of the recorder and will not store long without "bleed-through" garbling.

6. *Battery versus electricity.* Consider what your recording situations will be. One that runs on a battery as well as electricity is a plus, especially if you will be interviewing out of doors. There is a danger in depending totally on battery power. As the battery weakens, so does the sound, and you may end up with nothing, especially at the end. Whatever recorder you buy, *handle with care.*

Oral Interviewing

Don't expect to buy a recorder and go right off to interview a relative. Pre-interview considerations are:

1. *Practice makes perfect.* Know your equipment, and practice until you feel secure in getting good sound reproduction. Know the volume and tone level. Be sure you know how to operate the "Record" button properly, so you won't accidentally erase what has already been recorded.

Just for fun, practice with another person to get the feel of the interviewing experience. Then you can be more relaxed with the real thing.

2. *Be prepared for your interviewing.* Check to see what has already been done about your subject. Has a history already been written about the individual? Previous to the interview, learn everything you can about your interviewee and his background. Analyze your problem and make notes on what you hope to accomplish through the intended interview. What information do you hope he can supply you?

Make a list of the main points you expect to cover. Then formulate questions around those points. *Write down questions,* and you'll probably be more confident. This list will direct the interview and should prevent rambling. Without prior preparation, you waste the interviewee's time and will later experience frustration because you will have passed over a gold mine of material. However, the list is only an aid. If you find unexpected information, don't let the list stifle you. Get what is there.

Remember that your work may some day serve as source material for other recorded family and local history, so be as thorough and as accurate as possible.

Know your genealogical relationship to the interviewee and how he fits into the family whose history you are gathering. Listing family members on the Family Group Sheets clarifies the problem in your mind. Take that sheet and Pedigree Chart with you for reference. It's a timesaver in establishing common ground and may prevent misunderstandings. Let him see your genealogy sheets so he can add data if available.

If you are not previously acquainted with the interviewee, you may need someone to vouch for your integrity, so he will know your intent and not suspect you of being a prying gossip.

3. *Make an appointment* about a week ahead. Then check with him the day before or that day to make sure you're expected.

4. *Have an Interview Release form.* This might be unnecessary for your purposes, but in order to be legally protected, consider having your interviewee sign an Interview Release Form before you begin the interview. This is a bit touchy because your interviewee might be reluctant and even suspicious that you will take advantage of him. However, if the interview is to be filed with a historical society or other archives, they will require this protection and will provide a form, such as the one suggested below:

INTERVIEW RELEASE FORM

Because of the historical value of this oral history interview, I _____ grant all rights pertaining to this tape
     (interviewee)
and transcription to _____, in order to promote historical studies.
        (interviewer)

In return, the interviewer will supply me with a typed transcript of this interview.

Dated _____   Interviewee _____
                                     (name)
                Address _____
                Interviewer _____
                                       (name)
                Address _____

A checklist of necessary supplies will keep you from arriving with only half of your equipment, or leaving some of it at the place of interview. Carry the checklist with you.

—Recorder
—Take-up reel, if using a reel-to-reel recorder
—Sufficient blank tape or cassette tapes
—Microphone, if separate from machine
—List of questions to be covered, compiled during pre-interview preparation
—Notepad and pen
—Extension cord
—Interview Release form

For a pleasant, productive interviewing experience, you must be aware of a lot of precautions that would otherwise possibly come to mind after the experience when it is too late to rectify the mistakes and omissions.

Plan on an interview to last about one-and-a-half to two hours. Indicate this to your interviewee as you arrive, then he will know what to expect. Some people become tired easily, but that length of time should be quite safe. Watch for signs of fatigue, but usually he will let you know if he doesn't want to stop. Ordinarily, observe the time limit yourself. Don't stay longer unless he insists. You surely don't wish to impose. If a person seems to be a bit "fuzzy" the day of the appointment, by rescheduling at a later date, you may find him more responsive and alert. We all have our good and bad days, but this is especially true of older people. Make a subsequent appointment if you did not exhaust the subject initially.

Be genuinely interested. If you are too brusque and businesslike, he will sense disinterest. On the other hand, he will glow and respond to your sincere interest in him.

When you make the appointment, tell him what subjects you would like to cover so that he can be thinking and planning and can accumulate whatever records he has that will be helpful.

Usually an interviewee is more comfortable in familiar surroundings and would prefer being interviewed at home. However, there may be other questionable circumstances. He may feel inhibited by being interviewed around family members, or there may be too many distractions at home. Consider a possible alternative ahead of time.

Privacy is desirable. Try to have the interviewee alone with you, and he'll speak more freely. A kibitzing spouse can monopolize the interview or make the interviewee uneasy.

When you arrive, try to eliminate interruptions, such as telephone and visitors. Be aware of the physical arrangements of the area. Close windows and doors, if possible, to minimize possible outside noises such as buses, trucks, airplanes, screaming children, and barking dogs. Blaring radio or TV in the next room, vacuum and other household appliances, and chiming clocks all add up to an inaudible tape.

Place the recorder between you and the interviewee but close enough to you so you can operate it without noticeable movement. If the microphone is separate, never hold it. Put the mike on a flat surface (preferably padded) closer to the person with the softer voice. Any nervous fingertapping on a hard surface will be picked up by the sensitive mike.

Sit at a comfortable speaking distance from the interviewee in order to establish good rapport.

Your interviewee will probably be uneasy at first and not know what is expected of him. While setting up equipment, chat amiably to reduce uneasiness. Some people suffer from mike fright. However, as soon as good rapport is established, don't waste time. If he is reluctant to be taped, assure him he will get a copy of the transcript, and that you won't use the information contrary to his wishes.

Remember that an interview is not a dialogue. You may have to talk a little about your people as they relate to his possible subject. But after the ice is broken, let him do the talking. That's why you're there, isn't it? Speak only as necessary in asking questions to guide him and keep the interview moving.

Don't use an interview to show off your knowledge. Let your interviewee be the star.

Now you're ready to go. Speak an identifying heading for the tape: "This is John Doe interviewing Uncle Arthur Evans at his home in the small town of Scotia, Nebraska, May 15, 1977." Also include in this tape-heading the subjects to be discussed.

Retest the machine and the tape, to ensure proper recording. Make any necessary adjustments in the position of mike or volume control. Now you're on your way. Except for these preliminary necessities, try to call as little attention as possible to the machine. Some people cannot relax and talk freely when they realize their words are being recorded.

As you interrogate, remember the journalist's "who, what, where, when, why, and how." But be careful to create a casual conversational atmosphere instead of putting your subject "on the witness stand." Ask one question at a time. State it clearly and simply to avoid confusion.

As the interview progresses, don't interrupt. This connotes your respect and creates good rapport. Instead of interrupting, keep a notepad handy for jotting down questions that may arise, or note necessary clarifications to be made later. Don't try to put words in his mouth.

Avoid contradicting or correcting any misinformation he might give, or your interview may end abruptly. If you have already read or heard something on the subject being discussed, be tactful and say, "I've heard" or "I've read . . ." This gives him a chance to relate his side of the story. And he could be right, you know.

Questioning is an art. Ask "open" questions rather than "closed" questions. Examples:

OPEN QUESTION:

"Uncle Arthur, tell me about the circumstances of your birth."

Uncle Arthur: "Well, we were living in a log cabin and it was February. The wind whistled through the loose-fitting doors and windows. There was no doctor for miles, but the midwife was there . . ." (He will fill in all possible details.)

Nudge with a nod or "was that all?" until you have the complete story.

CLOSED QUESTION:

"You were living in the small town of Unionville, Ohio, I know. What's the closest big town?"

Uncle Arthur: "Cleveland."

If your interviewee is ill or has health or time problems that make an interview uncomfortable, ask preplanned closed questions. However, if your interviewee is mentally alert, by all means ask "open" or leading questions which lead the individual into memories contributing considerable detail.

There will be periods of silence, but don't panic or turn off the recorder. Be patient and let him have the necessary time to think. If you interrupt him, you may cut off something he is trying hard to recall.

Your own questions will not always be worded perfectly. Of course, you will have written out some questions as a part of your pre-interview preparation. But if you stumble occasionally over your own words, your interviewee will feel more comfortable and won't fear his own stumbles.

If your interviewee rambles too far off course, pull him back with a question such as, "Before we move on, would you back up and tell me how old you were at the time of the Depression?" Wait for his reply, then ask, "How did the Depression affect your family financially?"

Ask your interviewee to describe the person(s) you're discussing. As he tries to describe him physically, no doubt you'll get some character insights as well.

We hear much about maintaining a positive approach in our relationships with others. But in your questioning, sometimes try a negative approach and see what happens. It usually brings out honest, spontaneous reactions. For example, if you say, "I have heard that the Mine Superintendent where you worked was an honest man, but that he was a slave driver with the men," you might be surprised at the stories that erupt, in defense of or attacking the individual, and you'll get a picture of his working conditions.

Be responsive to your interviewee's brand of humor. Smile reassuringly and nod encouragement when he seems a bit hesitant.

Invariably your interviewee will want to insert some "off the record" comments and stories. Try to avoid this and keep the tape moving. Even if it must be erased later, at least it's there in case it turns out to be something relevant and useful. There's also the danger, if you've turned off the recorder as he suggested, that he will go right on to something pertinent and you will miss it because the machine is off.

Make the interview more than simple memories. Find the turning points in life. What principles guided his life?

When you think you're through, don't rewind and turn off the machine immediately. Chat briefly as you gather up your other equipment, and he may say, "Oh, I do remember something about working in the mine that I didn't tell you." The machine is still ready to continue without delay.

When you're finished, don't be abrupt. On the other hand, don't linger too long either. Bow out graciously on a friendly note. Leave the door open for another visit, if it becomes necessary. Let him know you consider him your friend. Before you leave, find out if he can introduce you to others who might be knowledgeable sources. Also inquire about his possible "home sources" and photos. One source can lead you to another.

If possible, make an appointment to return with the transcript for necessary clarifications or additions. This sets a projected goal for your transcription so you won't procrastinate. There is a strong temptation to let the tape sit, but you do have an obligation to let him correct the transcript and you promised him a copy. Also you do want him to still be around when those clarifications and corrections must be made. However, you could get bogged down if you have a number of tapes. Get your family history done and then complete the transcriptions for your interviewee.

Back at home, evaluate your interviewee. What were your own reactions to him? Was his information generally accurate or were there glaring discrepancies? Was he close to the subjects you discussed, or did he get it secondhand too? How much did he actually know? Was he old enough at the time of events discussed to be significantly aware of conditions then. How trustworthy is he? Some salty oldsters spin tall tales. Was your interviewee inclined to exaggerate and overstate? Did he try to color or slant the facts? A person's health condition is important, because it affects his viewpoint, whether he's pessimistic or optimistic. His state of health definitely affects his memory. Was he well enough to be reliable?

Since we're always working toward improvement, evaluate yourself and your interviewing techniques. Listen to the tape, and your weaknesses will literally jump at you. (I had no idea my laugh was so loud.) You may feel as if you're a failure, but be patient with yourself. You'll improve with practice and better preparation. There is no substitute for experience, and there's only one way to get it.

Immediately after the interview, write on the tape containers (and the spool, if using a reel-to-reel recorder) identifying notes similar to the tape heading, so you can keep them organized for speedy selection and playback.

Storing Tapes

If you intend to store the tapes, observe some precautions. Store reel tapes properly in their boxes, on edge, at room temperature (in the 70s) with humidity around 50. Avoid dampness.

Stored tapes should be rewound at least once a year to prevent "print through." If the tension is not steady, the tape may wind unevenly. No parts should protrude above the rest of the tape. If this happens, rewind the tape carefully so it is smooth and even before storing. Uneven winding and catching distorts the sound.

Dust destroys tape, so be sure they are stored in containers and are kept clean and dust free.

Handle carefully and avoid fingermarking the tape. Never mark your place on the tape with a grease or wax pencil. This collects dust.

Avoid eating, drinking, or smoking when taping, because of the possibility of damaging the tape. Smoke doesn't affect it, but fine ashes are destructive.

Keep tapes away from heavy machinery. Seldom in a home would there be a machine powerful enough to erase the tape. But if they were exposed to a generator or powerhouse, they could be erased. Or a demagnetizer, which is used for cleaning tape recorder heads, could also erase the tape, if closely exposed to it, while the demagnetizer is "on."

No particular precautions are necessary with cassette tapes except for room temperature and dampness, as noted above, and proximity to heavy machinery. A demagnetizer should be used occasionally on both reel-to-reel recorders and cassettes to clean heads and avoid build-up there. Consult your dealer about this.

Transcription

Longhand transcribing is extremely laborious. If you don't type, perhaps a family member will do it for you.

However, you do have another alternative. Some historical societies offer their facilities in exchange for tapes. The subjects do not need to be prestigious people for the society to be interested in them. Older people in all circumstances have insights to a different age and lifestyle, and perhaps their memories lend light on developments of historical significance.

For example, my husband's stepfather was the first cement contractor in his city. Yet he was a man of very ordinary means, as a result of the Depression. Fortunately, a local radio announcer conducted a series of broadcasts about these industry pioneers in that area. He was an important contributor to local history, but I was too close to recognize it. How fortunate that the radio announcer made that tape, even though it was short, before Dad had his stroke and could no longer communicate with us. The tape had local historical significance and so does its transcription.

For transcribing, use wide margins and double or triple space to allow ample room for corrections and notes. Leave a space where words are garbled or unclear.

If using a reel-to-reel tape recorder, a foot attachment can be purchased so that it operates similar to a dictaphone.

Allow the interviewee to go over the transcript. Frequently, he didn't intend the statement to sound the way it came out on tape, and clarifications must be made. Check for corrections and verify all names, dates, and places. Be sure they are spelled correctly. Try to prove the names, dates, and places from other existing records. Even though an individual may have records at his fingertips, they are subject to error. But a transcript cannot be corrected without returning it to the source.

We know of one particular tape that was made and transcribed and stored in a collection. The interviewer never returned to have it clarified. Because of hearing problems wrong names, dates, and other misunderstandings were included in the transcript. Yet anyone reading that transcript would naturally assume it was accurate because of the close relationship of the individuals involved, and it has been quoted erroneously in a number of books. When we checked the transcript against the father's record book and spoke aloud those names and dates, we could understand how the mistakes could slip through.

After transcribing the tape, read the typed copy and listen to the tape at the same time, in order to correct as many mistakes as possible. Our ears play tricks on us. Sometimes we hear something that is completely foreign to the subject. The following list is a perfect example:

AS TYPED	ACCORDING TO THE TAPE
1915	1950
heard a buffalo	a herd of buffalo
no muzzle loader gun	an old muzzle loader gun
when she was sick	when she was six
the world's fair	welfare
a man should not lie	the Maginot Line

After necessary clarifications and corrections are made and the family history is finished, give a copy of the finished interview to your interviewee in an attractive labeled folder in appreciation for his effort.

Editing

When you get the interview transcribed, you will see a need for editing. Make a carbon as you transcribe, then you can preserve one untouched for future reference, and have a working copy for revision. However, if you intend to use the interview, as such, for part of your family history, you may want to polish some rough edges. Fragments of sentences may be hanging in the air. Some interviewees become quite confused and repeat or say things they don't really mean or that are contradictory. This is where skillful editing comes in.

You do want it readable and coherent. This is also the reason for returning to consult your interviewee about obscure details.

As a rule of thumb, transcribe the tape exactly as spoken. Don't feel you have to make it grammatically correct. The charm of these old-timers is in their manner of speech.

Indicate "laugh" in parentheses where it occurs. You may have to do some condensing because of space, or you may have to leave out some of the detail for your compiled finished work. Where you interrupt a quote, note the omissions by ellipsis—three dots (. . .). Always retain a copy of the original interview as it stood since there may be details that will be useful to someone else for another purpose.

Taping Your Autobiography

Your "bone collection" (Chapter 2) is organized into chronological filing folders or manila envelopes. Your colored paper has a growing list of entries out of your past. But the task of writing it all down seems to be too big.

"If I could just tell it to someone," you say. You can. Beg, borrow, or buy a tape recorder. You can talk to yourself as long as you wish without feeling that it's a sign of senility because you're actually talking to your posterity.

But don't just start talking. In order to dictate an effective tape, you must prepare.

Take your first folder—birth to first grade perhaps—and go over all the items in it thoroughly. *Study* pictures. We repeat: A picture is worth a thousand words. Make notes widely spaced on your paper for rearranging as you think and plan, or outline with wide spaces to accommodate frequent insertions. Know what you want to cover so you will get it in proper order. For your high school and college years, go through your old yearbooks. That certainly triggers the memory process.

Note essential background information. Examine your birth certificate and see how many important details are recorded. In addition to those, tell about the house where you lived, the town, the mode of living, big or little house, painted or unpainted, rag carpets or scrubbed boards, horse and buggy, Model T, or '51

Chevy? All these details tell a story. Close your eyes and picture them, then paint them with words. If you don't preserve this information, who will? But do be selective. Don't record every meaningless memory that comes to your mind. Remember those "turning points?" This is the fine line of good judgment.

The sound of your own voice frightens you in the stillness? You may be one of those individuals who is afraid of silence and works better to background music. Go to the library and check out records for your stereo. Choose some of the old collections with tunes that were popular during the various stages of your life. You'll be surprised how this will turn the nostalgia wheels. The music usually enhances the final tape production. Be sure to test volume, so that the music is muted and your voice is just right. Place the mike where it will be comfortable and you can sit back in your easy chair and concentrate on what you're saying, instead of the machine.

With notes in hand, remember that you are going to talk about only one segment of your life on this particular tape. Know the length of your tape and plan accordingly. As you talk, you may want to make additions to the notes or outline you have made. Have additional scratch paper handy.

Turn down the telephone bell as low as possible and refuse to answer it during this private time. Concentrate only on the job at hand. Let other problems wait. This particular one—writing your autobiography—has been waiting all your life. Give it the priority it deserves and get it off your chest.

Plan a couple of hours of quiet time in your busy schedule for uninterrupted recording:

(a) When the children are napping,
(b) After work and the day is wrapped up,
(c) 4 A.M. one day a week until taping is completed,
(d) 6 A.M. Sunday morning instead of sleeping in.

But do find those extra time slots. Their length will depend on the quantity of your colored paper lists and other collected "bones." You may need a couple of hours for each folder or envelope. But you are the boss.

Turn the stereo on very softly, if you've planned this for background. Now you won't be so afraid of the hesitations as you speak.

Turn on the recorder. Begin the tape with the statement:

This is _____, recording my life story at my home _____ (address) in _____, on _____ (date). I am the son/daughter of _____ and _____.

You've started! Stop the recorder if you need to, in order to recover from the shock and to clear your throat, or listen to the quieting music for a few seconds while you gather the courage to continue.

> According to my mother, July 9, 1919, was the hottest day of the year, and she was extremely uncomfortable. Perspiration literally dripped off her face as she waited impatiently for my father's return with the doctor. Virginia, her first-born, not quite two, played in the corner with her doll. A boiler of water was heating on the coal stove—there must be plenty of hot water—and that was the only way to get it, even in the summer's heat.
>
> The little town of Kimberly, Idaho, near Twin Falls, boasted only one doctor, and of course babies were delivered at home. Papa had to run on foot to notify the doctor. He returned alone, puffing. Favoring his broken arm in the sling, he dropped into a straight chair and explained, "The doctor has left town, but a brand new one has arrived, and he's on his way here. You'll be his first maternity case."
>
> Mother, only 21, all but collapsed. As a matter of fact, that young doctor almost lost his first case . . .

Try to finish at least that "one-to-six" segment of your story before terminating your first recording session. Reference to your outline made from your cards and file folders will give you direction as you speak and will prevent aimless rambling into the tape recorder.

Continue this same process through each chronological segment of your life. Don't worry about whether or not it sounds professional. You are recorded for posterity—you are history, and as the years speed by, it will become "ancient history," believe it or not. But the very fact that it is recorded makes you a part of the tapestry of civilization, instead of the dropped threads.

You must decide whether to transcribe a segment as you go, or blaze right on through your whole life without going back. When you think about it, you'll realize advantages and disadvantages of either choice.

When your taped segments are completed, you'll experience a great exhilaration—at last it's out! And even if your life were prematurely snuffed out, you've beaten time and have left a part of yourself. You might want to close your tape by talking to your children or grandchildren, to leave them with your philosophy of life, or some counsel to guide them past some of your mistakes. Do it while you have the opportunity and you're in a reflective mood. You may not get back to it at a later date.

Label, date, and number your tapes as you complete them for ready reference and ease of playing the sequence.

If your time is extremely crowded, but you travel quite a bit alone, as you drive you can talk into a battery tape recorder with a built-in mike and have "company" to keep you alert. Of course this will work only if you have a quiet car and can keep the windows closed. Long evenings in a motel room, which would otherwise be wasted, can be utilized in working on your story.

But you're not through until it's transcribed, edited, and written the best way you can do it. Longhand transcription is painfully slow, but possible, if that's all you have. By all means, type it if you possess the skill. If not, LET one of your children or grandchildren type it for you. Remember the old adage: "If you want someone to love you, let him do something for you."

And do be appreciative, because it is a tedious job. This is why you should be selective in your recording sessions. Those words must all be typed. And two hours of taping could run into about fifty typed pages, depending on your talking speed. Your posterity should have your words on paper for reading. A tape recorder isn't always available for listening. Tape recorders are comparatively new and will continue to undergo improvements and model changes, making old tapes obsolete, but the printed word has been around quite a while. Reading is here to stay, in spite of statements that "Johnny can't read."

You may wish to use this transcription as your rough draft for your autobiography. But do save the tape, simply because it's you, and will be treasured by your posterity. The transcription may be only a stepping stone to a more comprehensive and skillfully written life story into which you will weave additions, changes, and shifts in sequence. But save the original and work from a carbon. You have achieved a milestone!

Suggested Chronological Checklist For Your Autobiography

(To ensure inclusion of important details. Use it as it applies to your life.)

NAME IN FULL:

BIRTH: Day, month, year, house or hospital where born, town, county, state or country, and surrounding circumstances.

PARENTAGE AND FAMILY BACKGROUND: Names, birthdates, birthplaces. (Only brief information as it relates to you.)

BLESSING and/or BAPTISM: Day, year, where (specific church building), and by whom.

GODPARENTS:

CHILDHOOD: Earliest memories with friends and relatives. Conditions under which I lived. Amusing anecdotes and incidents.

BROTHERS, SISTERS, ETC.: How they related to my life.

INFANTILE AND CHILDHOOD HEALTH CONDITION: Diseases, falls, accidents.

PLAY AND PLAYMATES: Amusements, unusual happenings with other children.

RELIGIOUS CONDITIONS IN THE CHILDHOOD HOME: Prayer habits. When and where special prayers were answered and experiences that built faith.

CHURCH ACTIVITY WHILE YOUNG: First Holy Communion, Bar Mitzvah, Guild, Circle, etc. Where and when.

ECONOMIC CONDITIONS IN THE HOME: Times when pennies were scarce. Perhaps when I wore patches. Compare with the present.

SCHOOL, TEACHERS, AND FAVORITE SUBJECTS:

MY HOME TASKS:

OTHER ORGANIZATIONS IN WHICH I PARTICIPATED:

YOUTHFUL AMUSEMENTS: The sports I enjoyed and the ones in which I actively participated. Other.

MY YOUTHFUL FRIENDS AND ASSOCIATES:

IMPORTANT ADVENTURES: Trips of outstanding interest, when and where.

FIRST INTERESTS IN OPPOSITE SEX:

COURTSHIP AND MARRIAGE:

SPOUSE'S PARENTAL BACKGROUND:

PEOPLE WHO HAVE MADE LASTING IMPRESSIONS ON MY LIFE:

VOCATIONS: Places of employment, by whom, tasks, wages, etc. (These make interesting comparisons with today.)

HEALTH: Diseases, accidents, operations, etc.

MY SPOUSE: The good things I looked for and found, new home conditions, moving from home to home.

NEIGHBORHOODS: How many different homes I have lived in during my life.

MY CHILDREN: Differences and traits, habits, character, talents, hobbies, achievements. Family relations.

TRAGEDY AND COMEDY IN THE HOME: The little things of life.

FAMILY PROBLEMS:

FAMILY RECREATION: Singing, dancing, sports, camping, etc.

RELIGION IN THE HOME WE ESTABLISHED: What part did it play, if any?

CELEBRATIONS, MEMORABLE CHRISTMASES AND OTHER HOLIDAYS, FAMILY GATHERINGS, BIRTHDAYS, ETC.:

GOOD BOOKS THAT HAVE INFLUENCED MY LIFE:

HOBBIES:

PUBLIC AND POLITICAL LIFE:

PERSONAL ACHIEVEMENTS:

APPRECIATION AND PHILOSOPHY OF LIFE:

FUTURE GOALS:

Chapter 20

THE FINISHED PRODUCT

Now that your autobiography/family history is written and ready for final polishing, you should choose the format for the finished product. At this point you should know what alternatives are open to you. Then decide what you will find the most comfortable form and what will fit best into your financial situation.

The format of your book is dependent largely on the type of binder you choose.

Binders and Paper

Be sure to check first your local stationery store to determine if supplies are available before you decide on your type of binder and paper, or you can order through the sources suggested in the Appendix.

A thick three-ring loose-leaf binder can be used, with 8½"×11" paper. The binder can be artfully covered with fabric, if desired, to personalize it and make it reflect you.

A legal-size post binder may appeal to you more. The legal-size sheet permits more photographs and other documents to be mounted on one page. Weigh the advantages of getting more on each long sheet against the ease of reading from a normal-size sheet.

For paper that will endure through the years, use one with rag content of at least 25 per cent. Never use onionskin or similar lightweight paper. For mounting pictures be sure you can buy heavier punched paper (at least 24-pound) for either the loose-leaf or the post binder.

Finished Copy

As long as you're putting forth the effort, do make your autobiography and family histories easily readable. Type if at all possible. We are geared to fast reading and tend to "turn off" anything
that slows down the pace. Your posterity will be more eager to
read a typed life story than a handwritten one. However, a diary
or journal is expected to be handwritten, unless, of course, you are
using loose paper, and prefer "writing at the typewriter." Of
course, the important thing is that you *do* record the events of
your life in some form.

Using the legal-size post binder presents three complications
not found with the three-ring binder:

The 8½"×14" paper will not fit on its side in a standard carriage typewriter. Therefore, it must be folded in the middle if a
long carriage is not available. Or it must be typed the narrow way
(vertically) which necessitates turning the binder for reading.
This is awkward. Handling a heavy post binder is cumbersome
when it grows to be thick. You may have difficulty finding, in
your locality, punched legal-size paper to fit the post binder and
would have to order by mail from sources listed in the Appendix.

If a long carriage machine is available, put the paper in the long
way and type in two columns for shorter eye span. You can then
readily flip through the book from typed pages to mounting pages,
without having to turn the binder.

Mounting

There are two ways of arranging pictures and other memorabilia. You can use mounting sheets separate from the typed text.
Or, decide where the visual material will be mounted as it relates
to the typed text and mount it on the same page. You will have
to trace around the picture to get the right size and know that it
synchronizes with the typed text.

The first is probably preferable because it saves much technical
figuring time and the trouble of typing around blocked areas for
visual material, which would first have to be outlined on the page.

Also the heavier mounting sheets support the pictures better. You can add as many pages of illustrations as desired wherever it relates to the story, even at a later date, without interrupting the flow of the story.

Undoubtedly some day your children each will want a copy of your autobiography, and many relatives may want your family history. You can't always find a machine that will satisfactorily reproduce a picture page. Reproduction quality of the pictures will probably be inferior. Also, visual material increases the number of pages until the cost runs high, sometimes prohibitively high. You don't want to retype for economy. That's a lot of unnecessary work. If picture pages are separate, you won't have to. Simply putting typed sheets through a photocopy machine is much easier to handle and more economical.

Guard your precious photos and other papers on your illustrated pages by using the proper mounting material. If the mounting is to be permanent, use Kodak's Rapid Mounting Cement. Follow instructions included in the box. This will not damage the paper or the photo. If you think you might be changing the photo to another spot in the future, then use patches of Double-Stick Adhesive Tape which can be purchased at the drugstore or art-supply shop. This is sticky on both sides so that it adheres to the photo and the mounting page at the same time. It can be pulled up without harm to the picture or page and placed elsewhere. *Don't* use rubber cement to mount pictures because it often bleeds through and can damage the picture. Photo-mounting corners can be used, but sometimes they're a nuisance, catching pages and coming unglued. Protective plastic covers for picture pages keep them safe from fingerprints and other accidents.

Have you had the thrill of finding a hundred-year-old photo of one of your ancestors? Perhaps yours will some day be considered as precious. But do label and date all photos on the back with a felt-tip pen. Digging with a reluctant ball-point pen can damage photos.

Perhaps you want to include an occasional picture of the locality of your family history at a particular time period. If you have found such a picture in a book with a credit line under it, such as

"Courtesy Sweetwater County Museum," write and ask for permission to use that picture and state your purpose. Ask what the charge is.

On the other hand, if you are simply seeking a picture for your particular subject, such as Fort Cumberland, Nova Scotia, around 1772, consider what public places are in the area that might have such a picture. In your library, check the Directory for Historical Societies and Agencies for a society or archives in the subject locale, where such a picture might be a part of their records. Public archives and bureaus of information might also have the desired pictures.

Photo duplication is expensive, so select your pictures carefully. Ask what the charge is, to be on the safe side. Some places, but not all, charge only for the reproduction cost. Give a credit line in your history to the supplying agency.

Labeling

A roll of gummed label paper, on which to type identifying information under pictures, is ideal. It can be rolled into the machine, typed, then cut to the necessary size and pasted under the picture.

Organize Photos

While we're considering photos, are you ever discouraged because you can't find the ones you want when you need them? Obviously, you won't include in your autobiography or family history every picture you ever took. But you will never know which ones to select unless you can collect and compare them—and organize them. You'll surely want to save the ones you don't include in your final manuscript.

Cardboard file boxes (3"×5", 4"×6", 5"×8"), in which to file your photos and negatives, can be purchased at a stationery or office-supply shop for a nominal fee. Put in dividers labeled for each year. File snaps and negatives chronologically or according to subject matter, then select the special ones you wish to include with your story. In this way, they don't become scattered and negatives will be with prints, which saves endless hours of searching when you need a reprint.

Suggested Extras for a Professional-looking Finished Manuscript

Every book has an order to it. Pull some off your own book shelf. Examine them and decide how you want yours to be arranged. Since you have put so much effort into the preparation of yours, you want it to look as professional and be as useful as possible to yourself and to your readers.

A Title Page
"My Autobiography" (Surely you can dream up a more appealing title.)
Compiled and written by

_____
(name)

_____
(place)

_____
(date)

Preface or Introduction (Optional)
Why have you written it and what do you hope to achieve through the effort?

Acknowledgments (Optional)
List the names and services of those who have been invaluable aids.

Contents
Preface i
Chapter 1 My Birth 2
2 (You may want to title each
3 chapter so the reader will know
4 what is contained therein.)
etc.

Appendices

    I Documents and other memorabilia (such as coat of arms, copies of ancestors' handwriting, pictures that have not been included in the narration, etc.)

    II Comments from my children

    III Favorite proverbs, poems, and other writings

    IV Maps (of moves and/or travels)

    V Family lineage

    VI Index

    (Or whatever else you wish to include.)

Indexing

Although this process is time-consuming, it is not difficult and will add greatly to the utility of your autobiography/family history as a reference. Indexing cannot be done until the final copy is typed so you know page numbers exactly. If your book is being printed, wait for the page proofs before indexing. Use $3'' \times 5''$ cards or uniform-size scrap paper. Go through the manuscript from beginning to finish, making a card for each name or idea that is mentioned, with page numbers where repeated.

A simple index lists only basic words, followed by the page numbers where this idea is treated. Example: Smith, Mary 4, 8, 15.

A more complete (and more informative) index lists an idea or subject. Then indent two spaces and list other subheadings of the key index word.

Example: Schooling 6, 10, 12, 15
        grade school 6
        junior high 9, 10

After all the ideas are entered on the cards, alphabetize them and type in that order.

Footnoting

When a member of your family picks up your family history and finds some bit of information that conflicts with what he has always understood, he will want to know where your information came from. Footnotes, in a sense, relieve you of the responsibility of making statements on your own authority. Footnotes are included in a manuscript: (1) to list the source of your material, (2) to make cross references, (3) to make acknowledgments, (4) to clarify points with additional comment or to qualify what is stated, without interrupting the flow of the story.

You have three alternatives for placing the footnotes: (1) at the bottom of the page, (2) at the end of each chapter, (3) at the end of history.

The advantage of listing footnotes at the bottom of each page is that the reader doesn't have to flip over several pages to the end of the chapter or paper to discover what the author wants you to know at that point, in addition to the text. The advantage of listing them at the end of the chapter or at the end of your history is that the typist does not have to worry about typing too far down the page to allow for the footnotes. If the material is typeset, the type can be changed for the footnotes, and they can be set all at once, at the end of the chapter or at the end of the story.

You have three alternatives for numbering footnotes. (1) If you plan to have footnotes at the bottom of each page, they can be numbered [1], [2], etc., and start over with [1] at the beginning of each subsequent page. (2) Footnotes can begin with [1] and advance numerically throughout each chapter. This is the preferred system if you plan to run the footnotes at the end of chapter. (3) They can begin with [1] and advance numerically through the whole history if your footnotes will appear at the end of the book. But this becomes a challenge to keep so many footnote numbers corresponding with the correct sources.

If you type your history, footnotes are single spaced with a double space between each one. But if you're preparing copy for a printer, you should double space text and footnotes.

For an example, if we were including in a history the marriage date of Joseph Burchell and Mary Llewellyn as shown on the forms in Chapter 18, it could appear in the text: Joseph Burchell married Mary Llewellyn 18 July 1839 in Birmingham, Warwickshire, England.[1]

Type the [1] part of a space above the line (or circle if handwriting), alerting the reader to the source for which the author wants to give credit. At the bottom of the same page, stop typing the text far enough up on the page to allow for a line to go part way across the page, separating text from footnote. Drop two spaces below the line and indent five spaces. Turn the typewriter platten back half a space and type [1]. Return the platten back to the normal typing line and write. Example:

---

[1] Original marriage certificate in Minnie Flack's trunk, along with many other documents and pictures, now in possession of Allie Flack Larsen, Vernon, Utah.

Quite a few sources were in that old trunk. They could be bunched together with a footnote at the end of the documents listed. If you refer to the contents of the trunk a few pages farther on, and if there are no other sources listed in between, at the bottom of that page, write: [2] Ibid. This is the abbreviation for the Latin word *Ibidem*, which means "in the same place."

If there were other source materials footnoted between the two references to Aunt Minnie's trunk, as an example, the second reference to the trunk would be listed: [5] and at the bottom of the page it would read:

[5] Flack, op. cit.

Many editors now prefer a short title system and avoid "op. cit."

If you were quoting from another book, you would add the page number where the footnoted material is recorded. Example:
[5] Flack, op. cit., p. 40.

In listing published books in footnotes, list the author's name first, in the order in which it is spoken, then a comma, followed by the name of the book, underscored, with bibliographic material following it in parentheses, then the page number following the close of the parentheses. Example: William G. Hartley, *Preparing a Personal History* (Salt Lake City, Utah: Primer Publications, 1976), p. 17.

If there are multiple authors, list them alphabetically according to surname. If there are two authors by the same surname, list them both. Example: Floren S. Preece and Phyllis P. Preece, *The*

Sure Guide to Genealogy Research (Mendon, Utah: Genealogy Club of America, 1969), p. 53.

If quoting from a periodical, the order is: George O. Zabriskie, "Systematically Climb Your Family Tree," *Genealogy Digest,* Vol. VII, No. 5, p. 135.

Of course there are many refinements of footnoting explained in style books for writers.[1]

Copyright

If your finished autobiography or family history is to be circulated at all or is to be placed in a library or historical society, you should copyright it as a protection against others lifting your material without your permission. To copyright your work, you must first of all put the appropriate notice in the history and then register the publication with the Library of Congress.

On the title page or the reverse side put the line, "Library of Congress Catalog Card Number . . ." (insert the number that appears on your copyright). On the next line write the word "Copyright" or the abbreviation "Copr." or the letter ©, followed by the year of copyright and your name as copyright owner. Example: "Copyright 1975 John Doe." This secures the copyright.

In order to register a copyright, write to Register of Copyrights, Library of Congress, Washington, D.C. 20559, requesting Form A, "Application of Registration of a Claim to Copyright in a Published Book Manufactured in the United States of America." Complete this form and return it, together with two copies of the best edition of the work and the registration fee of $6.00. Make your remittance payable to the Register of Copyrights.

Processing the form and material takes several months, but the copyright form reads: "It is the act of publication with notice that actually secures copyright protection. If copies are published without the required notice, the right to secure copyright is lost, and cannot be restored."

After processing, you will receive back the carbon copy of your

[1] *Words into Type* (Englewood Cliffs, N.J.: Prentice-Hall, Inc., 1974) and *A Manual of Style,* 12 ed. (Chicago and London: The University of Chicago Press, 1969).

application for your files, with the seal stamped, which makes it valid. A serial number is assigned to your work, noted in the upper right-hand corner. The Copyright Office keeps the original form and the books on file (see Appendix for Copyright Application form).

How Will You Reproduce Copies of Your Autobiography/Family History?

If you need fewer than fifty copies, then have it photocopied (Xerox or similar process). IBM Copier II does an excellent reproduction, even pictures. Of course, this is available only in major metropolitan areas. Call the IBM office nearest you to see where one is available. The field is always improving. Inquire and compare to get the best reproduction for your money. Permalife paper can be requested. It reproduces well and can be preserved indefinitely. Paper must then be punched to fit your binder. Shop around and compare prices. Permalife paper costs a little more per sheet.

Ditto is not the best method of reproduction, but may be the only way possible because of expense. Ditto masters are easy to type, but should be done carefully to ensure a better finished product. Take the time to correct properly as you type. If you need a few additional copies later, don't expect it to copy satisfactorily. For good quality, do not use a ditto master for more than one hundred copies.

Mimeographing is next best to ditto. Of course, special stencils must be cut for the purpose. Too many such jobs are of very poor quality, but it is possible to get a good product with care. Use a slow, even typing touch if not using an electric typewriter. Correct carefully with correction fluid made especially for stencils. Use mimeo bond for the paper. Don't plan on getting more than four or five hundred copies from a stencil. Some stencils won't hold up for that many, depending on how they're cut. But if you need that many, you should definitely consider some form of printing.

Offset printing is better than Xerography. This means that the printer will take your typed manuscript, photograph it, and make a plate from which the final printing is done. When photographs are included, this involves halftones (photographs), with additional cost for each. Be sure to start with a new ribbon so the duplication will be clear and sharp. Remember, the finished copy will look no better than what you submit.

In urban areas you may be able to find a printer set up for low-cost quick printing. Check the Yellow Pages of your telephone directory. The "quick print" method would reproduce one hundred copies per page, but quality may be substandard. After the initial plates are made, additional copies would be relatively inexpensive, but it's still costly.

Bids on printing are offered with three categories in mind:

1. *Excellent.* "Excellent" quality is a professional typeset printing job, which may be prohibitive for your purpose.

2. *Medium.* "Medium" quality means the "quick print" method with the negative being cleaned up and small blemishes being removed.

3. *Ordinary.* "Ordinary" quality means the "quick print" method, being reproduced as the printer receives it; blemishes and flaws will show up.

Prices will vary in different localities. If your autobiography/family history is extensive, you should obtain competitive bids from two or three printers. You're paying the bill, so you'll want the best possible price break. In seeking a bid, tell the printer how many copies you will need, the length of your manuscript, the number of pictures to be included, the binding desired, and the quality of paper to be used. When you receive the total bid, you can quickly compute the price per book. Remember that the larger the number to be printed, the lower the cost per individual book.

Paper selection is a price consideration. Since you want your work to be preserved indefinitely, don't skimp on the paper. You should know that Number 1 grade bond is more durable than Number 4 or Number 5, which is generally used in printing. The cost of Number 1 grade bond runs 15 to 20 per cent higher than Number 4 or 5.

Sheets are reproduced and then must be bound—either plastic

comb bound or adhesive bound (perfect bound). Having them hardbound, as in the case of regular books, is extremely expensive.

As an alternative, you could have the sheets run and given to you flat. Then they would have to be punched for your binder.

In spite of the inflationary cost of printing or duplicating, do find some method you can afford, so that those close to you can share the results of your effort.

If you are artistic, you may want to personalize some of the sheets with your own creations. If you use color drawings, you should know that it will reproduce only in black and white and halftones (shades of gray). Hand-lettering of chapter headings rather than typing them gives a distinctive personal flair.

Make your finished product reflect you.

Chapter 21

CONSERVING DOCUMENTS
AND MEMORABILIA

You are making history—for future generations—whether you like it or not. Family history is compiled from keepsakes and documents in the possession of individual families. So, in addition to writing your autobiography and/or family history, you will be collecting memorabilia and documents, interesting and valuable to you and to your posterity, records that have, or some day will have historic value.

For example, after a will has been probated, its value has not been exhausted. Genealogists probe wills and other documents for connecting links.

In a family trunk owned by my distant cousin Ethel in Buffalo, New York, valuable original family documents had been stored and handed down in the Pickle family, one of my ancestral lines. Some of the documents were over two hundred years old. The original will of John Pickle was there, listing his daughter Magdalena as the wife of Edmond Durpha. This had been misread and recorded in civil records as Edmond Dumpha.

Examination of the original will showed the r clearly but could have been easily misread as m or n. This is a good example of variable name spellings as discussed in Chapter 17, "Church Records." Although the name was written in the will as Durpha, by fitting together all other clues, we discovered that this truly was my third-great-grandfather, Edmond Durfee, connecting us with a long line of early American ancestry.

The will was beginning to crumble because the paper was now brittle. Each time it was handled, chips of paper broke off in our hands. As we copied data from that and other stored documents, we decided they must all be repaired for permanent preservation.

Naturally we began to mend with cellophane tape—what else? Fortunately Ethel consulted an expert at Grosvenor Library and discovered we were doing it all wrong.

Specific guidelines and precautions are necessary for mending and preserving records. A number of supply houses for document restoration and preservation are listed in the Appendix. Records conservation is becoming a highly specialized field.

Admit you're an amateur and don't touch that crumbling document until you know what you're doing. Well-intentioned "preservation" sometimes creates serious damage which cannot be undone. Below are some simple suggestions which will assist the amateur in preservation. Deterioration of records comes from people (that's right), air, light, darkness, heat, moisture, insects, rodents, fungi, acid. Please repair records only when really necessary and then only after checking correct methods. Prevent damage as much as possible by keeping the enemies listed above under control. Remember, you're preserving for permanency, for future generations.

Precautions in Preserving

1. Store papers flat, unfolded to avoid breaking at the folds.
2. Keep papers out of light. Light fades and destroys paper. Fluorescent light is especially hard on paper.
3. Protect against dust which causes paper deterioration. Acid-free archival boxes—available through Hollinger (see Appendix)—are good for storing your irreplaceable documents. See if your local librarian can sell you the small quantity you need.
4. Avoid heat which causes brittleness. Of course protect from fire.
5. Keep dry.
6. Protect from vermin, insects, and other pests.
7. Avoid handling.
8. Protect from theft.
9. Photocopy and film. For permanency, Xerox with Permalife paper.
10. Don't stick pins in papers.

11. Don't use "botch tape" (cellophane, masking, or similar tapes).
12. Don't use Elmer's glue or other white glues, mucilage, contact cement, etc. They stain and are brittle, acidic, and insoluble.
13. Don't use rubber cement, spray, or liquid. It is not permanent. It deteriorates, stains, and even bleeds through, damaging photos and papers.
14. Don't use self-adhering plastic laminates or heat-sealing lamination processes. They are "irreversible" even in solvent. Use them only for expendable materials, such as items that must be handled frequently. Some paper disintegrates under lamination.
15. Polyester sheets, which fit into a three-ring or legal-size binder, protect against direct finger contact and are usually sufficient protection for the items you wish to include with your autobiography or family history.
16. Clean pictures and papers CAREFULLY. Remove "rustables" such as paper clips, pins, staples, also rubber bands. Remove thick surface dust with a soft-hair brush, such as an artist's brush.
17. When using erasers, begin with soft ones, such as soap eraser, art gum, Opaline, Magic Rub, or Pink Pearl. Rub ever so lightly. Typewriter erasers are too harsh. Pencil erasers are unpredictable as to their composition, and you might make a streak that is permanent. Avoid tearing and skinning paper. Any cleaning process that is more complicated than outlined herein should be trusted to the experts only.

Flattening Ideas

1. If a paper can be easily unfolded, those folds can usually be flattened by simply placing the paper between clean paper or good blotters in a screw press, or between rigid pressing boards of masonite or plywood, then placing weights on top.
2. Rolled or folded items usually need humidity added in

order to unfold. A humidifier can be used to introduce moisture. Or place a pan of water in the bottom of a large, tightly-covered plastic container. Cover the pan with screen and set the documents on the screen so they are kept out of the water. Fasten the lid tightly to keep moisture inside, and let stand for twenty-four hours. The document will usually absorb sufficient moisture in that time. If not, let stand two or three days, but watch for mold formation.

After humidity has been absorbed, flatten as in ⚹1 above. Weights should not be too heavy, just sufficient to flatten but not to crush.

3. *Ironing with a warm iron or in a dry mount press should be avoided* because heat causes rapid acid deterioration and can be harmful to the document.

To Repair Simple Tears

1. Apply wheat paste or white-flour paste sparingly along the torn edges, just enough to hold it together.

   To make white-flour paste, add just enough cold water to one cup all-purpose flour to make the consistency of pancake batter. Add three-fourths cup boiling water and stir over heat until it bubbles—from five to six minutes— and becomes rather translucent.

   Apply paste and attach a piece of Japanese tissue or 100 per cent rag onionskin paper and let dry.

   (Wheat paste and Japanese tissue are available from Talas. See Appendix.)

2. *Dennison's Transparent Mending Tape* (glassine) won't stain. It is long lasting and is removed easily later on if necessary.

Encase

Place the document between two sheets of Mylar. Seal the edges together with polyester double-faced tape (Scotch brand, Double-coated Tape ⚹415—¼″ polyester film is wide enough).

The Library of Congress recommends this method. Mylar is available in sheets 11"×14" through Hollinger (see Appendix) or one of their suppliers. These and other conservation materials may be hard to find (see Appendix).

Professional conservators warn: Do nothing to a manuscript that cannot be undone without damaging, making it "irreversible." For example, if the document is already crumbling, don't patch it, but encase it. The paper is then protected against further handling or folding and will last indefinitely.

Now consider another aspect of old records. Referring back to my relative in Buffalo, even though Ethel owns the loaded trunk, it will remain with her for a limited time only, and, upon her death, will be bequeathed to one of her children or to some other relative who appreciates its value. No individual "owns" completely the records of the past. Even your own papers will some day be passed on to a descendant. At least you hope they'll be handed down and won't be burned. All too often that happens, because the heir is bewildered by the mass of disorganized material. This is another reason for you to compile it in an organized fashion which will be so interesting that your children will consider it their priceless "legacy" instead of "junk."

Preservation of Color Prints, Home Movies, and Slides

Home movies, colored slides, and colored prints were never intended for indefinite preservation. The dyes are not guaranteed. Keep them out of strong sunlight (or any light) in a dry, cool, dark place to ensure the best possible conservation. There is absolutely no way of guaranteeing that you can keep them a hundred years or longer, as can be done with black-and-white pictures. The colored picture will fade and the image will disappear in time.

Home movies should be run through occasionally to see if they are in good condition. Janice has one film which dates back forty years. The film shrank and had to be recopied by a specialist.

To preserve a colored print of real value, it would have to be lithographed. Such an expensive process would not be economically feasible unless one or two thousand copies were desired.

Cibichrome, a new process on the market, is the most permanent color process today for color prints. Of course, you must specify Cibichrome when film is left for development, and this is not available at all stations where you leave film.

Do have some black-and-white pictures taken occasionally. Otherwise this color-conscious generation may be blank to their descendants a hundred years from now because the pictures did not stand the test of time.

Chapter 22

PRESERVING CURRENT
FAMILY HAPPENINGS

Family history is being made every day. Important events slip by almost without notice unless we take the time to put them on paper or tape. Then as we are removed in time from the event, we recognize turning points and try to recall the details as they happened. Important events of our children, our brothers and sisters and parents sometimes pass unnoticed.

If you are young and your brothers and sisters are still at home, it's comparatively easy to record their interesting activities. If you can't motivate them to keep their own journals or diaries, then you keep a notebook and an envelope for each one, in which you can deposit newspaper clippings and other memorabilia as events occur, and make brief notations about their activities. Later in the chapter you'll see how this practice can become very important in your family relationships. Don't forget to jot down the amusing anecdotes that happen and the way you see a family member maturing under specific experiences.

On the other hand, if your brothers and sisters are married and gone from home, especially if they are scattered geographically, you may find it difficult to keep in touch. Unfortunately, the telephone has taken the place of letter writing in too many cases. But how much do you actually communicate in a telephone conversation? Not much? You're worrying about the mounting long-distance cost as you talk?

Perhaps you call your parents frequently, but the news you relate seldom filters out to the rest of the family. Brothers and sisters too often fail to communicate and, in so doing, lose interest in their extended families. If good rapport has been maintained through the years, sometimes grandparents, aunts, and uncles can straighten out a child with problems, when he can't be reached by parents.

Encourage your family to write letters—informative letters—rather than telephone so that events become a matter of record and family sheets can also be kept current. There are a number of communication methods.

Letters

Write frequent informative letters to your friends and family, and keep a carbon copy. This is one way to preserve a current history of your own immediate family's activities. If you don't have a typewriter, then keep carbon paper handy and write with a ballpoint pen, thus producing excellent carbon copies. Always date your letters. Invest in a three-hole punch and file those carbons in a loose-leaf notebook, which can become your immediate-family continuing history, or make your carbon copies on already-punched paper. Put an asterisk by a paragraph or particular note which you intend to extract later for inclusion in your autobiography. It's easy to spot quickly.

ROUND-ROBIN LETTERS

This is a good system for scattered brothers and sisters who procrastinate. Usually family members bend to the prodding of a round-robin letter. Of course, a few controls must be established to keep it moving fast enough to be newsworthy.

Encourage the oldest brother or sister to start the round robin, so the rotation is not confused. If they won't, then you start it. Write a page of the activities of spouse and children and mail it to the next rung down the family ladder, who adds a page and mails them both to the next step down. *Be sure to date all letters.* This goes the rounds of the family, with the stipulation that each person adds his page and mails it within a week so that it makes the rounds of the whole family before the news is outdated.

Mother and Dad may want to be included in this news exchange. When the letter returns to the person who started it, he removes his page, writes his latest family activities and mails it on again in the same order. Each time the letters reach YOU, photocopy them all or copy them on the typewriter, and this becomes your continuing family history. If it's photocopied you'll have the record in each one's handwriting, and that's a nice feature—provided everyone writes legibly. These round-robin letters become a Primary Source, available for reference when your family members become interested in writing their autobiographies.

FAMILY NEWSLETTERS

Occasionally a family won't co-operate even on a round robin. Then it may be necessary for one member to act as the family new clearinghouse. Face it, family togetherness requires effort. When these responsibilities are shared, it doesn't become too burdensome for one person. If you are trying to keep Family Record Sheets up to date and also working on your family history, your hands may be quite full.

My brother compiles a family newsletter periodically. He sets a deadline for others to send their news notes to him. Then he compiles them and calls his publication *Grandma's News Notes*. When Mother (Grandma) was alive, she was very proud of the accomplishments of her children and grandchildren as they were reported in the family letter. Occasionally something had slipped by without her knowledge, but not often. My brother edits it all in an interesting, humorous style—exaggerated journalistic reporting—so that everyone chuckles with the news.

As the grandchildren have married, he makes it a point to dig out biographical data about the new in-law and features that person. In this way all the cousins feel they have met the new family member, and the new in-law experiences an immediate sense of belonging.

If news from a particular couple is not funneled to the editor, he contrives a totally ridiculous news note about them, and the next time around, the input is improved.

Special days (Mother's and Father's Day) have been opportunities for tributes to the patriarch and matriarch contributed by their children. After Mother died, our editor included, among other things, some of her collected gems, so we all have copies of her handwriting.

Our editor has access to a copy machine, and pictures of impor-

tant family events are included. The minimal cost of production
and postage can be shared. The newsletter is mailed to all within
the family circle, even those away at school, and they anticipate it,
for they recognize this as a binding tie.

Most of us preserve these newsletters in a loose-leaf notebook.
Our family history is being well recorded as it happens, is great
fun in reminiscence, and it's in each home. It also becomes a good
reference source when questions arise because the events were
recorded near the time of happening.

Calendars and Date Books

Get a large calendar with big date squares, one in which the
number doesn't fill the whole space. Write very small and you
will be surprised how much you can crowd into that square—doctor's appointments, reminders of special events: Johnny's first
steps, the first time you presided at PTA meeting, etc. Save the
calendars, because even though this method leaves much to be desired, it is better than no diary at all.

Banks and insurance companies often give date books at the
end of the year. These have about half a page for appointments.
This is a quick journal. Make notes of the important events that
happened that day and your impressions and feelings. This is an
excellent reference.

Minutes of Family Gathering

Once a month our married children join those still at home for
dinner and family night. Since they all live within sixty miles of
home, this is not too difficult and surely is worth the effort. Following dinner, we have a variety of family-centered activities. One
daughter-in-law is especially clever at recording and reporting the
minutes. News is reported from each member of the clan. In this
way we not only keep up with each other's involvements, but they
become a matter of record. Sometimes the minutes are hilarious
and sometimes deeply moving, depending on the events of the
evening. Discussion about individual problems sometimes is a

means of working them out intelligently and objectively, and certainly each feels a sincere concern for every other member. This then becomes a continuing immediate-family history.

Scrapbooks

Scrapbooks are great fun. They are the "visual aids," as family history happens (see Chapter 21).

And now here's how you can effectively use what you have collected concerning your brothers and sisters, which was alluded to earlier in this chapter. Newly married, far from home and struggling financially, Paula wondered what she could do for Christmas gifts her first year. Her parents and brothers and sisters were all in affluent circumstances. Since she couldn't possibly reciprocate in a like monetary expenditure, hers must be meaningful gifts of intrinsic value.

Through the years she had kept a journal and had saved family mementos. So she sorted these into piles, one for each of her family members and made extensive notes of her memories regarding each one as they shared growing-up experiences and as they had influenced her life for good. Included were old pictures of those early years together, programs on which they had performed, newspaper clippings of achievements. Truly she gave of herself in her compilation. The gifts cost little monetarily, but required a great deal of time. That was all right—Paula had more time than money. She was homesick, and her concentrated effort helped that problem too.

All her life she had found it difficult to penetrate her father's brusque exterior. But in his gift book, she discovered she could tell him how much she truly loved and admired him and always respected his high principles and the good home he had provided.

Inexpensive loose-leaf notebooks held her finished products. At little expense she bought remnants of fabric to make decorative covers (some were brightly colored fake fur) suited to the recipients, but all were richly beautiful. These books proved to be the sweepstakes gift of each recipient. Each one expressed deep gratitude for an extra-special remembrance, which will only increase in value as the years fly.

Her father was deeply moved at her sincere expressions. This one effort crumbled the unseen barrier that had always held Paula at a distance.

This method could provide gifts spread out over a year's time, to be presented to each family member for birthdays or Christmas. Start early. It takes time!

What a lovely way to strengthen family ties.

Chapter 23

RECORDING CHILDREN'S BEGINNINGS

How many times have you heard a mother or father remark, "I could write a book about that child's sayings and the things she does. But when I try to remember them, I can't."

That's life. If you don't write it down—it's gone!

When Karla entered the hospital for the birth of each of her children, she took along a new baby book. While there, and knowing the awe and emotion of those first moments after birth would fade, she wrote a letter to her new baby, explaining her thrill and anticipation of rearing that child. She wanted that child to know, perhaps at a critical future moment in his life, how much she loved him and what high hopes she had for him. Never would there be another time when she could share the excitement of that first day, and perhaps her recorded emotional "high" would be a future anchor. After all, no parent has the assurance that he will still be on earth during the child's growing and maturing.

After returning home, Karla labeled a fresh large manila envelope, put the letter inside and deposited it in the decorative box, where she keeps envelopes for each child. The big box is placed in an accessible spot so she can conveniently file vital papers or notes as events occur. In a sense, this is the journal of each child before he is capable of keeping his own.

Periodically she adds another letter or sheet to the one she wrote in the hospital. When important events occur, she makes it a point to write them down at the time of happening. She dates each sheet as she writes. One boy is a Calamity Kid, and she records the humor or tragedy of his experiences, often as they occur.

Example:

Saturday, February 21, 1976. You and I were playing hide-and-seek. You ran out of your room. I heard a muffled cracking sound, and my first thought was that you had hit the wall and had split your head completely. You let out a terrible scream. I raced to pick you up. A bump about the size of a dollar in diameter began to swell and we started the ice packs.

Luckily you hadn't completely cracked your head open, but what an egg! With blurred eyes, I held up two fingers to see if you could focus and comprehend. "What am I holding up?" I asked.

Through your tears, you grinned sheepishly and mumbled, "Just your fingers, Mommie." Then you almost laughed aloud when I asked how many fingers there were. "Two, Mommie."

Suddenly you looked at the doorframe and laughed. "Look, I broke the door." Splinters of paint were sprinkled over the carpet and a twelve-inch crack split the doorframe.

You are a worry to me because of your many accidents, but you truly add a special spark to our home with your humor and loving ways. We love you.

Mom and Dad

As the child becomes old enough to enjoy the experiences in his envelope, Mother or Father sometimes write with the child present, and he helps to refresh their memory. At the beginning of each year, appointments are noted on the new calendar about every three months so that time is saved for these memory nights. Each child eagerly anticipates the remembering sessions.

Karla's record becomes a running journal from Day One and is a Primary Source. Nothing but a daily journal can supersede such a record. What fun and satisfaction the children experience when the parents reread to them some of the entries.

The parents anticipate the day—wedding days—when they will present a book to each grown child.

What goes in the envelope for each child?

Certificates of all kinds, church and civil.

Pictures (always date and put names on the back of every picture).

A minimum of two or three written papers and artwork per school year.

The firsts: first bankbook, first letter received, etc.

Newspaper pictures and notes of achievement.

Report cards.

Scout merit badges.

Printed programs of special events in which the child participated.

Judging sheets for competitive events.

Special letters written to him.

Meaningful concert programs.

Social-event mementos, such as dance programs.

Recognition certificates from school and church.

Health record. Then parents need never wonder, during a
measles epidemic, if Jimmie has had the measles, or
when did he have that measles shot?

Looking ahead, one can readily visualize the strong binding ties
of such a journal between parents and child. He feels the love and
unity, the security in such a home, the long-term goals, the striv-
ing so that worthy events may be recorded, how he turned his mistakes into stepping stones.

Karla anticipates the day when she and her husband can visit
their children's homes and hear their grandchildren exclaim,
"Guess what Daddy read to us! Out of the book—when he
cracked his head—" or some other such memory.

Of course, every child as he learns to write should be en-
couraged to keep his own private notebook in which he can record
his impressions and those ideas that are special to him.

For a young child who can't yet formulate his thoughts into
writing, his very own picture history can be kept by him, with a
little parental guidance. Get a separate three-ring binder and fill it
with plain paper. When something happens that he wishes to record, he can do it by drawing a picture of the event. The parent
can talk to the child about his picture and his memories of the
event. Then he can print a line or two to record concisely the
thoughts of the child regarding the event portrayed in his picture.

My youngest child showed precocious artistic ability. When she
reached kindergarten, her teacher and the principal were so
impressed that her imaginative large paintings, done with poster
paints and brush, were displayed all over the school. I have saved

many of those paintings in a huge envelope so they were not folded. It doesn't take storage space, but hides behind her chest of drawers—meaningful, irreplaceable reminders of her early artistic bent. How I wish I had made captions to accompany them to recapture her creative moments.

Another mother utilizes certain days, when the children are ill and bored, to visit with the child, nudging him to recall past and current happenings. She takes extensive notes and writes it down as nearly as possible the way he tells her.

One family which holds "home evening" every Monday night, schedules the last Monday of the year as a history night. Dad passes out paper and pencils and each individual writes down the important happenings during the past year. Since they have all anticipated this yearly event, they come somewhat prepared. After writing for a given length of time, the whistle blows and the paper is passed on to the next person, who writes down the things he remembers about the person whose paper he has received. This continues around the family circle. In this way some of the impressions of other family members add their insight. Mother is assigned the task of organizing their notes and finishing up the year's history for each one who is too young to do it himself.

A childless couple adopted two children—a brother and sister. Eager to share the humor and excitement of having these little ones, the mother posted a good-sized blackboard on her kitchen wall on which to jot down a reminding note, or the punch line of anecdotes, so that Daddy could share it too. Then after the children were in bed, she wrote the events in detail. The notations on the blackboard were not erased until this was done.

To make sure these children would always know they were loved and wanted, the parents started a family book in which were recorded such happenings, accomplishments, fun and pathos in the family. A copy of the family book was made for each child also. Of course, pictures were also a part of each book. In January during the lull that follows Christmas excitement, the mother always brought the books up to date.

One day their father gave each child—now adults—a copy of his philosophy of life. He said, "I want you always to know my convictions about the important principles of life, even when we're apart." These were added to the family book of each one.

Not long after this, the daughter was serving in the Peace Corps halfway around the world when delayed word reached her of her father's death. It was too late to return for the funeral. At her request, Mother sent her family book. The daughter said, "I would never have survived the trauma without my family book."

These books are tangible evidence to these children of family security, far more convincing than any spoken statements.

If you are the parent of an extraordinary child (hyperactive, handicapped, etc.) keep a special notebook about him. Extremely gifted children also deserve a special notebook. At meaningful intervals take frequent pictures—some black-and-whites too. Write down your own feelings, negative and otherwise. Date the entries. If the writing seems difficult, simply pretend you are talking to him. Depending upon his development, some day he will know what has gone into his rearing. But beyond that, you will be able to help other parents in similar situations. In serving them, you will also be benefited. Your doctor will undoubtedly know about Parents Anonymous, an organization of parents in your similar circumstances. You can give and receive help as needed.

Treasure Chests

The young are always our responsibility no matter what our age. Generations long past can have a part in shaping their lives. Grandmothers and grandfathers can link the past to the young ones with a treasure chest in which to display inherited treasures. Save some of your own special mementos, knowing that some day they'll be treasured by your descendants, reminders of the "olden days."

If you're young, start now. If you're older, start now. A drawer or special box will do until you find just the right container. My grandfather's treasures include an old Jew's harp; bone kerchief slides carved by his father; his father's rusty sheep shears; ancient horseshoes once worn by his favorite horse—man-to-man items.

My treasure chest includes, among other things, the gold heart locket sent by my husband when he was in the Navy; my mother's

tiny glass swan; my mother-in-law's toy kitchen utensils, the wood
rubbed and smooth, painstakingly carved by her Uncle Richard
when she was a little girl; the hundred-and-fifty-year-old water-
colored portrait of Great-grandmother Esther Burchell who lived
in England; the daguerreotype wedding likeness of her son Joseph
Burchell and his beautiful wife Mary.

Stories surrounding these keepsakes make them more than inan-
imate objects. The children are touched as I tell them how Joseph
and Mary Burchell were planning to emigrate to America with
their four children. One day before going to work in the mine, he
told Mary that if anything should happen to him, she should take
the children to America, as planned. That very day he was killed
in an explosion at work. Before Mary could make arrangements,
her baby son died, only to be followed by her eldest son a year
and a half later. She finally arrived in America with her surviving
son and one daughter. That daughter is my husband's grandmother.

Mementos in a treasure chest kindle a curiosity and respect in
the minds of small grandchildren, who may not have much to do
while visiting Grandma or Grandpa. In this way they learn family
history, and the stories become more cherished because of the tangible artifacts stored in the chest.

One grandmother mounts her treasures in small boxes inside
the chest so they can be seen but not handled or carried off. They
are never played with. These very items might otherwise be considered junk for discard, but they become the focus of precious
moments shared as grandparents talk and listen and weave strong
webs to hold descendants close—their legacy.

Select one of the many suggestions that fits your needs and circumstances, but don't tear another page off the calendar without
beginning your own history project.

Appendix

Library Helps

A few basic ideas for researching in the public library are helpful. The reference room of your local public library might disclose valuable specific manuscript information. Remember that the reference librarian is trained to assist you in solving your research problems. Consulting him immediately can save you many hours of unnecessary floundering in files and book stacks. For example, if you explain that you are looking for social life and customs of people in Nova Scotia from 1750–1800, he could probably quickly find the exact book for you.

However, if you wish to search out the material yourself, consider the following guides:

1. *Card Catalogue*, alphabetically arranged. Try looking under the country or state and then the title, "social life and customs," followed by the time period. If you belong to a minority group, you might find help listed under the racial or ethnic group, such as: Mexican-American social life and customs, date; Indians of North America, social life and customs, date; Negroes, state or city, social life and customs, date.

2. *Harvard Guide to American History*. This book lists all the sources according to times and places and is probably the most complete book of sources available.

3. *Bibliographic Index*. This is the index of all the source books in the United States. Look under United States Social Conditions, and the date.

4. *Dictionary of American Biography*. This book lists all of the important people of the day. Perhaps your ancestor was not famous, but if you knew who lived at the same time, it could lead you to concurrent biographies that could be helpful with background material.

5. *Time-Life Series*. These books give a general picture-narrative summary of time periods.

6. *The Readers Guide*. This index gives a complete listing of magazine articles printed in periodicals and indexed by the *Guide*. *The National Geographic* might have excellent pictures of the area of your search.

7. *Maps and Atlases*. You get more than geographical material from maps and atlases. Resources maps and historical maps and atlases trace peoples, conditions, geographical changes, etc.

8. *Historical Societies.* Most states and many counties have good historical societies that collect information of specific areas.
9. *Newspapers.* Local newspapers often maintain a history of the community.
10. *Monthly Catalog of U. S. Government Publications.*

   If you can't find needed information, but have pinpointed a town, write to the librarian in that town. Most librarians are willing to assist with a difficult problem. Enclose a self-addressed, stamped envelope for reply.

A list of abbreviations used in cataloguing will help you to understand the cards in the file:

D	Document (any manuscript except a letter, although sometimes brief notes are designated N and telegrams *Tel.*)
DS	Document signed (not necessarily by the writer, who may have been the signer's clerk.)
ADS	Autographed document signed (autograph meaning "self-written" by the person signing.)
TD	Typed document
TDS	Typed document signed
Df.	Draft
T.Df.	Typed draft
L	Letter
TL	Typed letter
LS	Letter signed (see DS above)
ALS	Autographed letter signed (see ADS above)

Use indexes in the library. Of course, indexes are not always complete, but if you can find a reference to the object of your search, you have saved endless hours of general searching. An article entitled "New England States Research," by Elizabeth L. Nichols, appeared in the November 1976 *Genealogical Helper.* It gives an excellent list of indexes that are available in most libraries. The whole article would be extremely valuable, especially if your people lived in or came from New England. Single copies of the *Genealogical Helper* may be purchased for approximately $2.00 from The Everton Publishers, Inc., Box 368, Logan, Utah 84321.

Other valuable sources include:

Adams, James Truslow, ed. *Atlas of American History* (New York: Charles Scribner's Sons, 1943). This is a companion volume to *Dictionary of American History.*

Almanacs—Canada, London, New York from 1848. Statistical information, covers factual material.

American Annual (an index that lists newspaper events chronologically).

Directory of Historical Societies and Agencies, 10th ed., 1976, published by American Association for State and Local History, 1400 Eighth Avenue S., Nashville, TN 37203. Should be available in your local library or historical society.

Directory of Microfilm Services in the U.S. and Canada, published by the Special Libraries Association, 235 Park Avenue S., New York, N.Y. 10003. Order the desired film through interlibrary loan.

Encyclopedia of Associations, ed. by Margaret Fisk, Gale Research Book
Tower, Detroit, MI 48226. Lists all fraternal and foreign interest and
ethnic groups. Paperbound supplements keep it up to date.
Sampling:

Brotherhood and Protective Order of Elks
2750 Lake View Avenue
Chicago, IL 60614

Veterans of Foreign Wars
VFW Building
Kansas City, MO 64111

Daughters of American Colonists
2205 Moss Avenue N.W.
Washington, D.C. 20008

(Most of the records of these organizations are not a source of genealogical
data, but the book will give you headquarters' addresses. Clubs' histories usually include data of individuals, only as they acted within the organization.)

Everyman's Dictionary of Dates (New York: International Publications,
1973). Makes useful dates easily accessible.
London Times. Alphabetically arranged by subject, name, etc. since 1790.
Lord, Clifford L. and Lord, Elizabeth H., eds., *Historical Atlas of the U.S.*
(New York: Henry Holt & Co., Inc., 1953). Includes political and eco-
nomic history maps, population statistics, and resources of the U.S. to
1950.
Museums Directory of the United States and Canada, 2nd ed., 1965, American Association of Museums and Smithsonian Institution, Washington,
D.C. This book lists historical societies in the U.S. and Canada. Look
under "Historic Agencies, Counsels, Commissions, Foundations and
Research Institutes," p. 906. Historical and Preservation Societies lists
historical societies alphabetically, pp. 926–31.
National Social Welfare Assembly, Inc. This is a service directory that gives
addresses and principal officers of the various agencies. Fields of interest
and territorial responsibility are included.
New York Times Index. On microfilm at most large libraries. Dates back to
1851. Article summaries may answer questions. In addition, specific references are given to date, page, and column.
*Rand McNally New Cosmopolitan World Atlas . . . Commercial Atlas and
Marketing Guide* (Chicago: Rand McNally & Co., 1968). Contains
data about solar system, world, U.S., and other regions: geographical facts
(climate, population, races, religions, languages); historical, political, and
physical maps.
The American Heritage Pictorial Atlas of U. S. History. A running commen-
tary tracing the history and geographical changes of the U.S. from prehistoric times to the present; illustrated.
The Encyclopediae of American Facts and Dates. Subjects covering politics
and government, sports, sciences, and books—arranged in chronological
order in parallel columns.
The National Union Catalog of Manuscript Collections, Index, 1967 (Library of Congress, Washington, D.C.). This book indexes vast unpublished manuscript collections and tells where they are filed.

Genealogical How-to Books

Many excellent books have been written on the subject. We list only a few as guides. Not much has been written about research in countries other than those listed.

BEGINNERS:

The Genesis of Your Genealogy, by Elizabeth L. Nichols (Logan, UT: The Everton Publishers, Inc., 2nd ed., 1973). A workbook for the very beginner.

Help Is Available, by Elizabeth L. Nichols (Logan, UT: The Everton Publishers, Inc., 1972). The second simplified instruction book.

The How Book for Genealogists, ed. George B. Everton, Sr., 7th ed. (Logan, UT: The Everton Publishers, Inc.).

INTERMEDIATE:

Family History for Fun and Profit, by Vincent L. Jones, Arlene H. Eakle, and Mildred H. Christensen (Salt Lake City: Publishers Press for The Genealogical Institute). General genealogical techniques are explained in considerable detail, including the calendar note-keeping system.

Know Your Ancestors, by Ethel Williams (Rutland, VT: Charles Tuttle Co., 1960). Covers the history of genealogy and basic instruction in scientific methods of tracing ancestry and compiling family history.

Search and Research, by Noel C. Stevenson (Salt Lake City: Deseret Book Co., rev., 1964). Where to write to find the various records in each state and some foreign countries.

Tracing Your Ancestry: A Step-by-Step Guide to Researching Your Family History (Birmingham, AL: Oxmoor House, 1976).

The Sure Guide to Genealogical Research, by Floren S. and Phyllis P. Preece, published by the Genealogy Club of America. General genealogical techniques are explained in considerable detail, including the calendar note-keeping system.

AMERICAN:

Genealogy in America, by Norman E. Wright, Vol. 1 (Salt Lake City: Deseret Book Co., 1968). Sources for research in Massachusetts, Connecticut, and Maine.

Historical and Genealogical Atlas of the Eastern United States, by Richard H. Jackson (Bountiful, UT: Horizon Publishers, 1976). Contains chronological maps from the Revolutionary period to the present for twenty-six states east of the Mississippi River.

Migration, Emigration and Immigration, by Olga K. Miller (Logan, UT: The Everton Publishers, Inc., 1974). Discusses the many migrations to the United States from the early colonial period, of many nationalities.

Researchers Guide to American Genealogy, by Val G. Greenwood (Baltimore: Genealogical Publishing Co., 1973).

Genealogical Research Methods and Sources, American Society of Genealogists (Washington, D.C.: American Society of Genealogists, 1960). Vol. 1 covers thirteen original colonies and major foreign countries. Vol.

2 covers Midwestern and Southern states, Ontario, Canada, and Huguenot and Jewish migrations. Each chapter is written by a specialist in that locality.

Handwriting of American Records for a Period of 300 Years, by E. Kay Kirkham (Logan, UT: The Everton Publishers, Inc., 1973). A guide to handwriting is indispensable, especially when your problem goes back a hundred years or more.

Simplified Genealogy for Americans, by E. Kay Kirkham (Salt Lake City: Deseret Book Co., 1968). Explains research in United States.

The U.S. Census Compendium, by John D. Stemmons (Logan, UT: The Everton Publishers, Inc., 1973).

BRITISH:

The Lives and Times of Our English Ancestors, by Frank Smith (Logan, UT: The Everton Publishers, Inc., 1969). This is a digest of a thousand years of the historical, social, economic, and religious activities of English ancestors.

Genealogical Research in England and Wales, Vols. 1, 2 3, by David E. Gardner and Frank Smith (Salt Lake City: Bookcraft, 1956–59).

A *Genealogical Atlas of England and Wales,* by David E. Gardner and Frank Smith (Salt Lake City: Deseret Book Co., 1960).

CANADA:

Tracing Your Ancestry in Canada, Public Archives of Canada (Ottawa: Queen's Printer, 1968).

NOVA SCOTIA:

Tracing Your Ancestry in Nova Scotia, Public Archives of Nova Scotia, 1967.

GERMAN:

The Atlantic Bridge to Germany, Vols. 1, 2, and 4, by Charles M. Hall (Logan, UT: The Everton Publishers, Inc.).

SCANDINAVIAN:

Scandinavian Genealogical Helper (Logan, UT: The Everton Publishers, Inc.).

Genealogical Guidebook and Atlas of Norway, by Frank Smith and Finn A. Thomsen (Logan, UT: The Everton Publishers, Inc., 1974).

Genealogical Guidebook and Atlas of Denmark, by Frank Smith and Finn A. Thomsen (Salt Lake City: Bookcraft, 1969).

Cradled in Sweden, by Carl-Erik Johansson (Salt Lake City, 1967). (Available through The Everton Publishers, Inc.)

SCOTTISH:

Sources for Scottish Genealogy and Family History, by D. J. Steele (London and Chichester: Phillimore & Co., Ltd., 1970).

In Search of Scottish Ancestry, by Gerald Hamilton-Edwards (London and Chichester: Phillimore Co., Ltd., 1972).

A *Genealogical Gazetteer of Scotland,* by Frank Smith (Logan, UT: The Everton Publishers, 1971).

Supplies

Choose the format you desire, then order supplies accordingly. Both of the houses listed below carry supplies to fit the three-ring and legal-size binders. The basic forms were devised by The Church of Jesus Christ of Latter-day Saints, who are recognized leaders in the field of genealogy. These have been modified to fit both binders.

For your binder, you will need:

Five-generation Pedigree Charts, on which you record your direct ancestry only.

Ancestral Photo Chart, on which you will mount the head photos of your direct ancestry.

Family Group sheets, on which you will record names, dates, and places of each family unit.

Mounting sheets for pictures and other documents that you wish to keep in your binder rather than in your reference files.

Division sheets are optional as your book grows in bulk.

Plain bond punched paper for your binder, on which to record your autobiography or family history.

When you get into genealogical research and set up your note-keeping system, you will find the following forms most helpful:

Work sheets. If you are "hooked" on genealogy and will be doing additional research, buy them by the ream for economy. They are indispensable in the note-keeping system outlined in this book.

Census sheets. Use these in copying census enumerations.

Calendar of Genealogical Research sheets.

The Genealogy Club of America, Suite 1007 Medical Arts Bldg., 54 East South Temple, Salt Lake City, Utah 84111, is a non-sectarian non-profit organization established to give assistance and clues to anyone in America who is interested in genealogy. They publish a monthly magazine called *Genealogy Digest*, as well as all necessary forms and supplies. Their current membership fee of $12 a year entitles members to a discount on all genealogical supplies purchased from them, as well as a subscription to the monthly magazine and the privilege of advertising in the magazine's "Query Corner," in an effort to locate others who might be working on your lines. Send for their price list.

The Everton Publishers, Inc., P.O. Box 368, Logan, Utah 84321, prints the supplies previously listed. In addition they publish *The Genealogical Helper*, a magazine devoted to assist amateur and professional genealogists around the globe. Current subscription rate is: $11 per year, $19 for two years, and $28.50 for three years. Anyone may advertise in the *Helper* for $.23 a word, typewritten copy.

They also have many genealogical "help" books available. Send for their free catalogue.

Records-conservation Supply Houses

Hollinger Corp., 3810 South Four Mile Run Road, Arlington, VA 22206. (Free catalogue of Mylar, acid-free papers, boxes, folders, envelopes, etc.)

Process Materials Corp., 329 Veterans Boulevard, Carlstadt, NJ 07072. (Adhesives, papers, mat board, etc.)

Talas, 104 Fifth Avenue, New York, NY 10011. (Send $1.00 for catalogue describing adhesives, paper, board, tools, equipment, etc.)

Photo Specialist for Copying Old Pictures

A photo specialist in copying old pictures is Simmons Photo, 111 East Broadway, Salt Lake City, UT 84111. If you are unable to find a photographer in your area who can copy pictures and reduce or enlarge them to suit the purpose of your book, or to make small head pictures (1"×1¼") for your Ancestral Photo Chart, this shop is your answer. They handle work for people all over the country, and they do some amazing copies, even from old, faded daguerreotypes, which you would suspect wouldn't show up at all.

Send for their photo-copying price list. You'll be pleasantly surprised at how reasonably you can have the work done. For example, the small head picture costs less than $1.00 for a negative including one print. Each additional copy is only about $.10, so you'll want to have copies done for each of your children's books at the same time.

Be sure to insure your pictures, and they will be returned to you insured.

Archives Branches of the National Archives and Records Service

For each of the following, address inquiries to: Chief, Archives Branch, Federal Archives and Records Center. Agencies in the District of Columbia, Maryland, Virginia, and West Virginia retire records to the Washington National Records Center, Washington, D.C. 20409.

Boston
380 Trapelo Road
Waltham, MA 02154
(Telephone 617-223-2657; hours 8:20 A.M.–4:50 P.M., Mon.–Fri. Serves Connecticut, Maine, Massachusetts, New Hampshire, Rhode Island, and Vermont.)

New York
Building 22—MOT Bayonne
Bayonne, NJ 07002
(Telephone 201-858-7245; hours 8 A.M.–4:30 P.M., Mon.–Fri. Serves New York, New Jersey, Puerto Rico, Virgin Islands.)

Philadelphia
5000 Wissahickon Avenue
Philadelphia, PA 19144
(Telephone 215-GE8-5200, ext. 588; hours 8 A.M.–4:30 P.M., Mon.–Fri. Serves Delaware and Pennsylvania; for the loan of microfilm also serves the District of Columbia, Maryland, Virginia, and West Virginia.)

Atlanta
1557 St. Joseph Avenue
East Point, GA 30344
(Telephone 404-526-7477; hours 8 A.M.–4:30 P.M., Mon.–Fri. Serves Alabama, Georgia, Florida, Kentucky, Mississippi, North Carolina, South Carolina, and Tennessee.)

Chicago
7358 South Pulaski Road
Chicago, IL 60629
(Telephone 312-353-8541; hours 8 A.M.–4:30 P.M., Mon.–Fri. Serves Illinois, Indiana, Michigan, Minnesota, Ohio, and Wisconsin.)

Denver
Building 48, Denver Federal Center
Denver, CO 80225
(Telephone 303-234-3187; hours 7:30 A.M.–4 P.M., Mon.–Fri. Serves Colorado, Montana, North Dakota, South Dakota, Utah, and Wyoming.)

San Francisco
1000 Commodore Drive
San Bruno, CA 94066
(Telephone 415-556-8452; hours 7:45 A.M.–4:15 P.M., Mon.–Fri. Serves California except southern California, Hawaii, Nevada except Clark County, and the Pacific Ocean area.)

Los Angeles
4747 Eastern Avenue
Bell, CA 90201
(Telephone 213-268-2548; hours 7:30 A.M.–4 P.M., Mon.–Fri. Serves Arizona; the southern California counties of Imperial, Inyo, Kern, Los Angeles, Orange, Riverside, San Bernardino, San Diego, San Luis Obispo, Santa Barbara, and Ventura; and Clark County, NV.)

Seattle
6125 Sand Point Way NE.
Seattle, WA 98115
(Telephone 206-442-4502; hours 8 A.M.–4:30 P.M., Mon.–Fri. Serves Alaska, Idaho, Oregon, and Washington.)

Kansas City
2306 East Bannister Road
Kansas City, MO 64131
(Telephone 816-926-7271; hours 8 A.M.–4:30 P.M., Mon.–Fri. Serves Iowa, Kansas, Missouri, and Nebraska.)

Fort Worth
4900 Hemphill Street (building address)
P.O. Box 6216 (mailing address)
Fort Worth, TX 76115
(Telephone 817-334-5515; hours 8 A.M.–4:30 P.M., Mon.–Fri. Serves Arkansas, Louisiana, New Mexico, Oklahoma, and Texas.)

Copyright Application Form

Application
for Registration of a Claim to Copyright
in a published book manufactured in
the United States of America

FORM A

REGISTRATION NO.

CLASS

A

DO NOT WRITE HERE

Instructions: Make sure that all applicable spaces have been completed before you submit the form. The application must be **SIGNED** at line 10 and the **AFFIDAVIT** (line 11) **must be COMPLETED AND NOTARIZED.** The application should not be submitted until after the date of publication given in line 4, and should state the facts which existed on that date. For further information, see page 4.

Pages 1 and 2 should be typewritten or printed with pen and ink. Pages 3 and 4 should contain exactly the same information as pages 1 and 2, but may be carbon copies. Mail all pages of the application to the Register of Copyrights, Library of Congress, Washington, D.C. 20559, together with 2 copies of the best edition of the work and the registration fee of $6. Make your remittance payable to the Register of Copyrights.

1. Copyright Claimant(s) and Address(es): Give the name(s) and address(es) of the copyright owner(s). Ordinarily the name(s) should be the same as in the notice of copyright on the copies deposited.

Name ....

Address ....

Name ....

Address ....

2. Title: ....
(Give the title of the book as it appears on the title page)

3. Authors: Citizenship and domicile information must be given. Where a work was made for hire, the employer is the author. The citizenship of organizations formed under U.S. Federal or State law should be stated as U.S.A. Authors may be editors, compilers, translators, illustrators, etc., as well as authors of original text. If the copyright claim is based on new matter (see line 5) give requested information about the author of the new matter.

Name . . .. Citizenship ....
(Give legal name followed by pseudonym if latter appears on the copies) *(Name of country)*

Domiciled in U.S.A. Yes .... No .... Address ....

Name . . . . Citizenship ....
(Give legal name followed by pseudonym if latter appears on the copies) *(Name of country)*

Domiciled in U.S.A. Yes .... No .... Address ....

Name .... Citizenship ....
(Give legal name followed by pseudonym if latter appears on the copies) *(Name of country)*

Domiciled in U.S.A. Yes .... No .... Address ....

4. Date of Publication of This Edition: Give the complete date when copies of this particular edition were first placed on sale, sold, or publicly distributed. The date when copies were made or printed should not be confused with the date of publication. **NOTE:** The full date (month, day, and year) must be given. For further information, see page 4.

....
(Month) (Day) (Year)

➤➤ (NOTE: Leave line 5 blank unless the following instructions apply to this work.) ◄◄

5. New Matter in This Version: If any substantial part of this work has been previously published anywhere, give a brief, general statement of the nature of the new matter published for the first time in this version. New matter may consist of compilation, translation, abridgment, editorial revision, and the like, as well as additional text or pictorial matter.

....

➤➤ NOTE: Leave line 6 blank unless there has been a PREVIOUS FOREIGN EDITION in the English language. ◄◄

6. Book in English Previously Manufactured and Published Abroad: If all or a substantial part of the text of this edition was previously manufactured and published abroad in the English language, complete the following spaces:

Date of first publication of foreign edition ....
(Year)

Was registration for the foreign edition made in the U.S. Copyright Office? Yes .... No ....

EXAMINER

If your answer is "Yes," give registration number ....

Complete all applicable spaces on next page

7. If registration fee is to be charged to a deposit account established in the Copyright Office, give name of account:

....

8. Name and address of person or organization to whom correspondence or refund, if any, should be sent:

Name .... Address ....

9. Send certificate to:

(Type or
print   Name ....
name and
address) Address ....

| (Number and street) |
| (City) | (State) | (ZIP code) |

10. Certification: (NOTE: Application not acceptable unless signed)

    I CERTIFY that the statements made by me in this application are correct to the best of my knowledge.

....
(Signature of copyright claimant or duly authorized agent)

11. Affidavit (required by law). Instructions: (1) Fill in the blank spaces with special attention to those marked **"(X)."** (2) Sign the affidavit before an officer authorized to administer oaths within the United States, such as a notary public. (3) Have the officer sign and seal the affidavit and fill in the date of execution.

    NOTE: The affidavit must be signed and notarized only *on or after* the date of publication or completion of printing which it states. The affidavit *must* be signed by an individual.

STATE OF .... }

COUNTY OF .... } *ss:*

I, the undersigned, depose and say that I am the
☐ Person claiming copyright in the book described in this application;
☐ Duly authorized agent of the person or organization claiming copyright in the book described in this application;
☐ Printer of the book described in this application.

That the book was published or the printing was completed on: **(X)** ....
(Give month, day, and year)

That, of the various processes employed in the production of the copies deposited, the setting of the type was performed within the limits of the United States or the making of the plates was performed within the limits of the United States from type set therein; or the lithographic or photoengraving processes used in producing the text were wholly performed within the limits of the United States, and that the printing of the text and the binding (if any) were also performed within the limits of the United States. That such typesetting, platemaking, lithographic or photoengraving process, printing, and binding were performed by the following establishments or individuals at the following addresses:
(GIVE THE NAMES AND ADDRESSES OF THE PERSONS OR ORGANIZATIONS WHO PERFORMED SUCH TYPESETTING OR PLATEMAKING OR LITHOGRAPHIC PROCESS OR PHOTOENGRAVING PROCESS OR PRINTING AND BINDING, ETC.)

Names **(X)** .... Addresses **(X)** ....

....

....
(Signature of affiant)

(Sign and notarize only on or after date given above)

                       sworn to
Subscribed and   before me this ....
                    affirmed

PLACE
NOTARIAL SEAL
HERE

day of ...., 19......

....
(Signature of notary)

FOR COPYRIGHT OFFICE USE ONLY	
Application and affidavit received	
Two copies received	
Fee received	
Renewal	

Certificate

Registration of a Claim to Copyright
in a published book manufactured in
the United States of America

FORM A

REGISTRATION NO.	CLASS
DO NOT WRITE HERE	**A**

This Is To Certify that the statements set forth on this certificate have been made a part of the records of the Copyright Office. In witness whereof the seal of the Copyright Office is hereto affixed.

Register of Copyrights
United States of America

1. Copyright Claimant(s) and Address(es):

Name ....

Address ....

Name ....

Address ....

2. Title: ....
(Title of book)

....

3. Authors:

Name .... Citizenship ....
(Legal name followed by pseudonym if latter appears on copies) (Name of country)

Domiciled in U.S.A. Yes .... No .... Address ....

Name .... Citizenship ....
(Legal name followed by pseudonym if latter appears on copies) (Name of country)

Domiciled in U.S.A. Yes .... No .... Address ....

Name .... Citizenship ....
(Legal name followed by pseudonym if latter appears on copies) (Name of country)

Domiciled in U.S.A. Yes .... No .... Address ....

4. Date of Publication of This Edition:

....
(Month)   (Day)   (Year)

5. New Matter in This Version:

....

....

6. Book in English Previously Manufactured and Published Abroad: If all or a substantial part of the text of this edition was previously manufactured and published abroad in the English language, complete the following spaces:

Date of first publication of foreign edition .... Was registration for the foreign edition made in the U.S.
(Year)   Copyright Office? Yes .... No ....

If your answer is "Yes," give registration number ....

EXAMINER

Complete all applicable spaces on next page

23

7. Deposit account:

8. Send correspondence to:

Name .... Address ....

9. Send certificate to:

(Type or
print   Name ....
name and
address) Address ....
                                        (Number and street)

....
                (City)   (State)   (ZIP code)

Information concerning copyright in books

When to Use Form A. Form A is appropriate for published books which have been manufactured in the United States.

What Is a "Book"? The term "books" covers not only material published in book form, but also pamphlets, leaflets, cards, and single pages containing text. Books include fiction, nonfiction, poetry, collections, directories, catalogs, and information in tabular form.

Unpublished Books. The law does not provide for registration of "book" material in unpublished form. Unpublished books are protected at common law against unauthorized use prior to publication.

Duration of Copyright. Statutory copyright in published books lasts for 28 years from the date of first publication, and may be renewed for a second 28-year term.

How to secure statutory copyright in a book

First: Produce Copies With Copyright Notice. Produce the work in copies by printing or other means of reproduction. To secure copyright, it is essential that the copies bear a copyright notice in the required form and position, as explained below.

Second: Publish the Work With Copyright Notice. The copyright law defines the "date of publication" as ". . . the earliest date when copies of the first authorized edition were placed on sale, sold, or publicly distributed by the proprietor of the copyright or under his authority, . . ."

Third: Register Your Copyright Claim. Promptly after publication, mail to the Register of Copyrights, Library of Congress,

Washington, D.C. 20559, two copies of the work as published with notice, an application on Form A, properly completed and notarized, and a fee of $6.

The Copyright Notice. The copyright notice for books shall appear on the title page or verso thereof, and shall consist of three elements: the word "Copyright," or the abbreviation "Copr.," or the symbol ©, accompanied by the name of the copyright owner and the year date of publication. Example: © John Doe 1974. Use of the symbol © may result in securing copyright in countries which are members of the Universal Copyright Convention.

> NOTE: It is the act of publication with notice that actually secures copyright protection. If copies are published without the required notice, the right to secure copyright is lost, and cannot be restored.

Books manufactured abroad

In General. Form A is not appropriate for books which have been manufactured outside the United States.

Foreign-Language Books. Applications covering foreign-language books by foreign authors, manufactured abroad, should be submitted on Form A–B Foreign.

English-Language Books. Books in English manufactured abroad may be registered for "ad interim" copyright (Form A–B Ad Interim); or, if they are protected under the Universal Copyright Convention they are eligible for full-term registration on Form A–B Foreign:

(1) *Ad Interim Copyright.* Ad interim registration is necessary for protection in the United States unless copyright has been secured

under the Universal Copyright Convention. To secure ad interim copyright a claim must be registered within 6 months of first publication abroad. Ad interim copyright lasts for 5 years or until an American edition is published within the 5-year period and registered.

(2) *Universal Copyright Convention.* An English-language work by a foreign author first published abroad is eligible for full-term U.S. copyright if: (a) its author is a citizen or subject of a country which is a member of the Universal Copyright Convention, or the work was first published in such country, and (b) all published copies bear the copyright notice provided under the Universal Copyright Convention.

FOR COPYRIGHT OFFICE USE ONLY	
Application and affidavit received	
Two copies received	
Fee received	

Where to Write for Vital Statistics
Birth and Death Records

A record of every birth, death, marriage, and divorce in the United States should be on file (at least in the twentieth century) either in the state or local record-keeping agencies. Certificates are prepared by physicians, funeral directors, other professional attendants, or hospital authorities, or clerks. The Federal Government does not maintain files or indexes of these records. A certified copy of a certificate can be obtained by writing or going to the vital statistics office in the state, county, or in some cases, city where the event occurred.

Always include return postage with your request. When writing for a certified copy, enclose a money order or certified check, since the office cannot refund cash lost in the mail. Fees as shown in the following charts are subject to change, as well as addresses. The information on the following charts is current for 1977. Updated pamphlets for a later date can be obtained by writing to Superintendent of Documents, U. S. Government Printing Office, Washington, D.C. 20402. According to your specific need, ask for: *Where to write for birth and death records, Where to write for marriage records,* or *Where to write for divorce records.*

In the United States, each state became a vital statistics repository at a different time. Prior to the establishment of the state offices, births and deaths were kept by county or city authorities. Marriages have always been kept by county or city offices, and divorces follow the same pattern generally. Therefore, if the event occurred before state offices began keeping the records, write to the appropriate county or city authority.

For certified copies of birth or death certificates, your letter should include the following data, typed or printed:

1. Full name of the person whose record is being requested.
2. Sex and race.
3. Parents' names, including maiden name of mother.
4. Month, day, and year of the birth or death.
5. Place of birth or death (city or town, county, and state; and name of hospital, if any).
6. Purpose for which copy is needed.
7. Relationship to person whose record is being requested.
   NOTE: Births occurring before birth registration was required or births not registered when they occurred may have been filed as "delayed birth registrations." Keep this in mind when seeking copy of a record.

Of course, you may not know all the above information, and if you do, you probably feel there is no need to obtain the certificate. If there is a question in your mind about any specific item, indicate it, so the searcher can be guided. A certificate is desirable because it is OFFICIAL PROOF of the event, and may verify or give additional details you do not have.

Where to Write for Birth and Death Records
in the United States and Outlying Areas

Place of birth or death	Cost	Address of vital statistics office	Remarks
Alabama	$3.00	Bureau of Vital Statistics State Department of Public Health Montgomery, Alabama 36104	Additional copies at same time $1.00 each. Records in State office since January 1, 1908. $3.00 per hour for special searches.
Alaska	$3.00	Bureau of Vital Statistics Department of Health & Welfare Pouch H Juneau, Alaska 99801	State office has records since 1913.
American Samoa	$1.00	Office of Territorial Registrar Government of American Samoa Pago Pago American Samoa 96799	Registrar has records since before 1900.
Arizona	$2.00	Division of Vital Records State Department of Health P.O. Box 3887 Phoenix, Arizona 85030	State office has records since July 1, 1909, and abstracts of records filed in counties before that date.
Arkansas Birth Death	$2.00 $3.00	Division of Vital Records Arkansas Department of Health 4815 West Markham Street Little Rock, Arkansas 72201	State office has records since February 1, 1914, as well as some original Little Rock and Fort Smith records from 1881.
California	$2.00	Vital Statistics Section State Department of Health 410 N Street Sacramento, California 95814	State office has records since July 1, 1905. For prior records write to County Recorder where event occurred.

Place of birth or death	Cost	Address of vital statistics office	Remarks
Canal Zone	Short Form Only $2.00	Vital Statistics Clerk Health Bureau Balboa Heights, Canal Zone	Central office has records since May 1904.
Colorado	$2.00	Records and Statistics Section Colorado Department of Health 4210 East 11th Avenue Denver, Colorado 80220	State office has deaths since 1900, births since 1910, also births for some counties for years before 1910.
Connecticut	$2.00	Public Health Statistics Section State Department of Health 79 Elm Street Hartford, Connecticut 06115	State office has records since July 1, 1897. For prior records, write to Registrar of Vital Statistics in town or city where event occurred.
Delaware	$2.50	Bureau of Vital Statistics Division of Public Health Department of Health & Social Services Jesse S. Cooper Memorial Building Dover, Delaware 19901	State office has records for 1861–63 and since 1881, but no records for 1864 through 1880.
District of Columbia	$1.00	Department of Human Resources Room 1022, Vital Records Section 300 Indiana Avenue, NW Washington, D.C. 20001	Death records on file beginning with 1885. Births beginning with 1871. Deaths beginning with 1885. No death records were filed during Civil War.
Florida	$2.00	Department of Health & Rehabilitative Services Division of Health Bureau of Vital Statistics P.O. Box 210 Jacksonville, Florida 32201	State office has some birth records since April 1865 and some death records since August 1877. Majority date from January 1917. (If exact date is unknown, fee is $2.00 for first year and $1.00 each additional year searched up to maximum of $25. Fee includes copy of record, if found.)

Georgia	$3.00	Vital Records Unit State Department of Human Resources Room 217-H 47 Trinity Avenue, SW Atlanta, Georgia 30334	State office has records since January 1, 1919. For prior records in Atlanta or Savannah, write to County Health Department where event occurred.
Guam	$1.00	Office of Vital Statistics Department of Public Health & Social Services Government of Guam P.O. Box 2816 Agana, Guam, M.I. 96910	Records on file since October 26, 1901.
Hawaii	$2.00	Research and Statistics Office State Department of Health P.O. Box 3378 Honolulu, Hawaii 96801	State office has records since 1853.
Idaho	$2.00	Bureau of Vital Statistics State Department of Health & Welfare Statehouse Boise, Idaho 83720	State office has records since 1911. For records from 1907-11, write County Recorder where event occurred.
Illinois	$3.00	Office of Vital Records State Department of Public Health 535 W. Jefferson Street Springfield, Illinois 62761	State office has records since January 1, 1916. For prior records write to County Clerk where event occurred.
Indiana	$3.00	Division of Vital Records State Board of Health 1330 West Michigan Street Indianapolis, Indiana 46206	State office has birth records since October 1, 1907, death records since 1900. For prior records, write to Health Officer in city or county where event occurred.
Iowa	$2.00	Division of Records and Statistics State Department of Health Des Moines, Iowa 50319	State office has records since July 1, 1880.

Place of birth or death	Cost	Address of vital statistics office	Remarks
Kansas	$2.00	Bureau of Registration & Health Statistics 6700 S. Topeka Avenue Topeka, Kansas 66620	State office has records since July 1, 1911. For prior records write County Clerk where event occurred.
Kentucky	$2.00	Office of Vital Statistics State Department of Health 275 East Main Street Frankfort, Kentucky 40601	State office has records since January 1, 1911, and for Louisville and Lexington before that date. If event occurred in Covington before 1911, write to City Health Department.
Louisiana	$2.00	Office of Vital Records State Department of Health P.O. Box 60630 New Orleans, Louisiana 70160	State office has records since July 1, 1914. City of New Orleans has their birth records from 1790 and death records from 1803.
Maine	$2.00	Office of Vital Records State Department of Health & Welfare State House Augusta, Maine 04333	State office has records since 1892. For prior records write to Town Clerk where event occurred.
Maryland	$2.00	Division of Vital Records State Department of Health State Office Building 201 West Preston Street P.O. Box 13146 Baltimore, Maryland 21203	State office has records since 1898. Baltimore records are available from January 1, 1875.
Massachusetts	$2.00	Registrar of Vital Statistics Room 103, McCormack Building 1 Ashburton Place Boston, Massachusetts 02108	State office has records since 1841. For prior records, write City or Town Clerk where event occurred. Earliest Boston records available are for 1848.

Michigan	Office of Vital & Health Statistics Michigan Department of Public Health 3500 North Logan Street Lansing, Michigan 48914	$2.00

State office has records since 1867. Also in County Clerk's office since 1867. Birth records since 1893 and deaths since 1897 in Detroit are in City Health Department.

Minnesota	Minnesota Department of Health Section of Vital Statistics 717 Delaware Street, SE Minneapolis, Minnesota 55440	$2.00

State office has records since January 1908. For prior records write to Clerk of District Court where event occurred. For Minneapolis or St. Paul, write to City Health Department.

Mississippi	Vital Records Registration Unit State Board of Health P.O. Box 1700 Jackson, Mississippi 39205	$2.00

State office has records since November 1, 1912.

Missouri	Bureau of Vital Records Division of Health State Department of Public Health & Welfare Jefferson City, Missouri 65101	$1.00

State office has records from January 1910. If event occurred in St. Louis (city), St. Louis County, or Kansas City before 1910, write to City or County Health Department. Copies of these records are $2.00.

Montana	Bureau of Records & Statistics State Department of Health & Environmental Sciences Helena, Montana 59601	$2.00

State office has records since late 1907.

Nebraska	Bureau of Vital Statistics State Department of Health Lincoln Building 1003 "O" Street Lincoln, Nebraska 68508	$3.00

State office has records since late 1904. If event occurred before that date, write the State office for information.

Place of birth or death	Cost	Address of vital statistics office	Remarks
Nevada	$2.00	Department of Human Resources Division of Health, Vital Statistics Office of Vital Records Capitol Complex Carson City, Nevada 89710	State office has records since July 1, 1911. For prior records, write to County Recorder where event occurred.
New Hampshire	$2.00	Department of Health & Welfare Division of Public Health Bureau of Vital Statistics 61 South Spring Street Concord, New Hampshire 03301	Write to State office or City or Town Clerk where event occurred.
New Jersey	$2.00	State Department of Health Bureau of Vital Statistics Box 1540 Trenton, New Jersey 08625	State office has records since June 1878. (When exact date is not known, a fee of $.50 is charged for each additional year searched.)
New Mexico	$2.00	Vital Records New Mexico Health & Social Services Department PERA Building, Room 118 Santa Fe, New Mexico 87501	State office has records since 1880.
New York (except New York City)	$2.00	Bureau of Vital Records State Department of Health Empire State Plaza Tower Building Albany, New York 12237	State office has records since 1880. For records prior to 1914 in Albany, Buffalo, and Yonkers or before 1880 in any other city, write Registrar of Vital Statistics in city where event occurred. For rest of state, except New York City, write to State office.

New York (all boroughs) birth death	$3.00 $2.50	Bureau of Records and Statistics Department of Health of New York City 125 Worth Street New York, New York 10013	Records on file since 1898. For Old City of New York (Manhattan and part of the Bronx) birth and death records from 1865–97, write to Municipal Archives and Records Retention Center, New York, 23 Park Row, New York 10038.
North Carolina	$2.00	Department of Human Resources Division of Health Services Vital Records Branch P.O. Box 2091 Raleigh, North Carolina 27602	State office has records since October 1, 1913, and some delayed records prior to that date.
North Dakota	$2.00	Division of Vital Records Office of Statistical Services State Department of Health Bismarck, North Dakota 58505	State office has some records from July 1, 1893; years from 1894–1920 are incomplete.
Ohio	$1.00	Division of Vital Statistics Ohio Department of Health G-20 Ohio Departments Building 65 S. Front Street Columbus, Ohio 43215	State office has records since December 20, 1908. For prior records, write to Probate Court in county where event occurred.
Oklahoma	$2.00	Vital Records Section State Department of Health Northeast 10th Street & Stonewall P.O. Box 53551 Oklahoma City, Oklahoma 73105	State office has records since October 1908.
Oregon	$3.00	Vital Statistics Section Oregon State Health Division P.O. Box 231 Portland, Oregon 97207	State office has records since July 1903, and some earlier records for City of Portland, dating from approximately 1880.

Place of birth or death	Cost	Address of vital statistics office	Remarks
Pennsylvania	$2.00	Division of Vital Statistics State Department of Health Central Building 101 South Mercer Street P.O. Box 1528 New Castle, Pennsylvania 16103	State office has records since January 1, 1906. For prior records, write to Register of Wills, Orphans Court, county seat where event occurred. For births in Pittsburgh from 1870–1905 or in Allegheny City (now part of Pittsburgh) from 1882–1905, write to Office of Biostatistics, Pittsburgh Health Department, City-County Building, Pittsburgh, Pennsylvania 15219. For City of Philadelphia births and deaths from 1860–1915, write to Vital Statistics, Philadelphia Department of Public Health, City Hall Annex, Philadelphia, Pennsylvania 19107.
Puerto Rico	$.50	Division of Demographic Registry & Vital Statistics Department of Health San Juan, Puerto Rico 00908	Central office has records since July 22, 1931. For prior records, write to local Registrar (*Registrador Demografico*) in municipality where event occurred or to central office.
Rhode Island	$2.00	Division of Vital Statistics State Department of Health Room 101, Health Building Davis Street Providence, Rhode Island 02908	State office has records since 1853. For prior records, write to Town Clerk where event occurred.
South Carolina	$2.00	Division of Vital Records Bureau of Health Measurement S.C. Department of Health & Analysis Environmental Control 2600 Bull Street Columbia, South Carolina 29201	State office has records since January 1, 1915. For City of Charleston births from 1877 and deaths from 1821 write to Charleston County Health Department. Florence City births and deaths from 1895–1914 are on file at Florence County Health Department.

		Newberry City births and deaths from late 1800s are on file at Newberry County Health Department. For prior records, write to County Health Departments where event occurred.
South Dakota	$2.00	Division of Public Health Statistics State Department of Health Pierre, South Dakota 57501	State office has records since July 1, 1905, and some prior births and deaths.
Tennessee	$2.00	Division of Vital Statistics State Department of Public Health Cordell Hull Building Nashville, Tennessee 37219	State office has births from entire state from January 1, 1914, and Nashville birth records from June 1881, Knoxville birth records from July 1881, Chattanooga birth records from January 1882. Nashville death records from July 1, 1874, Knoxville death records from July 1, 1887, Chattanooga death records from March 6, 1872. Birth and death enumeration records by school districts from July 1, 1908, through June 30, 1912. Memphis birth records are from April 1, 1874 through December 1887. Records continue November 1, 1898, to January 1, 1914. Death records date from May 1, 1848, to January 1, 1914. Write to Memphis-Shelby County Health Department, Division of Vital Statistics, Memphis, Tennessee.
Texas	$2.00	Bureau of Vital Statistics Texas Department of Health Resources 410 East Fifth Street Austin, Texas 78701	State office has records since 1903.

Place of birth or death	Cost	Address of vital statistics office	Remarks
Trust Territory of the Pacific Islands	$.25 plus $.10 per 100 words	Clerk of Court of district where event occurred. (If not sure of district, write to the Director of Medical Services, Department of Medical Services, Saipan, Mariana Islands 96950, to have inquiry referred to correct district.)	Courts have records since November 21, 1952. Beginning 1950 a few records for various islands are temporarily filed with the Hawaii Bureau of Vital Statistics.
Utah	$3.00	Division of Vital Statistics Utah State Department of Health 554 South Third East Salt Lake City, Utah 84113	State office has records since 1905. If event occurred from 1890 through 1904 in Salt Lake City or Ogden, write to City Board of Health. Elsewhere in State from 1898 through 1904, write to County Clerk where event occurred.
Vermont	$2.00	Town or City Clerk of town where birth or death occurred. Secretary of State Vital Records Department Statehouse Montpelier, Vermont 05602 Public Health Statistics Division Department of Health Burlington, Vermont 05401	For information on vital statistics laws, how to correct, etc., write to Department of Health.
Virginia	$2.00	Bureau of Vital Records & Health Statistics State Department of Health James Madison Building P.O. Box 1000 Richmond, Virginia 23208	State office has records from January 1853 through December 1896 and since June 4, 1912. For records between those dates, write to Health Department in city where event occurred.

Virgin Islands (U.S.) St. Thomas	$2.00	Registrar of Vital Statistics Charlotte Amalie St. Thomas, Virgin Islands 00802	Registrar has birth records on file since July 1, 1906, and death records since January 1, 1906.
St. Croix	$2.00	Registrar of Vital Statistics Charles Harwood Memorial Hospital St. Croix, Virgin Islands 00820	Registrar has birth and death records since 1840.
Washington	$3.00	Bureau of Vital Statistics Health Services Division Department of Social & Health Services P.O. Box 709 Olympia, Washington 98504	State office has records since July 1, 1907, in Seattle, Spokane, and Tacoma. Copy also available from City Health Department. For prior records, write to Auditor in county where event occurred.
West Virginia	$1.00	Division of Vital Statistics State Department of Health State Office Building No. 3 Charleston, West Virginia 25305	State office has records since January 1917. For prior records write to Clerk of County Court where event occurred.
Wisconsin	$4.00	Bureau of Health Statistics Wisconsin Division of Health P.O. Box 309 Madison, Wisconsin 53701	State office has some records since 1814. Early years are incomplete.
Wyoming	$2.00	Vital Records Services Division of Health & Medical Services State Office Building West Cheyenne, Wyoming 82002	State office has records since July 1909.

Marriage Records

An official record of every marriage should be available in the place where the event occurred. These records may be filed permanently either in a state vital statistics office or in a city, county, or other local office.

A copy may be obtained by writing to the appropriate office listed below. Fees listed are subject to change.

In writing for a copy, it is suggested that a money order or certified check be enclosed since the office cannot refund cash lost in transit. In your request, include the following information as a guide to the search. Type or print all names and addresses.

1. Full names of bride and groom (including nicknames).
2. Residence addresses at time of marriage.
3. Ages at time of marriage (or dates of birth).
4. Date and place of marriage.
5. Purpose for which copy is needed.
6. Relationship to person whose record is on file.

Place of marriage	Cost of copy	Remarks. For certified copies write to:
Alabama	$2.00	Records since August 1936: Bureau of Vital Statistics, State Department of Public Health, Montgomery, Alabama 36104. Fee includes search and copy, if found.
	$1.00	Probate Judge in county where license was issued.
Alaska	$3.00	Records since 1913: Bureau of Vital Statistics, Department of Health & Welfare, Pouch H, Juneau, Alaska 99801.

Place of marriage	Cost of copy	Remarks. For certified copies write to:
American Samoa	$1.00	Registrar of Vital Statistics, Pago Pago, American Samoa 96799.
Arizona	Varies	Clerk of Superior Court in county where license was issued.
Arkansas	$2.00	Records since 1917: Division of Vital Records, Arkansas Department of Health, 4815 W. Markham Street, Little Rock, Arkansas 72201.
	$2.00	Full certified copy may be obtained from County Clerk in county where license was issued.
California	$2.00	Vital Statistics Section, State Department of Public Health, 410 N Street, Sacramento, California 95814.
Canal Zone	$2.00	License Section, Civil Affairs Bureau, Box L, Balboa Heights, Canal Zone.
Colorado	*	Statewide index of records for all years except 1940–67: Records and Statistics Section, Colorado Department of Health, 4210 East 11th Avenue, Denver, Colorado 80220. Inquiries will be forwarded to appropriate county office.
	Varies	County Clerk in county where license was issued.
Connecticut	$2.00	Records since July 1, 1897: Public Health Statistics Section, State Department of Health, 79 Elm Street, Hartford, Connecticut 06115.
	$2.00	Registrar of Vital Statistics in town where license was issued.
Delaware	$2.50	Bureau of Vital Statistics, Division of Public Health, Department of Health & Social Services, Jesse S. Cooper Memorial Building, Dover, Delaware 19901.
District of Columbia	$2.00	Marriage Bureau, Room 337, 440 G Street, NW, Washington, D.C. 20001. Fee for proof of marriage, $1.00. Fee for application only, $1.00. Complete record $2.00.
Florida	$2.00	Records since June 6, 1927: Bureau of Vital Statistics, State Division of Health, P.O. Box 210, Jacksonville, Florida 32201. If year is unknown, the fee is $2.00 for the first year

* Apply to county where license was issued if known. Certified copies not available from State Health Department.

Place of marriage	Cost of copy	Remarks. For certified copies write to:
		searched and $1.00 for each additional year up to a maximum of $25. Fee includes a copy of the record if found.
	$2.00	Clerk of Circuit Court in county where license was issued.
Georgia	*	Centralized State records since June 9, 1952: Vital Records Unit, State Department of Human Resources, Room 217-H, 47 Trinity Avenue, SW, Atlanta, Georgia 30334. Inquiries will be forwarded to appropriate office.
	$2.00	County Ordinary in county where license was issued.
Guam	$1.00	Office of Vital Statistics, Department of Public Health & Social Services, Government of Guam, P.O. Box 2816, Agana, Guam, M.I. 96910.
Hawaii	$2.00	Research and Statistics Office, State Department of Health, P.O. Box 3378, Honolulu, Hawaii 96801.
Idaho	$2.00	Records since 1947: Bureau of Vital Statistics, State Department of Health & Welfare, Statehouse, Boise, Idaho 83720.
	Varies	County Recorder in county where license was issued.
Illinois	*	Records since January 1, 1962: Office of Vital Records, State Department of Public Health, Springfield, Illinois 62761. All items may be verified (fee $2.00).
	$2.00	County Clerk in county where license was issued.
Indiana	*	Records since 1958: Division of Vital Records, State Board of Health, 1330 West Michigan Street, Indianapolis, Indiana 46206. No certification. Inquiries will be forwarded to appropriate office.
	Varies	Clerk of Circuit Court, or Clerk of Superior Court, in county where license was issued.
Iowa	$2.00	Division of Records & Statistics, State Department of Health, Des Moines, Iowa 50319.

* Apply to county where license was issued if known. Certified copies not available from State Health Department.

Place of marriage	Cost of copy	Remarks. For certified copies write to:
Kansas	$2.00	Records since May 1913: Bureau of Registration & Health Statistics, Kansas State Department of Health and Environment, 6700 S. Topeka Avenue, Topeka, Kansas 66620.
	Varies	Probate Judge in county where license was issued.
Kentucky	$2.00	Records since July 1, 1958. Office of Vital Statistics, State Department of Health, 275 East Main Street, Frankfort, Kentucky 40601.
	Varies	Clerk of County Court in county where license was issued.
Louisiana	*	Records since 1946: Bureau of Vital Statistics, State Department of Health, P.O. Box 60630, New Orleans, Louisiana 70160. Inquiries will be forwarded to appropriate office.
	$2.00	Certified copies are issued by Clerk of Court in parish where license was issued.
Maine	$2.00	Office of Vital Records, State Department of Health & Welfare, Statehouse, Augusta, Maine 04333.
	$2.00	Town Clerk in town where license was issued.
Maryland	$2.00	Records since June 1, 1951: Division of Vital Records, State Department of Health & Mental Hygiene, State Office Building, P.O. Box 13146, 201 West Preston Street, Baltimore, Maryland 21203.
	Varies	Clerk of Circuit Court in county where license was issued or Clerk of Court of Common Pleas of Baltimore.
Massachusetts	$2.00	Records since 1841: Registrar of Vital Statistics, Room 103, McCormack Building, 1 Ashburton Place, Boston, Massachusetts 02108. Earliest Boston records are for 1848.
Michigan	$2.00	Records since April 1867: Office of Vital & Health Statistics, Michigan Department of Public Health, 3500 North Logan Street, Lansing, Michigan 48914.
	$2.00	County Clerk in county where license was issued.

* Apply to county where license was issued if known. Certified copies not available from State Health Department.

Place of marriage	Cost of copy	Remarks. For certified copies write to:
Minnesota	*	State-wide index since January 1958: Section of Vital Statistics, State Department of Health, 717 Delaware Street, SE, Minneapolis, Minnesota 55440. Inquiries will be forwarded to appropriate office.
	$2.00	Clerk in District Court in county where license was issued.
Mississippi	$2.00	Statistical Record only from January 1926 to July 1, 1938, and from January 1, 1942 to present: Vital Records Registration Unit, State Board of Health, P.O. Box 1700, Jackson, Mississippi 39205.
	$2.00	Circuit Clerk in county where license was issued.
Missouri	Free	Indexes since July 1948. Division of Health, Bureau of Vital Records, Jefferson City, Missouri 65101. Correspondent will be referred to appropriate Recorder of Deeds of the county where the license was issued.
	Varies	Recorder of Deeds in county where license was issued.
Montana	*	Records since July 1943: Bureau of Records & Statistics, State Department of Health & Environmental Sciences, Helena, Montana 59601. Inquiries will be forwarded to appropriate office.
	Varies	Clerk of District Court in county where license was issued.
Nebraska	$3.00	Records since January 1909: Bureau of Vital Statistics, State Department of Health, Lincoln Building, 1003 O Street, Lincoln, Nebraska 68508.
	Varies	County Court in county where license was issued.
Nevada		Indexed since January 1, 1968. Department of Human Resources, Division of Health, Vital Statistics, Capitol Complex, Office of Vital Records, Carson City, Nevada 89710. Inquiries will be forwarded to appropriate office.
	Varies	County Recorder in county where license was issued.

* Apply to county where license was issued if known. Certified copies not available from State Health Department.

Place of marriage	Cost of copy	Remarks. For certified copies write to:
New Hampshire	$2.00	Records since 1640. Department of Health & Welfare, Division of Public Health, Bureau of Vital Statistics, 61 South Spring Street, Concord, New Hampshire 03301.
	$1.00	Town Clerk in town where license was issued.
New Jersey	$2.00	State Registrar, State Department of Health, P.O. Box 1540, Trenton, New Jersey 08625. If year is unknown, the fee is an additional $.50 for each year to be searched.
	No fee	For records from May 1848 through May 1878 write to the Archives and History Bureau, State Library Division, State Department of Education, Trenton, New Jersey 08625.
New Mexico	Varies	County Clerk in county where marriage was performed.
New York (except New York City)	$2.00	Records from January 1880 to December 1907 and since May 1915: Bureau of Vital Records, State Department of Health, Empire State Plaza, Tower Building, Albany, New York 12237.
	Varies	Records from January 1908 to April 1915: County Clerk in county where license was issued.
	$2.00	Records from January 1880 to December 1907: Write to City Clerk in Albany or Buffalo and Registrar of Vital Statistics in Yonkers, if marriage occurred in these cities.
New York City	$4.00	Records from 1847–65: Municipal Archives and Records Retention Center, New York Public Library, 23 Park Row, New York, New York 10038, except Brooklyn records for this period, which are filed with County Clerk's Office, Kings County, Supreme Court Building, Brooklyn, New York 11201. Additional copies of the same record ordered at the same time all $2.00 each.
	**	Records from 1866–1907: City Clerk's Office in borough in which marriage was performed.

** $4.00 when exact year of marriage submitted. (Add $.50 for the second year of search and $.25 for each additional year.) Certificate will show names, ages, dates of birth, and date and place of marriage. For additional information—names and countries of birth of parents, matrimonial history, etc.—express request must be made. Mail request must also include cost of return postage.

Place of marriage	Cost of copy	Remarks. For certified copies write to:
	**	Records from 1908 to May 12, 1943: Residents-City Clerk's Office in borough of bride's residence; non-residents-City Clerk's Office in borough in which license was obtained.
	**	Records from May 13, 1943, to date: City Clerk's Office in borough in which license was issued.
Bronx Borough		Office of City Clerk, 1780 Grand Concourse, Bronx, New York 10457. Records for 1908–13 for Bronx are on file in Manhattan Office.
Brooklyn Borough		Office of City Clerk, 208 Joralemon Street, Brooklyn, New York 11201.
Manhattan Borough		Office of City Clerk, Chambers and Centre Streets, New York 10007.
Queens Borough		Office of City Clerk, 120–55 Queens Boulevard, Borough Hall Station, Jamaica, New York 11424.
Richmond Borough		Office of City Clerk, Borough Hall, St. George, Staten Island, New York 10301.
North Carolina	$2.00	Department of Human Resources, Division of Health Services, Vital Records Branch, P.O. Box 2091, Raleigh, North Carolina 27602.
	Varies	Registrar of Deeds in county where marriage was performed.
North Dakota	$1.00	Records since July 1, 1925: Division of Vital Records, State Department of Health, Bismarck, North Dakota 58505. Inquiries will be forwarded to appropriate office.
	Varies	County Judge in county where license was issued.
Ohio	*	Records since September 1949: Division of Vital Statistics, Ohio Department of Health, G-20 Ohio Departments Building, 65 S. Front Street, Columbus, Ohio 43215. Inquiries will be forwarded to appropriate office. All items may be verified.
	Varies	Probate Judge in county where license was issued.

** $4.00 when exact year of marriage submitted. (Add $.50 for the second year of search and $.25 for each additional year.) Certificate will show names, ages, dates of birth, and date and place of marriage. For additional information—names and countries of birth of parents, matrimonial history, etc.—express request must be made. Mail request must also include cost of return postage.

* Apply to county where license was issued if known. Certified copies not available from State Health Department.

Place of marriage	Cost of copy	Remarks. For certified copies write to:
Oklahoma	Varies	Clerk of Court in county where license was issued.
Oregon	$3.00	Records since January 1907: Vital Statistics Section, State Health Division, State Board of Health, P.O. Box 231, Portland, Oregon 97207. Fee includes search and first copy. Additional copies of the same record ordered at the same time are $2.00 each.
	Varies	County Clerk of county where license was issued.
Pennsylvania	*	Records since January 1941: Division of Vital Statistics, State Department of Health, Central Building, 101 South Mercer Street, P.O. Box 1528, New Castle, Pennsylvania 16103. Inquiries will be forwarded to appropriate office.
	Varies	Marriage License Clerks, County Court House in County seat where license was issued.
Puerto Rico	$.50	Division of Demographic Registry & Vital Statistics, Department of Health, San Juan, Puerto Rico 00908.
Rhode Island	$2.00	Records since January 1853: Division of Vital Statistics, State Department of Health, Room 101, Health Building, Davis Street, Providence, Rhode Island 02908.
	$1.00	Town Clerk in town, or City Clerk in city where marriage was performed.
South Carolina	$2.00	Records since July 1, 1950: Division of Vital Records, Department of Health & Environmental Control, 2600 Bull Street, Columbia, South Carolina 29201.
	Varies	Records since July 1, 1911: Probate Judge in county where license was issued.
South Dakota	$2.00	Records since July 1, 1905: Division of Public Health Statistics, State Department of Health, Pierre, South Dakota 57501.
	$2.00	County Treasurer in county where license was issued.
Tennessee	$2.00	Records since July 1945: Division of Vital Records, State Department of Public Health, Cordell Hull Building, Nashville, Tennessee 37219.
	Varies	County Court Clerk in county where license was issued.

* Apply to county where license was issued if known. Certified copies not available from State Health Department.

Place of marriage	Cost of copy	Remarks. For certified copies write to:
Texas	Varies	County Clerk in county where license was issued.
Trust Territory of Pacific Islands	Varies	Clerk of Court in district where marriage was performed.
Utah	Varies	County Clerk of county where license was issued.
Vermont	$1.50	Records since 1857: Secretary of State, Vital Records Department, Statehouse, Montpelier, Vermont 05602.
	$2.00	Town Clerk in town where license was issued. For information on vital statistics laws, how to correct a record, etc. write to Public Health Statistics Division, Department of Health, Burlington, Vermont 05401.
Virginia	$2.00	Records since January 1853: Bureau of Vital Records & Health Statistics, State Department of Health, James Madison Building, P.O. Box 1000, Richmond, Virginia 23208.
	Varies	Court Clerk in county or city where license was issued.
Virgin Islands (U.S.)	*	Bureau of Vital Records & Statistical Services, Virgin Islands Department of Health, Charlotte Amalie, St. Thomas, Virgin Islands 00802. Inquiries will be forwarded to appropriate office.
St. Croix	$1.00	Clerk of Municipal Court, Municipal Court of the Virgin Islands, Christiansted, St. Croix, Virgin Islands 00820.
St. Thomas & St. John	$1.00	Clerk of Municipal Court, Municipal Court of the Virgin Islands, Charlotte Amalie, St. Thomas, Virgin Islands 00802.
Washington	$3.00	Records since January 1, 1968: Bureau of Vital Statistics, Health Services Division, Department of Social & Health Services, P.O. Box 709, Olympia, Washington 98504.
	$2.00	County Auditor in county where license was issued.
West Virginia	*	Records since 1921: Division of Vital Statistics, State Department of Health, State Office Building No. 3, Charleston, West Virginia 25305. Inquiries will be forwarded to appropriate office. Some items may be verified (fee $1.00).

* Apply to county where license was issued if known. Certified copies not available from State Health Department.

Place of marriage	Cost of copy	Remarks. For certified copies write to:
	Varies	County Clerk in county where license was issued.
Wisconsin	$4.00	Records since April 1835: Bureau of Health Statistics, Wisconsin Division of Health, P.O. Box 309, Madison, Wisconsin 53701.
Wyoming		Records since May 1941: Vital Records Services, Division of Health & Medical Services, State Office Building West, Cheyenne, Wyoming 82002.
	Varies	
	$2.00	County Clerk in county where license was issued.

Divorce Records

An official record of every divorce or annulment of marriage should be available in the place where the event took place. These records may be filed permanently either in a state vital statistics office or in a city, county, or other local office.

A copy may be obtained by writing to the appropriate office listed below. Fees listed are subject to change.

When writing for a copy, it is suggested that a money order or certified check be enclosed since the office cannot refund cash lost in transit. The following information will also be needed (type or print all names and addresses):

1. Full names of husband and wife (including nicknames).
2. Present residence address.
3. Former addresses (as in court records).
4. Ages at time of divorce (or dates of birth).
5. Date and place of divorce or annulment of marriage.
6. Type of final decree.
7. Purpose for which copy is needed.
8. Relationship to persons whose record is on file.

Place of divorce	Cost of copy	Remarks and address
Alabama	$3.00	Records since January 1950: Bureau of Vital Statistics, State Department of Public Health, Montgomery, Alabama 36104. Fee includes search and report, or copy of record, if found.
	$1.50	Clerk or Registrar of Court of Equity in county where divorce was granted.

Place of divorce	Cost of copy	Remarks and address
Alaska	$3.00	Records since 1950: Bureau of Vital Statistics, Department of Health & Welfare, Pouch H, Juneau, Alaska 99801.
	Varies	Clerk of the Superior Court in judicial district where divorce was granted: Juneau and Ketchikan (First District), Nome (Second District), Anchorage (Third District), Fairbanks (Fourth District), Alaska.
American Samoa	$.50	Registrar of Vital Statistics, Pago Pago, American Samoa 96799.
Arizona	Varies	Clerk of Superior Court in county where divorce was granted.
Arkansas	$2.00	Coupons since 1923: Division of Vital Records, Arkansas Department of Health, 4815 West Markham Street, Little Rock, Arkansas 72201.
	Varies	Full certified copy may be obtained from Circuit or Chancery Clerk in county where divorce was granted.
California	$2.00	For final decree entered since January 1, 1962 or initial complaint filed since January 1, 1966: Vital Statistics Section, Department of Health, 410 N Street, Sacramento, California 95814.
	Varies	Clerk of Superior Court in county where divorce was granted.
Canal Zone	$2.00	License section, Box L, Balboa Heights, Canal Zone. Cristobal Division (Atlantic Area), Clerk, U.S. District Court, Box 1175, Cristobal, Canal Zone.
Colorado	*	State-wide index of records for all years except 1940–67: Records and Statistics Section, Colorado Department of Health, 4210 East 11th Avenue, Denver, Colorado 80220. Inquiries will be forwarded to appropriate county office.
	Varies	Clerk of District Court in county where divorce was granted.
Connecticut	*	Index of records since June 1, 1947: Public Health Statistics Section, State Department of Health, 79 Elm Street, Hartford, Connecticut 06115. Inquiries will be forwarded to appropriate place.

* Certified copies not available.

Place of divorce	Cost of copy	Remarks and address
	$3.00	Clerk of Superior Court in county where divorce was granted.
Delaware	*	Records since March 1932: Bureau of Vital Statistics, Division of Public Health, Department of Health & Social Services, State Health Building, Dover, Delaware 19901. Inquiries will be forwarded to appropriate office. Search made and essential facts of divorce verified (fee $2.50).
	$2.00	Prothonotary in county where divorce was granted.
District of Columbia	Varies	Records since September 16, 1956: Clerk, Superior Court for the District of Columbia, Family Division, 451 Indiana Avenue, Washington, D.C. 20001. Records prior to September 16, 1956: Clerk, U.S. District Court for the District of Columbia, Washington, D.C. 20001.
Florida	$2.00	Records since June 6, 1927: Bureau of Vital Statistics, State Division of Health, P.O. Box 210, Jacksonville, Florida 32201. If year is unknown, the fee is $2.00 for the first year searched and $1.00 for each additional year to a maximum of $25. Fee includes a copy of the record found.
	Varies	Clerk of Circuit Court in county where divorce was granted.
Georgia	*	Centralized State records since June 9, 1952: Vital Records Unit, State Department of Human Resources, Room 217-H, 47 Trinity Avenue, SW, Atlanta, Georgia 30334. Inquiries will be forwarded to appropriate office.
	Varies	Clerk of Superior Court in county where divorce was granted.
Guam	Varies	Clerk, Superior Court of Guam, Agana, Guam, M.I., 96910.
Hawaii	$2.00	Records since July 1, 1951: Research and Statistics Office, State Department of Health, P.O. Box 3378, Honolulu, Hawaii 96801.
	Varies	Circuit Court in county where divorce was granted.

* Certified copies not available.

Place of divorce	Cost of copy	Remarks and address
Idaho	$2.00	Records since January 1947: Bureau of Vital Statistics, State Department of Health & Welfare, Statehouse, Boise, Idaho 83720.
	Varies	County Recorder in county where divorce was granted.
Illinois	*	Records since January 1, 1962: Office of Vital Records, State Department of Public Health, 535 W. Jefferson Street, Springfield, Illinois 62761. Some items may be verified (fee $2.00).
	Varies	Clerk of Circuit Court in county where divorce was granted.
Indiana	Varies	County Clerk in county where divorce was granted.
Iowa	*	Brief statistical record only since 1906: Division of Records and Statistics, State Department of Health, Des Moines, Iowa 50319. Inquiries will be forwarded to appropriate office.
	Varies	County Clerk in county where divorce was granted.
Kansas	$2.00	Records since July 1951: Bureau of Registration & Health Statistics, 6700 S. Topeka Avenue, Topeka, Kansas 66620.
	Varies	Clerk of District Court where divorce was granted.
Kentucky	$2.00	Records since July 1, 1958: Office of Vital Statistics, State Department of Health, 275 East Main Street, Frankfort, Kentucky 40601.
	Varies	Clerk of Circuit Court in county where divorce was granted.
Louisiana	*	Records since 1946: Division of Public Health Statistics, State Board of Health, P.O. Box 60630, New Orleans 70160. Inquiries will be forwarded to appropriate office. All items may be verified.
	Varies	Clerk of Court in parish where divorce was granted.
Maine	$2.00	Records since January 1, 1892: Office of Vital Statistics, State Department of Health & Welfare, Statehouse, Augusta, Maine 04333.
	$1.00	Clerk of District Court in the judicial division where divorce was granted.

* Certified copies not available.

Place of divorce	Cost of copy	Remarks and address
Maryland	*	Records since January 1961: Division of Vital Records, State Department of Health & Mental Hygiene, State Office Building, 201 West Preston Street, P.O. Box 13146, Baltimore, Maryland 21203. Inquiries will be forwarded to appropriate office. Some items may be verified.
	$2.00	Clerk of the Circuit Court in county where divorce was granted.
Massachusetts	$1.50	Index only from 1952: State Registrar of Vital Statistics, Room 103, McCormack Building, 1 Ashburton Place, Boston, Massachusetts 02108. Inquirer will be directed where to forward request.
	$1.50	Registrar of Probate Court in county where divorce was granted.
Michigan	$2.00	Records since 1897: Office of Vital & Health Statistics, Michigan Department of Health, 3500 North Logan Street, Lansing, Michigan 48914.
	Varies	County Clerk in county where divorce was granted.
Minnesota	*	Index since January 1, 1970: Minnesota Department of Health, Section of Vital Statistics, 717 Delaware Street, SE, Minneapolis, Minnesota 55440.
	Varies	Clerk of District Court in county where divorce was granted.
Mississippi	*	Records since January 1, 1926: Division of Public Health Statistics, State Board of Health, P.O. Box 1700, Jackson, Mississippi 39205. Inquiries will be forwarded to appropriate office.
	$2.00	Chancery Clerk in county where divorce was granted.
Missouri	*	Indexes since July 1948. Division of Health, Bureau of Vital Records, State Department of Public Health & Welfare, Jefferson City, Missouri 65101. Inquiries will be referred to appropriate Circuit Clerk of the county in which the decree was granted.
	Varies	Clerk of Circuit Court in county where divorce was granted.

* Certified copies not available.

Place of divorce	Cost of copy	Remarks and address
Montana	*	Records since July 1943: Division of Records & Statistics, State Department of Health, Helena, Montana 59601. Inquiries will be forwarded to appropriate office. Some items may be verified.
	Varies	Clerk of District Court in county where divorce was granted.
Nebraska	$3.00	Records since January 1909: Bureau of Vital Statistics, State Department of Health, Lincoln Building, 1003 O Street, Lincoln, Nebraska 68508.
	Varies	Clerk of District Court where divorce was granted.
Nevada	*	Indexed since January 1, 1968: Department of Human Resources, Division of Health, Vital Statistics, Office of Vital Records, Capitol Complex, Carson City, Nevada 89710. Inquiries will be forwarded to appropriate office.
	Varies	County Clerk in county where divorce was granted.
New Hampshire	$2.00	Records since 1880: Department of Health & Welfare, Division of Public Health, Bureau of Vital Statistics, 61 South Spring Street, Concord, New Hampshire 03301. Fee includes search and one copy.
	Varies	Clerk of the Superior Court which issued the decree.
New Jersey	$2.00	Superior Court, Chancery Division, State House Annex, Room 320, Trenton, New Jersey 08625.
New Mexico	Varies	County Clerk in county where divorce was granted.
New York	$2.00	Records since January 1, 1963: Bureau of Vital Records, State Department of Health, Empire State Plaza, Tower Building, Albany, New York 12237.
	Varies	County Clerk in county where divorce was granted.
North Carolina	$2.00	Department of Human Resources, Division of Health Services, Vital Records Branch, P.O. Box 2091, Raleigh, North Carolina 27602.
	Varies	Clerk of Superior Court where divorce was granted.

* Certified copies not available.

Place of divorce	Cost of copy	Remarks and address
North Dakota	*	Index of records since July 1, 1949: Division of Vital Records, State Department of Health, Bismarck, North Dakota 58505. Inquiries will be forwarded to appropriate office. Some items may be verified.
	Varies	Clerk of District Court in county where divorce was granted.
Ohio	*	Records since 1948: Division of Vital Statistics, Ohio Department of Health, G-20 Ohio Departments Building, 65 S. Front Street, Columbus, Ohio 43215. Inquiries will be forwarded to appropriate office. All items may be verified.
	Varies	Clerk of Court of Common Pleas in county where divorce was granted.
Oklahoma	Varies	Court Clerk in county where divorce was granted.
Oregon	$3.00	Records since May 1925: Vital Statistics Section, State Health Division, P.O. Box 231, Portland, Oregon 97207. Fee includes search and first copy. Additional copies of the same record ordered at same time are $2.00 each.
	Varies	County Clerk in county where divorce was granted.
Pennsylvania	*	Records since January 1946: Division of Vital Statistics, State Department of Health, Central Building, 101 South Mercer Street, P.O. Box 1528, New Castle, Pennsylvania 16103. Inquiries will be forwarded to appropriate office.
	Varies	Prothonotary, Court House, in county seat where divorce was granted.
Puerto Rico	$.60	Superior Court where divorce was granted.
Rhode Island	*	Records since January 1962: Division of Vital Statistics, State Department of Health, Room 101, Health Building, Davis Street, Providence, Rhode Island 02908. Inquiries will be forwarded to appropriate office.
	$1.00	Clerk of Family Court in county where divorce was granted.
South Carolina	$2.00	Records since July 1, 1962: Division of Vital Records, Department of Health & Environmental Control, 2600 Bull Street, Columbia, South Carolina 29201.

* Certified copies not available.

Place of divorce	Cost of copy	Remarks and address
	Varies	Records since April 1949. Clerk of county where petition filed.
South Dakota	$2.00	Records since July 1, 1905: Division of Public Health Statistics, State Department of Health, Pierre, South Dakota 57501.
	Varies	Clerk of Court in county where divorce was granted.
Tennessee	$2.00	Records since July 1945: Division of Vital Statistics, State Department of Public Health, Cordell Hull Building, Nashville, Tennessee 37219.
	Varies	Clerk of Court where divorce was granted.
Texas	Varies	Clerk of District Court in county where divorce was granted.
Trust Territory of Pacific Islands	Varies	Clerk of Court in District where divorce was granted.
Utah	Varies	County Clerk in county where decree was granted.
Vermont	$1.50	Records since January 1860: Secretary of State, Vital Records Department, Statehouse, Montpelier, Vermont 05602.
	$3.00	Clerk of County Court where divorce was granted.
Virginia	$2.00	Records since January 1918: Bureau of Vital Records & Health Statistics, State Department of Health, James Madison Building, P.O. Box 1000, Richmond, Virginia 23208.
	Varies	Clerk of Court in county or city where divorce was granted.
Virgin Islands (U.S.)		
St. Croix	$2.40	Deputy Clerk of District Court, Christiansted, St. Croix, Virgin Islands 00820.
St. Thomas & St. John	$2.40	Clerk of District Court, Charlotte Amalie, St. Thomas, Virgin Islands 00802.
Washington	$3.00	Records since January 1, 1968: Bureau of Vital Statistics, Health Services Division, Department of Social & Health Services, P.O. Box 709, Olympia, Washington 98504.
	Varies	County Clerk in county where divorce was granted.
West Virginia	Varies	Clerk of Circuit Court, Chancery Side, in county where divorce was granted.

* Certified copies not available.

Place of divorce	Cost of copy	Remarks and address
Wisconsin	$4.00	Records since October 1, 1907: Bureau of Health Statistics, Wisconsin Division of Health, P.O. Box 309, Madison, Wisconsin 53701.
Wyoming	$2.00	Records since May 1941: Vital Records Services, Division of Health & Medical Services, State Office Building West, Cheyenne, Wyoming 82002.
	Varies	Clerk of District Court in county where divorce was granted.

Bibliography

Autobiography Section

Bruening, Sylvia. *The Story of Your Life*. Published by the author. Salt Lake City, 1974.

DeMille, Cecil B. *The Autobiography of Cecil B. DeMille*. Edited by Donald Hayne. Englewood Cliffs, N.J.: Prentice-Hall, Inc., 1959.

Dunaway, Philip, and Evans, Mel. *A Treasury of the World's Great Diaries*. Garden City: Doubleday & Company, Inc., 1957.

Franklin, Benjamin. *The Autobiography of Benjamin Franklin*. New York: Walter J. Black, 1941.

Franklin, Benjamin. *The Autobiography of Benjamin Franklin*. New York: Everymans Library; Dutton, 1968.

Hartley, William G., *Preparing a Personal History*. Salt Lake City: Primer Publications, 1976.

Heslop, J. Malan, and Orden, Dell Van. *How to Write Your Personal History*. Salt Lake City: Bookcraft, Inc., 1976.

Johnson, Edgar. *One Mighty Torrent*. New York: The Macmillan Company, 1955.

Keller, Helen. *The Story of My Life*. Garden City: Doubleday & Company, Inc., 1954.

Lagemann, John Kord. "Don't Be Afraid to Let Your Feelings Show," *Reader's Digest*, May 1976.

Mallery, Richard D., edited by. *Masterworks of Autobiography*. Garden City: Doubleday & Company, Inc., 1946.

Perrin, Porter G. *Writer's Guide and Index to English*. New York: Scott, Foresman and Company, 1950.

Schwerin, Doris. *Diary of a Pigeon Watcher*. New York: William Morrow and Company, Inc., 1976.

Tanner, Annie Clark. *A Mormon Mother*. Published by Tanner Trust Fund, University of Utah Library, Salt Lake City, Utah, 1976.

Twain, Mark. *The Autobiography of Mark Twain*. Edited by Charles Neider, New York: Harper & Brothers, 1959.

White, William Allen. *The Autobiography of William Allen White*. New York: The Macmillan Company, 1946.

Yogananda, Paramhansa. *Autobiography of a Yogi*. Los Angeles: Self-Realization Fellowship Publishers, 1956.

Family History Section

Bowen, Catherine Drinker. *Biography, the Craft and the Calling*. Boston: Little, Brown and Company, 1968.

―――. *Family Portrait*. Boston: Little, Brown and Company, 1970.

Clifford, James. *From Puzzles to Portraits*. Chapel Hill: University of North Carolina Press, 1970.

Coultron, G. G. *Medieval Panorama*. 1938.

Dixon, James D. *History of Charles Dixon*. Rockford, Ill.: Forest City Publishing Company, 1891.

Felt, Thomas E. *Researching, Writing and Publishing Local History*. Nashville: American Association for State and Local History, 1976.

Haley, Alex. *Roots*. Garden City: Doubleday & Company, Inc., 1976.

Homans, Abigail Adams. *Education by Uncles*. Boston: Houghton Mifflin Company, 1966.

Nangle, B. *The Monthly Review*. First Series, Oxford, 1934.

Modern Short Biographies and Autobiographies. Edited by Marston Balch. New York: Harcourt, Brace and Company, 1945.

Rawlyk, George A. *Nova Scotia's Massachusetts*. Montreal: McGill-Queens University Press, 1973.

Diary Section

Anne Frank: The Diary of a Young Girl. Edited by Otto H. Frank. Garden City: Doubleday & Company, Inc., 1952.

Kennedy, Rose Fitzgerald. *Times to Remember*. Garden City: Doubleday & Company, Inc., 1974.

The Diary of Samuel Pepys. Edited with additions by Henry Whealley. New York: Random House, 1946.

Searching, Organizing, and Preserving Section

Baum, Willa K. *Oral History for the Local Historical Society*. Nashville: American Association for State and Local History, 1974.

Felt, Thomas E. *Researching, Writing and Publishing Local History*. Nashville: American Association for State and Local History, 1976.

Foulger, Paul (personal interview). Historical Department, Church of Jesus Christ of Latter-day Saints, 50 East North Temple, Salt Lake City, Utah, 1976.

Gardner, David E.; Harland, Derek; Smith, Frank. *A Basic Course in Genealogy*, Vol. 1. Salt Lake City: Bookcraft, Inc., 1958.

Haley, Alex (a tape recording made by, and in the possession of the author, of Alex Haley's address before the League of Utah Writers at the University of Utah, Salt Lake City, Utah, November 17, 1976).

Harland, Derek. *A Basic Course in Genealogy*, Vol. 2. Salt Lake City: Bookcraft, Inc., 1958.

Hartley, William G. *Oral History Program Handbook*. Church of Jesus Christ of Latter-day Saints, Historical Department, Salt Lake City, Utah, 1973.

Jones, Vincent L.; Eakle, Arlene H.; and Christensen, Mildred H. *Family History for Fun and Profit*. Salt Lake City: Publishers Press, 1972.

Marston, Doris. *A Guide to Writing History*. Cincinnati, Ohio: Writer's Digest, 1976.

Preece, Floren F., and Phyllis T. *The Sure Guide to Genealogy Research*, Mendon, Utah: Genealogy Club of America, 1969.

Shumway, Gary L. and Hartley, William G. *An Oral History Primer*. Salt Lake City, Utah: by the Authors, 1976.

"Roots: A Major Break-Through for Black Genealogy." *Genealogy Digest*, August 1976.

Where to Write for Births, Deaths, Marriages, Divorces. Superintendent of Documents, U. S. Government Printing Office, Washington, D.C. 20402, 1976.

929
Di

Dixon, Janice T.

Preserving your past

DATE